Parti**c**ipatory Democ )e

Brigitte Geißel
Marko Joas (eds.)

Participatory Democratic Innovations in Europe

Improving the Quality of Democracy?

Barbara Budrich Publishers
Opladen • Berlin • Toronto 2013

A CIP catalogue record for this book is available from
Die Deutsche Bibliothek (The German Library)

© 2013 by Barbara Budrich Publishers, Opladen, Berlin & Toronto
www.barbara-budrich.net
ISBN   978-3-8474-0113-1
eISBN   978-3-8474-0371-5

Die Deutsche Bibliothek – CIP-Einheitsaufnahme
Ein Titeldatensatz für die Publikation ist bei der Deutschen Bibliothek erhältlich.

Verlag Barbara Budrich ⓑ Barbara Budrich Publishers
Stauffenbergstr. 7. D-51379 Leverkusen Opladen, Germany

86 Delma Drive. Toronto, ON M8W 4P6 Canada
www.barbara-budrich.net

Jacket illustration by Bettina Lehfeldt, Kleinmachnow, Germany
Printed in Europe on acid-free paper by
paper&tinta, Warsaw

Table of Contents

Preface

Democracy as form of governance is constantly under pressure from its environment, including its 'users'. Therefore it is also constantly changing, to follow the popular attitudes, ways of behavior by the public, academic research results and technological options in the society. Some changes are introduced deliberately by the political actors in our societies; others are just appearing, without any action by the contemporary political system.

The research society has taken up to follow these changes more closely during the last ten years. The view of s' democratic systems has changed into a picture of a vivid democracy that is – at least to some extent – responsive to the changes in our societies. This volume is showing and analyzing what is going on in Europe regarding democratic innovations.

We focus on institutionalized innovations in this volume, often based on examples already used in other countries. It is clear that diffusion of innovations, projects and good practices is the way how new models to act are introduced. It is also notable that many new democratic innovations are active at the local level of the society – the government level closest to the people.

We want to present a number of European cases with this volume, mostly based on empirical work on case studies, but also some experiments in the field of research.

The starting point for this volume was a workshop on democratic innovations at the ECPR Joint Sessions in Potsdam 2009. We have added to this base some additional articles, giving the book an in-depth view on all major innovations used today.

We want to thank Barbara Budrich Verlag for giving us the opportunity to publish the book. We also want to thank our authors for very responsive mode to the work during the last hectic phase before publishing. Dr Iris Lindahl-Raittila has made excellent work with our linguistic problems as many of us are non-native English speakers. Likewise, Michele Ferrari has been of invaluable help to finalize the technical lay-out. We want also to thank the economic support for the book by Goethe University Frankfurt, Research Unit 'Democratic Innovations' and the Department of Political Science at Åbo Akademi University, with the 'Democracy: A Citizen Perspective - A Centre of Excellence on Democracy Research'.

Åbo and Frankfurt, August 31, 2013,

Brigitte Geissel and Marko Joas

Introduction:
On the Evaluation of Participatory Innovations -
A Preliminary Framework

Brigitte Geissel

Despite the world-wide triumph of democracy, the quest for an optimal 'politike' has not yet reached the "end of history" (Fukuyama). It turned out that representative democracies do not necessarily satisfy the citizenries. A few examples may suffice here to demonstrate current democratic malaises (e.g. Dalton 2004). The perception that politicians care about what people think has declined dramatically in countries like Germany, France, Sweden, Finland and Austria – all stable democracies – since the 1970s. Many citizens are convinced that their governments aim to serve 'big interests' and they doubt the abilities of their representatives to govern complex societies. While these malaises – some authors even speak of disenchantments, ills, demystification or deconsolidation Dalton et al. 2006; Offe 2003; Habermas 1973) – do not necessarily lead to far-reaching political crises, they are viewed as cause for concern. This concern is the breeding-ground for discussions about new forms of democratic decision-making. As Diamond and Morlino (2005: ix) put it, there is a high level of consensus that also "long-established democracies must reform … to attend to their own gathering problems of public dissatisfaction and … disillusionment".

More and more citizens as well as political scientists pin their hopes on participatory innovations as a means to cure the malaises. They are convinced that "the cure for democracies' ills is more democracy" (Dalton et al. 2006: 251; also: Warren 2006; Offe 2003). Several national and subnational governments followed this route and implemented various kinds of participatory innovations, i.e. the inclusion of citizens into processes of political will-formation and decision-making. In fact, current democracies are constantly changing, finding new forms and adapting to societal challenges and pressures.

However, up to now there is a striking imbalance between the amount of time, money and energy invested in participatory innovations and the amount of attention paid to assess them empirically (OECD 2005: 10). With few exceptions, published in recent years, the case-study approach is still prevailing. Case studies assess each innovation within its own setting and according to its own goals providing detailed descriptions and rich understanding of the individual cases. However, with case studies alone a scientific patchwork remains, leaving too many questions open. Therefore, in this edition we apply a criteria-based approach for analyzing participatory innovations (similar: Smith 2009). The price for criteria-based approaches is the lack of detailed information ignoring the special features of individual cases – for the benefit of creating more comprehensive insights (Mathur and Skelcher 2007).

Recently some scholars applied systematic criteria-based approaches, most notably Smith (2009), Fung (2003, 2006) and Papadopoulos and Warin (2007). However, these studies mainly focus on the Americas –for example the British Columbia Citizens' Assembly on Electoral Reform (Canada), Participatory Budgeting in Porto Alegra (Brasil), or community policing in Chicago (USA). Systematic research comparing the impacts of different innovations in *Europe* is still missing and our edition is starting to fill this gap by evaluating benefits and disadvantages of participatory procedures tried out in European states. We hope to shed light on the puzzle of which innovation is useful, useless, or even harmful when it comes to addressing different 'democratic malaises' in the European context.

The outline of this chapter is as follows: First, participatory innovations are categorized and explained. In the main part of the introduction, we develop the analytical framework for evaluating participatory procedures all contributors in this edition will adhere to in their evaluation. Finally, we describe the outline of the edition.

(Democratic) Innovations

'Innovation' is a complex term, which is used mostly in technology and economics but is also attracting increasing interest in the context of politics (Considine and Lewis 2007; Papadopoulos and Warin 2007; Casper and van Waarden 2005; Smith 2005). It is difficult to delineate the term 'innovation' with any precision. What makes the definition even more challenging is the fact, that innovations are often not invented, but reinvented or copied. In technology and economics, about 70-80 percent of what firms interpret as innovations are not really new for the sector, but are actually imitations (Unger 2005: 21). This is also true in the world of politics. An innovation can be new in one country, but widespread in another. Thus given the fact that, for example, direct democracy is common in Switzerland, direct democratic elements in other countries could be considered as imitation - or as an innovation in a different 'sector' (for processes of diffusion, see e.g. Grönholm 2000: 63).[1]

---

1   The literature on democratic innovations covers for example checks and balances between the branches of representative government or new forms of top-down communication (e.g. Offe 2003). However, for the most part, the literature has focused on popular participation in processes of political will-formation and

Accordingly, we refer to participatory innovation as new procedures consciously and purposefully introduced with the aim of mending current democratic malaises and improving the quality of democracy. If a new procedure is tried out in a country, we call it innovation irrespective of whether the innovation in question has already been tried out in another country. Similar political terms, such as 'strong democracy', 'deep democracy', and 'participatory democracy' refer to participatory innovations as well, but are often utilized as normative concepts portraying 'more participation' as a desirable project with many utopian features. In contrast, *this edition aims at evaluating existing participatory procedures empirically.*

Which Innovations?

Which innovations are now worth considering? Based on a comprehensive literature survey conducted at the Social Science Research Center Berlin in 2006, using over 200 publications, three types of participatory innovations can be identified:

- cooperative governance,
- deliberative procedures,
- direct democratic procedures.

All types will be discussed in the following paragraphs. Since "the newest are the experiments with co-governance, ... and deliberative assemblies" (Newton 2012: 16) we start with cooperative governance and deliberative procedures and finally discuss direct democracy. Additionally we take e-democracy into account. Although we consider e-democracy as a technical innovation providing novel ways of political interaction we add one chapter and evaluate the impacts of e-democracy (for a detailed discussion of the varieties of participatory procedures, see also Geissel and Newton 2012; Fung 2006).

Cooperative Governance

According to authors like Smith (2005: 56–60) or Talpin (2012) cooperative governance is distinguished from other participatory innovations by direct citizen influence on political decisions. "The main specificity of co-governance[2] institutions, in comparison with other participatory innovations, is their

---

decision-making. These participatory innovations are regarded as a cure for current malaises of representative democracy (see Geissel 2009).

2   The terms cooperative governance and co-governance are used interchangeably.

level of empowerment." Innovations of this type mean "that power is shared between citizens and elected officials." (Talpin 2012: 184). Other terms used in the literature are 'collaborative governance' or 'empowered participatory governance' (e.g. Fung and Wright 2001): state actors and non-state actors work jointly to decide on a policy (Geißel 2009).

Forms of cooperative governance with state actors and non-state actors are wide spread and exist probably since the beginning of modern democracy. In corporatist democracies inclusion of major economic interests in public decision-making is by definition ensured. However, cooperative governance goes beyond this concept, because it means more than the inclusion of trade unions and employers' representatives. Cooperative governance involves institutionalized citizens' and often organized groups' involvement in political will formation and decision-making to a broader extent.

Cooperative governance procedures are initiated for a variety of reasons. Mostly they are expected to improve problem-solving capacities and to develop effective and legitimate decisions. The recruitment of participants varies considerably, as well. Some procedures try to guarantee the involvement of all relevant stakeholder groups and affected citizens, other procedures rely on self-selected participants and interest groups (e.g. Fung 2003).

Deliberative Procedures

Deliberation emphasizes discursive will-formation – in contrast to the aggregative modus of voting (see Setälä in this edition). The definition of deliberation, however, is controversial (e.g. Delli Carpini et al. 2004: 316-219; Talpin, Fiket and Memoli, Strandberg and Grönlund, Himelroos in this edition). Many European proponents of deliberative democracy refer to Habermas' concept of deliberation which includes strict rules, for example rational exchange of arguments among free and equal citizens (Habermas 1992). Only communication in compliance with these rules is regarded as deliberative. In contrast, US American proponents apply lower standards and regard most kinds of discussion as deliberation (e.g. Fishkin and Luskin 2004; Fishkin 1995). In this edition we suggest a similar, broad definition. According to our broad definition deliberative procedures can have many different faces – ranging on a 'continuum of deliberative procedures' from minimum to extensive deliberation (see also Himelroos in this edition). The most widespread forms are information-exchanging events with a minimum of discussion, e.g. public meetings. They can be located on the 'deliberation-continuum' at the 'least deliberative, information-exchanging side'. On the 'most deliberative side', high-quality deliberative procedures can be found with well organized deliberative processes, well-recruited participants, well-prepared background materials, including invited experts, facilitators, and mediators, for example the Deliberation Day in Finland in 2006 or Deliberative Polls (Fishkin and Luskin 2004).

Generally deliberative procedures are consultative. They produce and provide elaborate advice which is submitted to decision-making bodies. The decision-making bodies decide whether they accept or reject the advice.[3] Deliberative procedures are often adopted in small-scale units and are initiated for different reasons, for instance to negotiate compromises in contentious situations, to identify collective goals, or to generate new ideas. The recruitment of the participants reflects the multitude of forms. Some deliberative procedures comprise of self-selected participants, in other procedures participants are selected carefully to mirror the social composition of the constituency.[4]

Direct Democratic Procedures

Direct democracy is currently popular in many countries as an additional and complementary form of decision-making within representative democracies.[5] Direct democratic procedures include casting votes on policies and rules or dismissing officials (recall). They can be consultative or binding, mandatory, e.g. constitutionally required, as well as initiated top-down by political representatives (e.g. parliament, city council, president, mayor) or bottom-up by citizens ('popular initiative' or 'petition').[6] Some procedures are decision-controlling, referring to a law(-proposal), or decision-promoting, putting is-

---

3   The Danish consensus conference on gene-technology (1987), for example, contributed significantly to the decisions of the parliament (for more examples, see Goodin/Dryzek 2006; Delli Carpini et al. 2004: 329-330).

4   Examples of deliberative procedures include 'Planungszellen' (planning cells), 'Round Figures', 'Cooperative Discourse', 'Citizen Juries', and 'Focus Groups'. All of these different terminologies insinuate unambiguous differences between the different procedures and clear-cut procedural structures. However, this is not the case: similar procedures may be named differently and dissimilar procedures can have the same labels. Thus the field remains chaotic with respect to terminology and semantics.

5   Over 20 institutional changes offering improved options for direct democracy have been introduced in OECD countries within the last decades and the trend is continuing (Scarrow 2001).

6   The terminology used in the literature is rather blurred and intricate. Some authors use, for example, the term 'referendum' for all forms of direct democratic procedures including popular initiatives (e.g. Setälä 2006); other authors differentiate between popular initiatives initiated by the citizens and referenda initiated by representatives.

sues on the political agenda (see Setälä in this edition; Kriesi 2008). Direct democratic procedures also differ vastly in terms of the number of signatures required to launch a citizens' petition or the minimum quota of participants casting their votes for a popular vote to be accepted as valid.[7]

Motives for initiating a top-down or a bottom-up popular vote vary vastly (see Setälä in this edition). Governments often promote a referendum to improve legitimacy or to gain a mandate from the citizens especially if their parties or coalitions are divided on an issue. The Swedish government, for example, launched a referendum on nuclear energy (1980) because the major parties could not find a consensus on the issues. Non-state actors use the popular vote to push topics on the political agenda, or to control political decisions.

E-Democracy

E-democracy became famous with the rise of information and communication technology. It covers a variety of novel tools and channels of communication, information and participation, for example online-platforms. E-democracy had raised lofty hopes in the 1990s. It was expected to make political communication and participation easier, faster and more equal. However, real-life experiences have revealed the limited benefits. New technologies – as far as we know to date – do not necessarily improve democracy – and sometimes even have opposing impacts. Involvement and participation, for example, often did not become more inclusive, but even more biased (see Lidén, Strandberg and Grönlund in this edition). The term "digital divide" illustrates this bias.

How to Evaluate Participatory Innovations – Framework

Frameworks for evaluating participatory innovations within consolidated democracies have been spelled out rarely. Although the call for a "concise research agenda" was made as early as 1979 (Sewell and Philips) and continued to echo in the following years, it remained almost unheard of for years (Rowe and Frewer 2004: 521 ff.). During the 1990s, few publications discussed the problem, referring to for example "fairness and competence"

---

7   Petitions for referenda are applied seldom if a high number of signatures is required, whereas low quota lead to a more intensive use (see Mittendorf 2008).

(Renn et al. 1995). A couple of years later Chess and Purcell's (1999) and Rowe et al.'s (2004: 93) studies might be regarded as starting signals for the next generation of frameworks (see Table 1.1). And they already differentiated between theory-based criteria and criteria based on participants' goals (Chess and Purcell 1999: 2686). Referring to the criteria presented by Rowe et al. (2004), Abelson and Gauvin (2006) evaluated context, process, and outcome using sub-categories such as deliberative quality (similar: Burgess/Chilvers 2006). In the following years similar yardsticks could be found and are compiled in Table 1.1: some authors focus on inclusion and equality (equal access[8], equal consideration, equal opportunities to participate), on efficiency and effectiveness, or on aspects of legitimacy and accountability. In his seminal book on "Democratic Innovations" Smith (2009) applied the following criteria: inclusiveness, popular control, considered judgement, publicity, efficiency, and transferability. And finally, Geissel (2012, also 2009) summarizes the contributions of a recent edition on 'Evaluating Democratic Innovations'.[9] She identified the following recurring criteria in current research on participatory innovations: inclusive participation, improvement of citizens' democratic skills, impact on public policies, quality of deliberation, legitimacy and political satisfaction, and transparency (almost identical: Michels 2011). Table 1.1 summarizes the different generations of frameworks in form of a synopsis.[10]

---

8   This is often defined as expanded opportunities for citizens and/or to increased citizen usage of these opportunities (e.g. Dalton et al. 2006:14).

9   Geissel and Newton 2012 with articles by Budge, Kriesi, Beetham, Fishkin, Smith, Rucht, Talpin

10   Although other studies on democratic, participatory innovations have been conducted in recent years, the studies collected in the figure are among those publications discussing their framework of analysis explicitly.

Table 1.1 Frameworks and Criteria Applied in Evaluation Studies on Participatory Innovations

	Renn et al. 1995	Chess & Purcell 1999	Rowe et al. 2004	Abelson & Gauvin 2006	Dalton et al. 2006	Holtk. et al. 2006	Papadop. & Warin 2007	Fung 2008	Smith 2009	Geissel 2009	Michels 2011	Geissel 2012
Inclusive participation	(x)	(x)	x	x	x		x	x	x	x	x	x
Meaningful participation			x	x	(x)		(x)	x	x	(x)	x	x
Legitimacy		(x)		x		x				x	x	x
Quality of Deliberation	(x)			x			x	x	x	x	x	x
Effectiveness		x	x	x		x	x	x	x	x	(x)	(x)
Citizens' Enlightenment	(x)	(x)							(x)	x	x	(x)
Other criteria (examples)	Fairness		many[1]	process rules	trans-parency		publicity, account-ability		trans-ferability			trans-parency

x = *mentioned explicitly, although terms differ*

(x) = *mentioned implicitly*

15

Based on the described literature, we suggest a framework including the following dimensions: 1) inclusive and meaningful participation, 2) legitimacy, 3) deliberation, 4) effectiveness, and 5) enlightened citizens. This framework is in line with current developments (Geissel 2012; Michels 2011) and avoids pitfalls of former agendas.[11]

The identified criteria are complex concepts requiring further clarification. They are outlined in the remaining part of this chapter. For each criterion we start with a short description of its meaning and its malaise in current representative democracies. Then we discuss whether and how participatory innovations are expected to mend this malaise and provide some ideas about how to evaluate their impacts. However, some words must be said about measurements beforehand. In this introduction we can just tackle the question of how to measure the different criteria empirically and give some ideas about which indicators might be applied. The authors themselves decided which indicators are useful for their specific cases. [12] And the authors also decide which criteria are most important in the context of the innovation they are examining. Thus, not all authors are able to cover all criteria in their empirical work, but choose the adequate and applicable ones.

1) Inclusive and Meaningful Participation

Inclusive participation seems to be guaranteed in representative democracies - at least de jure - via election of political representatives with the notion of 'one man one vote'. However, two democratic malaises are currently discussed in the context of voter turnout. First, participation in elections has been declining

---

11   Three pitfalls can be mentioned: First, several criteria mentioned in other frameworks are problematic, as for example 'openness' (see Papadopoulos/Warin 2007). 'Open' innovations might provide less inclusive participation than innovations with selected participants. Or, as Dalton et al. (2006: 262) put it: "Equality of access is not sufficient if equality of usage is grossly lacking". Second, ex ante and ex post impacts have often not been differentiated properly, i.e. impacts which are predisposed by design, and impacts which can only be measured after the end of the procedure are lumped together (e.g. Abelson/Gauvin 2006). For example, the fact that consultative procedures are without decision making competency is part of the design and not an ex post impact. And third, criteria for the evaluation of success and prerequisites for success are often confused: for example, "access to resources" or "early involvement" (Rowe et al. 2004) might be favorable conditions for a successful procedure. However, they cannot serve as criteria for the evaluation of the impact.

12   The same is true for the time frame of evaluation – weeks, months or years. Each author works with the time frame which is useful in his or her case. However, the contributions in this edition are surprisingly coherent (see conclusion).

in most consolidated democracies for years with sometimes less than 40% of the electorate casting a ballot. Many politicians as well as political scientists regard this as an alarming sign. Second, participation in elections became de facto more exclusive because underprivileged strata of society refuse to take part (Schäfer 2009). The promise of 'one man one vote' does not suffice to guarantee inclusive, equal input into the political system.

These malaises need to be addressed and many authors demand a cure arguing for more 'equality in input', 'representative input' or 'inclusive participation' via participatory innovations. Participatory innovations, so goes the argument, provide more inclusive input options – especially for those citizens who are not engaged in traditional forms of participation such as elections. However, opponents of participatory innovations claim the converse: participatory forms would undermine inclusive and equal participation. Participatory innovations are used – and misused – by politically already active social strata of society, i.e. the well-off and better-educated strata of society, especially middle-aged and middle class males with time, money, and political know-how. Their interests would be pushed through under the cover and rhetoric of 'participatory democracy' – to the detriment of the common good (Raymond, 2002: 183). According to these voices, participatory innovations impede inclusive participation (Papadopoulos 2004: 220).

The question whether participatory procedures provide *inclusive and equal participation* has become a crucial topic in empirical research in the last years. Authors use different terms such as representativeness, equal access, political equality, equal opportunities to participate, inclusiveness in presence and voice or inclusion (of those affected) – but they all refer to the same idea of inclusive and equal participation. In the context of this edition we leave it to the authors to define and analyse 'inclusive participation' in line with the participatory procedure under research.

Not only inclusiveness of participation is a malaise of current representative democracies, but also the notion of *meaningful* participation. Meaningful participation seems to be guaranteed in democracies – again with the notion of "one man one vote". Every vote counts the same and has the same influence on the composition of the government. However, citizens increasingly regard participation as meaningless. They feel that their participation does not make a difference and that most politicians do not care much about what their constituencies want. Proponents argue that participatory innovations would mend these malaises, because they give citizens more say. In contrast, some authors emphasize that most participatory procedures are symbolic anyway and without influence on political decision – and there is some controversy whether the symbolic character is to be considered as fortune or as misfortune (Geissel 2012). However, many studies on participatory innovations refer to this criterion, applying terms like influence, transformation of citizen preferences into public policies, responsiveness or popular control. The conceptual umbrella of all these different terms is the impact of participatory procedures on political decisions.

However, how can *meaningful participation* be measured in the context of participatory innovations? Co-governance and direct democratic procedures lead by definition more often to public policies. Thus it can be easily evaluated whether and how outcomes of these procedures are transferred into policies. In contrast, deliberative procedures are seldom connected to decision-making bodies and have had little or even no impact on public policies. In our edition, authors evaluate in different ways whether and to what degree participation in the cases they are examining have been meaningful.

2) Legitimacy and Political Support

Legitimacy is one of the core notions of democracies and is defined in many different ways (e.g. legal legitimacy, input-legitimacy, output-legitimacy; for details, see Geißel 2008). In this edition, we refer to legitimacy derived by citizens' political support, i.e. 'perceived legitimacy'. Perceived legitimacy is declining in many representative democracies. Citizens still support the idea of democracy, but they are less satisfied with their political system, and especially with their representatives. Participatory innovations are expected to meet some of these malaises. Several proponents argue that citizens would accept the political system, decisions, or even politicians with more enthusiasm, if they were involved in the political process. Opponents in contrast argue that impacts on perceived legitimacy are doubtable. There are, for example, no reasons to assume more positive attitudes towards politicians after involvement in a participatory procedure. And Easton (1965: 58) already highlighted the danger of "demand input overload". Demands might be created and enforced by participatory involvement, while the state has insufficient capacity and means to fulfill them. Frustration and discontent rather than improved legitimacy might be the result of participatory procedures.

Trying to support one hypothesis or the other, research on participatory innovations has often taken (perceived) legitimacy into account – from the perspective of the participants and/or the wider public. Indicators applied in this context are, for example, acceptance (of decisions and of decision-making procedures) or trust in public institutions and decision-makers.

3) Deliberation

Representative democracies depend on elections, e.g. on the aggregation of citizens' preferences. However, this aggregative mode is increasingly regarded as 'too simplistic', because citizens' preferences are often "raw, crude", unsophisticated, and not well thought out. Proponents of deliberative procedures argue that this malaise of current representative democracies can be solved via deliberative procedures. Only by means of deliberation can citizens reflect and transform their preferences and make reasoned decisions.[13] Accordingly, the quality of *deliberation* is raised in many studies on participatory innovations. Authors of these studies are concerned about whether participatory procedures really involve high-quality deliberation, applying concepts such as "reflective judgements" (Smith 2009: 24), constructive conflict management or thoughtfulness (see Talpin, Setälä and Himmelroos in this edition).

4) Effectiveness

In politics effectiveness means attainment of shared, collective goals of a constituency, for example, economic growth, social equality, or low criminality (Roller 2005; Lijphart1999). Effectiveness is often regarded as one of the advantages of democracies. Democracies seem to work more effectively than any other kind of political system (see e.g. Government-Effectiveness-Index of World Bank). However, this looks quite different from the perspective of citizens. Citizens in representative democracies are not necessarily satisfied with the performance of their systems, but increasingly discontent because the outcome does not meet their needs and interests. Participatory innovations are often expected to mend these malaises and lead to the attainment of collective goals.

In contrast to 'meaningful participation' the main question concerning effectiveness is, whether collective problems are actually solved – whereas meaningful participation just measures whether participants' statements are taken into account by policy-makers. It might, for example, happen that suggestions made by a participatory procedure are transformed into policies, but the actual outcome largely missed the collective goal.[14]

How can effectiveness of participatory procedures be measured? The easiest way would be to evaluate, whether collective goals are more often reached

---

13 Deliberation has always played an important role in theories of democracy. However, it was limited to the political elite for a long time. In contrast, current democratic theories demand deliberation within civil society and among citizens.

14 Output means policies and public spending, outcome refers to the actual resolution of the problem. For example, studies on output ask about policies and public spending concerning the health care or education systems, whereas studies on outcome look at the actual achievement, e.g. low infant mortality or high educational level of the population. From this perspective, (output) legitimacy is achieved when a political system provides these goods. Or, in the words of Scharpf, political decisions are legitimate if and because they effectively promote the collective goals of the constituency in question (Scharpf 1999: 6).

via participatory procedures than via decisions of political representatives. However, empirical research is not that easy. First, there are methodological problems and lack of data. In most cases it is not possible to compare the effectiveness of decisions made by citizens' and by political representatives directly. Second, in complex societies collective goals are more often than not contested or vague.[15] Thus, it is problematic to assess whether a 'collective goal' was actually reached. In these cases collective goals must be compromised or identified, before they can be 'translated' into policies. Actually, many participatory innovations are designed to support the process of identifying or compromising collective goals. Thus participatory innovations might also be evaluated on the basis of whether they are helpful to identify or to compromise collective goals of a constituency.

5) Enlightened Citizens and Democratic Education

As already stated by Thomas Jefferson (1776), democracy should not only generate common welfare, but also an enlightened democratic citizenry. Almond and Verba (1963) have demonstrated the importance of enlightened citizens' attitudes, skills, and behaviour for thriving democracies (see also Inglehart and Welzel 2005). Democracies can only consolidate and stay stable, if their citizens accept democratic principles and perform democratic skills. However, democratic skills and virtues seem to stagnate in current representative democracies or even to worsen, for example participation in elections. Again, proponents hope that participatory innovations mend this malaise. In fact, *citizens' enlightenment* is often regarded as a major advantage of participatory procedures. Democratic virtues and skills are expected to improve via participation. Some authors even anticipate that "participating in democratic decisions makes participants better citizens", enhances tolerance, public spiritedness, or the ability to listen and to compromise (Fung and Wright 2001; Mansbridge 1999; Gundersen 1995: 6, 112; Renn et al. 1995; Pateman 1970). However, it is unlikely that all civic skills can be enhanced at the same pace and to the same extent. Some skills, such as knowledge, for example, might be improved easily while democratic skills like tolerance might be more difficult to acquire. And some opponents even doubt that participatory innovations have any educative impacts at all. Accordingly, the final yardstick to measure im-

---

15 In a few cases, of course, the collective goals are undisputed and the effectiveness of participatory innovations can be measured straightforwardly. An innovation is effective, for example, if it attains a collective local goal, such as the reduction of water pollution (e.g. Geissel/Kern 2000) or low public debt (e.g. Freitag/Wagschal 2007).

pacts of participatory innovations is citizens' enlightenment, i.e. the improvement of citizens' democratic skills.

The framework with the discussed dimensions is summarized in the following table (Table 1.2).[16] The criteria portrayed in Table 1.2 are intertwined in many ways. Some criteria might be so densely related – conceptually and empirically – that improvement of one criterion may diffuse benefits to the other criteria. High quality of deliberation and enlightenment of citizens might go hand in hand, for example. If citizens have the chance to deliberate in a highly qualified way, they probably enhance political knowledge and even democratic skills. However, potential trade-offs can also be mentioned.[17] For example, there could be a trade-off between inclusive involvement and deliberation – depending on the applied innovation and its design (e.g. Talpin in this edition). Generally up to now, interconnectedness and trade-offs are surely no 'iron laws' but a matter for empirical research. Or, as Warren (2006: 245) already observed, many trade-offs "happen under some circumstances but not under others" and it is still a challenge for empirical research to elaborate Warren's finding.

One Framework for all Innovations?

The objective of the introduction was to develop a framework for the evaluation of participatory innovations, which can be applied by the contributors. However, in terms of the variety of innovations, should the criteria and the framework not differ from innovation to innovation because different innovations might aim to solve different democratic problems? Should each innovation not be assessed according to its own goals and objectives?

The answer to this question is: no. First, it is the intention of this edition to provide a criteria-based evaluation of several innovations – not a case study approach. Second, it is in most cases hardly possible to identify clear goals of a

---

16 Some criteria will not be taken into account in this edition. Transferability, for example, is a useful criterion, but in this edition we are trying to evaluate democratic evaluations considering their impacts. And criteria such as "access to resources" or "early involvement" (see Rowe et al. 2004) are necessary for evaluating prerequisites for success. However, they cannot serve as criteria for the evaluation of the impacts of participatory innovations. Impacts and prerequisites are linked without doubt, but for a clear analysis the distinction is crucial.

17 Some authors might state that a trade-off might exist between comprehensive inclusion and effectiveness. In the wake of Schumpeter (1950) or Dahl (1994) they suspect that 'too much' participation hinders effectiveness. However, they follow a different definition of effectiveness, which includes for example the speed of decision-making. Since this is not a malaise that participatory innovations are expected to improve, this argument does not fit.

participatory procedure, because different political actors pin different hopes on an innovation. One example is Participatory Budgeting: local councils launched it with the aim of cutting local expenses and decreasing local debts. Other actors, however, were hoping to improve citizens' civic skills or to enhance meaningful participation (Sintomer et al. 2005). And some initiators of direct democratic procedures, to mention another example, intend not only to support effectiveness, but to increase deliberation (see LeDuc 2006; Setälä in this edition). Also, organizers of deliberative procedures do not only expect to improve deliberation and to enlighten citizens, but also to achieve meaningful participation (Goodin and Dryzek 2006). Most participatory procedures are expected to treat several democratic malaises and it is a task of empirical research to find out which hopes are actually fulfilled.

Table 1.2 Framework to Evaluate Participatory Innovations

Criterion	Intentions of Procedure	Possible Indicators (Examples)
Participation	Inclusive participation	Inclusive participation of affected groups and stakeholders, participation of minorities
	Meaningful participation	Agenda-setting options for participants, transformation of participants' preferences into policies
Legitimacy	Improvement of perceived legitimacy	Attitudes towards - political representatives - the political system
Deliberation	High-quality public deliberation	Rational debate, willingness to listen, respectful exchange of arguments
Effectiveness	Improvement of effectiveness	Identification of collective goals, achieving collective goals, output in line with collective interests
Democratic citizenries	Enlightenment of citizens	Improvement of knowledge, improvement of tolerance, enhanced public spiritedness

Outline of the Edition

This edition covers many European countries, which were active in the field of citizens' participation within the last decades – implementing co-governance procedures (e.g. Spain), fostering deliberative procedures (e.g. France) or improving direct democratic options drastically (Poland, Finland, Germany) (Scarrow 2001). Some of the experiences discussed in this edition are exemplary for specific regions. Participatory Budgeting, for example, became famous in the Western European Romance-speaking countries (Italy, France, and Spain) (Sintomer et al. 2006; Röcke and Putini in this edition). Accordingly these countries are discussed in this edition. Other types of innovations can be found in post-socialist democracies. Several of these rather new democracies have addressed their typical malaises of corruption and non-transparent decision-making by introducing recalls to a larger extent than older democracies (see Smith in this edition). In this publication recalls in Poland and Slovakia thus serve as examples of this general trend in post-communist countries.

Several countries are neglected in this edition. They are partly left out because they do not provide any participatory innovations and reforms, for example Greece. Other countries well-known for their participatory innovations are missing as well, i.e. Denmark, the Netherlands, and the UK.[18] Denmark became famous through the invention of the 'Danish Consensus Conferences' and a huge number of publications are already available discussing this innovation. In the Netherlands, several participatory procedures, e.g. urban 'interactive policy making', have been en vogue since the 1990s. These Dutch examples have been examined in several recent publications and are already quite well-known (Hendriks and Michels 2011; Michels 2011). Finally the UK: Since most literature on participatory innovations focuses on the English-speaking world, British examples have already been widely discussed (e.g. Geissel and Newton 2012: Hansen 2006).

Our edition takes research a step forward by presenting new empirical cases. It highlights participatory innovations in less well-known regional settings and does not intend to be a systematic coverage of all European states. The edition proceeds as follows.

---

18   Switzerland is left out since most of all publications on direct democracy focus on Switzerland anyway.

Cooperative Governance

This chapter highlights procedures of cooperative governance. Currently, Participatory Budgeting is the most famous co-governance procedure: three of the four contributions examine Participatory Budgeting in France, Germany and Italy (Röcke, Putini, Talpin); the fourth paper scrutinizes local participatory procedures in Spain (Font and Navarro).

Anja Röcke analyses Participatory Budgeting processes considering their impacts on participation and effectiveness, but also takes aspects of deliberation, citizens' enlightenment and legitimacy into account. After a short description of Participatory Budgeting and its distribution within Europe, she develops a typology of Participatory Budgeting procedures. Two cases, a French example (Poitou-Charentes) and a German example (Berlin Lichtenberg), serve as models for her analysis. The very different PB designs in both cities lead to partly diverse impacts, but partly also similar results. For example, participation was more meaningful in the French than in the German case, but in both cases the percentage of active participants was relatively small. And in both cases, as PBs are situated at the local level, links to "the overall political agenda-setting-process" at higher political levels were missing – meaningful participation and effectiveness was strictly limited to small-scale issues.

Antonio Putini evaluates four Italian cases of Participatory Budgeting (Grottammare, Modena, Novellara, Priverno). These cases were selected based on a general survey on Italian Participatory Budgeting experience because of their most heterogenic contexts. Thus the four examples provide a broad variety of designs as well as contexts and involve different findings. Inclusive and meaningful participation, deliberation, effectiveness, and citizens' enlightenment are significantly shaped by designs and contexts of co-governance procedures.

Also Julien Talpin assesses Participatory Budgeting procedures. His main questions are what quality and discursive interactions among ordinary citizens look like and under what conditions collective discussions can become deliberative. To find out he compares two Participatory Budgeting procedures, Rome Municipio XI (Italy) and Morsang-sur-Orge (in the Paris banlieue, France), because these procedures are "among the most empowered in Europe, in terms of the proportion of budget directly decided by citizens". Applying direct observation and ethnographic research he detected that the quality of deliberation was low in both procedures, or in other words, deliberation was scarce. High quality deliberation seems to require "a deep procedural organization of the discussion – small groups, systematic facilitation, etc.". Furthermore, "the emergence of disagreement" is helpful, which can then be transformed into deliberation if sufficient support is provided.

Joan Font and Clemente Navarro scrutinize one specific criterion, inclusive participation, in Spanish participatory innovations. First, they debate about the differences between participatory procedures in the different European states and explain the "Spanish case". Then they describe their research design and the cities as well as the participatory instruments under research (Neighbourhood Councils, Policy Councils, Local Agenda 21, Local Ombudsman, Participatory Budgeting and Citizen Juries). The authors checked for differences in participation with emphasis on gender, age, education, social class and children living in the household. The findings are as expected; participation in participatory procedures is biased "towards men, dissatisfied citizens, more ... involved individuals and, above all, members of associations". However, the authors do not end with descriptions of unequal participation, but try to find reasons leading to these inequalities. Based on comprehensive and in-depth empirical research they identified three causal mechanisms "responsible for the unequal outcomes of participatory processes". And, furthermore, they discuss whether and how institutional design of participatory procedures matter. Thus this article is one of the very few ones which examines participatory biases in different participatory procedures – a necessary enterprise which will hopefully have many followers.

Deliberative Procedures

Three following articles focus on deliberative democratic procedures. Two of them highlight European small-scale deliberative procedures in one southern European country, Italy (Fiket and Memoli), and one northern country, Finland (Strandberg and Grönlund). The third paper has a conceptual approach.

Irena Fiket and Vincenzo Memoli examine a Deliberative Poll held in Turin, Italy (2007). Deliberative Polls, invented by Fishkin, generally "bring together a statistical microcosm of citizens". The organizers or the Turin Deliberative Poll, however, added an additional component and arranged meetings between the participants and political decision makers. Fiket and Memoli evaluate the impact of the Turin Deliberative Poll on inclusive participation, legitimacy, quality of deliberation and citizens' enlightenment. Additionally, they analyzed the perceived legitimacy of this Deliberative Poll throughout its different phases. Some of the most surprising and interesting findings are that "participants' satisfaction with how democracy works increase(d) after deliberation" and that "the increase is undoubtedly higher after the direct interaction with decision makers". These findings are indeed novel. In contrast to most studies which could not find an increase in perceived legitimacy (see Strandberg and Grönlund in this edition) the Turin case was different. The most obvious explanation is that deliberative procedures do generally not imply direct communication with decision-makers – and that obviously this communication is the most influential part for enhancing legitimacy. This is surely an important finding for organizers of future deliberative procedures.

Kim Strandberg and Kimmo Grönlund explore a 'Virtual Polity Experiment in Citizen Deliberation' (Finland, 2008) focussing on the criteria inclusive participation (including "technical obstacles"), legitimacy, and citizens' enlightenment. Strandberg and Grönlund's experiment deals with the question, whether and how deliberation can be "made manageable in large scale societies" and apply information and communication technology to meet this challenge. Their experiment is "one of the first full-scale on-line experiments in citizen deliberation using live video (webcam streaming) and audio conducted in Europe" with several surveys at different stages of the experiment to assess the impacts of deliberation and to measure knowledge gains.[19] Their findings are "ambiguous". The experiment was rather inclusive in terms of participants, but had no impacts on perceived legitimacy and only few ramifications on citizens' enlightenment.

Most of the contributions in this edition are empirical, with one exception: Staffan Himmelroos discusses in his conceptual contribution how to measure and to operationalize deliberation. Himmelroos rightly argues that to evaluate deliberation "we need to have a good understanding of what citizen deliberation entails and what the standards of a qualitative deliberative procedure are". Accordingly, he provides us with helpful tools. Starting with a discussion of the "ideal process", mainly the Habermasian ideal speech situation, he introduces current critical comments ("too rational – too rigid?") and asks how Habermas' concept can be expanded to capture "real world deliberation". Himmelroos suggests an approach that "emphasises the underlying notion of dialog inherent in all forms of inter-subjective deliberation". To do so he complements the currently most advanced instrument for measuring deliberation, the Discourse Quality Index, with a measurement called Initiative/Response-Analysis, understanding dialog as initiatives and responses. The combination of the Discourse Quality Index with the Initiative/Response-Analysis provides a useful tool, because it covers equally well rational discourses and other "dynamics of interactive communication". We are convinced that this tool will be very helpful for future analysis of the deliberative quality of participatory innovations.

19 Since the experiment was not connected to political decision-making procedures, the criteria of meaningful participation and effectiveness could not be taken into account. This limitation is more or less in line with many studies on deliberative procedures since deliberative experiments seldom influence policies directly (e.g. Delli Carpini et al. 2004) – even if political decisions-makers are invited as in the case of the Turin Deliberative Polls.

Direct Democratic Procedures

In this part of the edition two different forms of direct democracy are scrutinized, one analysing different forms of referenda (Setälä) and the other looking at recall instruments (Smith).

Maija Setälä disentangles different forms of direct democracy and discusses their diverse advantages and disadvantages. In her contribution she asks whether direct democratic procedures enhance inclusive participation, deliberation and citizens' enlightenment. Her theoretical point of departure is deliberative democratic theory. This is a rather innovative approach, since direct democracy has rarely been scrutinized from this perspective. She illustrates that different forms of direct democracy have vastly different impacts when considering deliberation as well as inclusion. This is an important contribution because it clarifies that direct democracy can imply a wide range of impacts, depending on the specific design. Although Setälä's paper is not an empirical examination, she applies European real-life examples to illustrate her conceptual findings. Thus, she provides necessary insights for the evaluation of direct democratic procedures not published before.

Michael Smith discusses local recalls as 'old tools' for inclusive and meaningful participation in Poland and Slovakia. Recalls have been actively used in Poland and Slovakia at the local level and are "one of the most important innovations in citizen empowerment". Smith evaluates the recall process in terms of four main criteria: 1) whether citizen participation in the process is *meaningful*, 2) whether it is *inclusive*, 3) whether the recall helps restore *legitimacy*, and 4) the *effectiveness* of the recall process. His in-depth analysis is novel since research on local recalls is scarce and little is known about its impacts. Smith concludes that recall is a powerful tool for meaningful and effective participation "due to its binding outcomes". He shows that recalls are often used by poor, marginalized and minority populations. Recalls also restored perceived legitimacy of public office. Altogether recalls are "most effective in helping resolve extreme and highly divisive situations in a transparent, inclusive and legitimate manner".

E-Democracy

Since we consider e-democracy as an innovation which had raised high hopes but had soon revealed its limited potential for enhancing democracy, one article will discuss the topic. Gustav Lidén scrutinizes the 'qualities of e-democracy' and exemplifies his findings for the case of Sweden. Not surprisingly, one of his main conclusions is that e-democracy struggles with the same problems and challenges as democracy generally. E-democracy does, for example, not necessarily make participation more inclusive or meaningful; and the emergence of high-quality deliberation depends, as in the off-line world, on supporting facilitators and structures. E-democracy seems to have little impacts on citizens' enlightenment or improvement of civic skills. All in all, his study confirms former findings: E-democracy provides novel channels for information exchange, participation and communication, but its potential for improving the quality of democracy is low.

Conclusions

In the final synopses and concluding chapter Marko Joas summarizes the findings presented in this edition against the framework presented in the introduction.

Acknowledgement

The author is most grateful to Marko Joas, Michael Smith, Joan Font and especially the anonymous reviewers for valuable comments on earlier versions.

References

Almond, Gabriel A. & Sidney Verba, 1963: *The Civic Culture: Political Attitudes and Democracy in Five Nations*. Newbury Park, CA.: Sage Publications.

Abelson, Julia & Francois-Pierre Gauvin, 2006: *Assessing the Impacts of Public Participation: Concepts, Evidence and Policy Implications*. Ottawa, Canada: Canadian Policy Research Networks CPRN.

Baiocchi, Gianpaolo, 2001: Participation, Activism, and Politics: The Porto Alegre Experiment and Deliberative Democratic Theory. In: *Politics and Society* 29: 1, 43-72.

Burgess, Jacquelin & Chilvers, Jason (2006): Participatory assessment, in: *Science and Public Policy*, vol. 33, nr. 10, 713-728.

Casper, Steven & Frans van Waarden, 2005: *Innovations and Institutions*, Glos: Edward Elgar .

Chess, Caron &Kristen Purcell. 1999. Public Participation and the Environment: Do we Know What Works? In: *Environmental Science & Technology* 33:2685-2692.

Considine, Mark & Lewis Jenny M. 2007: Innovation and Innovators Inside Government: From Institutions to Networks. In: *Governance: An International Journal of Policy, Administration, and Institutions*, vol. 20, no. 4, 581-607.

Dalton, Russell J., 2004: *Democratic Challenges, Democratic Choices. The Erosion of Political Support in Advanced Industrial Democracies*. Oxford: Oxford University Press.

Dalton, Russell J., Bruce E. Cain, & Susan E. Scarrow. 2006: Democratic Publics and Democratic Institutions, in: *Democracy Transformed?*, edited by B. E. Cain, R. J. Dalton, and S. E. Scarrow. Oxford: Oxford University Press, 250-275.

Delli Carpini, Michael X., Fay Lomax Cook & Lawrence R. Jacobs, 2004: Public deliberation, discursive participation, and citizen engagement: A review of the empirical literature. In: *Annual Review of Political Science*, 7, 315-44.

Diamond, Larry & Leonardo Morlino (Hg.), 2005: *Assessing the Quality of Democracy*. Baltimore: The Johns Hopkins University Press.

Dryzek, John S., 2002: *Deliberative Democracy and Beyond*, Oxford Scholarship Online Monographs.

Easton, David, 1965: *A Systems Analysis of Political Life*. New York et al.: Wiley.

Fishkin, James S., 1995. *The Voice of the People. Public Opinion and Democracy*. New Haven, CT, CT, London, U.K.: Yale University, New Haven, CT, CT Press.

Fishkin, James & Robert C. Luskin, 2004 : Experimenting with Democratic Ideal: Deliberative Polling and Public Opinion. Paper presented at the Swiss Chair's Conference on Deliberation, European University Institute, Florence, Italy, May 21-22.

Freitag, Markus & Uwe Wagschal (ed.), 2007: Direkte Demokratie - Bestandsaufnahmen und Wirkungen im internationalen Vergleich. Berlin: LIT Verlag.

Fung, Archon, 2008: Pragmatic Conception of Democracy, paper presented at the Conference "Democratic Innovations", Feb. 2008, Berlin.

Fung, Archon, 2006: Varieties of Participation in Complex Governance, in: *Public Administration Review*, Special Issue, Dec. 2006, 66-75.

Fung, Archon. 2003: Survey Article: Recipes for Public Spheres: Eight Institutional Design Choices and Their Consequences. In: *The Journal of Political Philosophy*, vol. 11, no: 3, 338-367.

Fung, Archon & Erik Olin Wright 2001. Deepening Democracy: Innovations in Empowered Participatory Governance. In: *Politics and Society* 29, 1, 5-41.

Geissel, Brigitte, 2009: How to Improve the Quality of Democracy? Experiences with Participatory Innovations at the Local Level in Germany, in: *German Politics and Society*, Issue 93, Vol. 27, No. 4, p. 51-71.

Geißel, Brigitte, 2008: Zur Evaluation demokratischer Innovationen – die lokale Ebene, in: Heinelt, Hubert and Vetter, Angelika (Hg.): Lokale Politikforschung heute, 227-248.

Geissel, Brigitte, 2012: Democratic innovations: theoretical and empirical challenges of evaluation, in: Geissel, Brigitte and Kenneth Newton (ed.): *Evaluating Democratic Innovations*, London and New York, Routledge, 209-214

Geissel, Brigitte & Newton, Kenneth (ed.) 2012: *Evaluating Democratic Innovations*, London and New York, Routledge.

Geissel, Brigitte & Kristine Kern, 2000: Soziales Kapital und Lokale Agenda 21. Lokale umweltpolitische Initiativen in den U.S.A. In: Heinelt, Hubert and Mühlich, Eberhard (ed.), Lokale Agenda 21-Prozesse, Erklärungsansätze, Konzepte, Ergebnisse. Opladen: Leske + Budrich, 257-76.

Goodin, Robert E. & John S. Dryzek, 2006: Deliberative Impacts: The Macro-Political Uptake of Mini-Publics. In: *Politics & Society* 34: 2, 219-44.

Gundersen, Adolf G. 1995: *The Environmental Promise of Democratic Deliberation*. The University of Wisconsin Press.

Grönholm, Björn 2000: Diffusion of Models. In Joas, Marko: *Local Agenda 21 – Models and Effects: An Analysis of LA21 Activities in Finland and the Baltic Sea Region*, Åbo Akademi, Åbo, 63-86.

Habermas, Jürgen, 1973: Legitimationsprobleme im Spätkapitalismus. Frankfurt a.M.: Suhrkamp.

Habermas, Jürgen, 1992: Faktizität und Geltung, Frankfurt a.M., Suhrkamp.

Hansen, Janus, 2006: Public Participation, in: *Science and Public Policy*, vol. 33, nr. 8, 571-584.

Hendriks, Frank & Michels, Ank, 2011: Democracy Transformed? Reforms in Britain and The Netherlands (1990—2010), in: *International Journal of Public Administration*, 34:5, 307-317.

Jefferson, Thomas, 1776: Declaration of Independence,

Kriesi, Hanspeter, 2008: Direct democracy – the Swiss experience, Paper presented at the International Workshop-Conference: Democratic Innovations – Theoretical and Practical Challenges of Evaluation, WZB-Berlin, 7-9 February 2008.

LeDuc, Lawrence, 2006: Referendums and Deliberative Democracy, paper prepared for presentation at the International Political Science Association, Fukuoka, 2006.

Lijphart, Arend, 1999: *Patterns of Democracy. Government Forms and Performance in Thirty-Six Countries.* New Haven, CT, CT, London, U.K.: Yale University, New Haven, CT, CT Press.

Mansbridge, Jane, 1999: On the Idea That Participation Makes Better Citizens. In: Elkin, Stephen L. and Soltan, Karol Edward (ed.), *Citizen, Competence, and Democratic Institutions.* University Park, PA: Pennsylvania State University, 291-325.

Mathur, Nevdeep & Skelcher, Chris, 2007: Evaluating Democratic Performance, in: *Public Administration Review* March and April 2007: 228-237.

Michels, Ank, 2011: Innovations in democratic governance, in: *International Review of Administrative Sciences* 77(2): 275-293.

Mittendorf, Volker, 2008: Auswirkungen von Quoren und Themenrestriktionen bei kommunalen Bürgerbegehren im Ländervergleich, in: Vetter, Angelika (Hg.): Erfolgsbedingungen lokaler Bürgerbeteiligung, Wiesbaden: VS Verlag, S. 73-103.

Newton, Ken, 2012: Curing the democratic malaise with democratic innovations, in: Geissel, Brigitte and Kenneth Newton (ed.): *Evaluating Democratic Innovations*, London and New York, Routledge, 3-20.

OECD, 2005: Evaluating Public Participation in Policy Making, OECD Publications.

Offe, Claus (ed.), 2003: Demokratisierung der Demokratie. Diagnosen und Reformvorschläge. Frankfurt a.M., New York: Campus.

Papadopoulos, Yannis, 2004: Governance und Demokratie. In: Benz, Arthur (ed.), Governance - Regieren in komplexen Regelsystemen. Eine Einführung. Wiesbaden: VS Verlag für Sozialwissenschaften, 215-38.

Papadopoulos, Yannis & Warin, Phillippe, 2007: *European Journal of Political Research* 46, Special Issue.

Pateman, Carole: 1970: *Participation and Democratic Theory.* Cambridge et al.: Cambridge University Press.

Raymond, Leigh, 2002: Localism in environmental policy: New insights from an old case. In: *Policy Sciences* 35, 179-201.

Renn, Ortwin, Thomas Webler & Peter Wiedemann, 1995: *Fairness and Competence in Citizen Participation: Evaluating Models for Environmental Discourse.* Dordrecht, The Netherlands:

Roller, Edeltraud, 2005: *The Performance of Democracies. Political Institutions and Public Policies.* Translated by Bendix, John. Oxford: Oxford University Press.

Rowe, Gene & Lynn J. Frewer, 2004: Evaluating Public-Participation Exercises: A Research Agenda. In: *Science, Technology, and Human Values* 29, 4, 512-56.

Rowe, Gene, Roy Marsh and Lynn J. Frewer, 2004: Evaluation of a Deliberative Conference a. In: *Science, Technology, and Human Values* 29, 1, 88-121.

Scarrow, Susan E. 2001. Direct Democracy and Institutional Chance. A Comparative Investigation. In: *Comparative Political Studies* 34, 6, 651-65.

Schäfer, Armin, 2009: Alles halb so schlimm? Warum eine sinkende Wahlbeteiligung der Demokratie schadet, in: MPIfG Jahrbuch 2009-2010. Max-Planck-Institut für Gesellschaftsforschung. Köln, 5-10.

Scharpf, Fritz W. 1999. Regieren in Europa. Effektiv und demokratisch? Frankfurt a.m.: Campus.

Schumpeter, Joseph A. 1950. Kapitalismus, Sozialismus und Demokratie. Bern: A. Francke.

Setälä, Maija, 2006: On the problems of responsibility and accountability in referendums, in: European *Journal of Political Research* 45: 699-721.

Sewell, Derrick. and Susan. Philips 1979. Models for the Evaluation of public participation programmes. In: *Natural Resources Journal* 19, 337-58.

Sintomer, Yves, Carsten Herzberg and Anja Röcke (eds.), 2005: Participatory Budgeting in a European comparative approach- perspectives and chances of the cooperative state at the municila level in Germany and Europe, Final report, Volume II (Documents).

Smith, Graham, 2005: Beyond the Ballot: 57 Democratic Innovations from around the World, http://www.makeitanissue.org.uk/Beyond%20the%20Ballot.pdf.

Smith, Graham, 2009: Democratic Innovations: Designing Institutions for Citizens Participation, manuscript, to be published Cambridge University Press.

Talpin, Julien, 2012: When democratic innovations let the people decide, in: Geissel, Brigitte and Kenneth Newton (ed.): *Evaluating Democratic Innovations*, London and New York, Routledge, 184-206.

Unger, Brigitte, 2005: Problems of measuring innovative performance, in: Casper, Steven and Frans van Waarden, 2005: *Innovations and Institutions*, Glos: Edward Elgar, 19-51.

Warren, Mark E., 2006: A Second Transformation of Democracy, in: *Democracy Transformed?*, edited by B. E. Cain, R. J. Dalton, and S. E. Scarrow. Oxford: Oxford University Press: 223-249

Forms of Democratic Innovations in European Participatory Budgeting
The Examples of Poitou-Charentes (France) and Berlin Lichtenberg (Germany)

Anja Röcke

Introduction

Participatory Budgeting (PB) is widely seen as an innovative democratic procedure aiming to involve ordinary citizens in the allocation of municipal budgets (e.g. Abers 2000; Avritzer 2002; Baiocchi 2005; Fung 2011, Gret & Sintomer 2005; Smith 2009). Developed in Porto Alegre, Brazil, at the end of the 1980s, PB has since around the year 2000 spread to Europe (Sintomer et al. 2008a), where it is part of a broad movement to introduce more participatory instruments to policy-making. For Rosanvallon (2008: 301), the "development of procedures that involve citizens in the making of decisions that concern them is one of the major features of the recent evolution of democratic regimes", and many other scholars have stressed the theoretical and empirical developments and innovations induced through the spreading of participatory instruments during the last 20 years (e.g. Bacqué et al. 2005; Fung & Wright 2003; Geissel & Newton 2012; Smith 2009). Yet, one should not underestimate the parallel spreading of populist or "media" democracy (Manin 1996) and a growing disillusion with institutional democracy (e.g. Tocal & Montero 2006). Some observers have even made the diagnosis that democratic structures continue to exist only formally, but are in reality hollowed out by the dominance of economic elites (Crouch 2004). In this chapter, however, the focus lies on procedures that deliberately pursue the aim to enhance the democratic quality of policy-making. The criteria of democratic innovation developed in the introductory chapter of this book allow for an empirical and critical analysis of the degree to what the democratic intentions have been met in practice.[20]

---

20   The empirical analysis only includes the criteria of participation and effectiveness (and, to a lesser degree, deliberation). Statements in relation to the other two criteria, legitimacy and enlightened citizens, remain at the level of hypotheses, because they were not in the focus of my research on these cases (Röcke 2013).

Two cases are analyzed in detail for this undertaking: the PB processes in the French region of Poitou-Charentes and in a district of the German capital, Berlin Lichtenberg. Both examples have strong political visibility and are exceptional rather than typical cases in their respective national context;[21] they are interesting in that they allow the highlighting of different dynamics of democratic innovation, especially as regards the question of effectiveness of participation. The French process takes place in all regional high schools. All members of the high school community are invited to take part in two meetings, to develop and vote for project priorities (in the domains of culture, construction or equipment in high schools), of which the first one will then be approved and financed by the regional Parliament (in total 10 million euros per year for all high schools). Whereas the initial impetus was clearly political (the goal of a "participatory democracy"), the strongest impact so far concerned the regional administration, which has undergone an important reform process due to the participatory initiative. The other case, Berlin Lichtenberg, consists of a range of different meetings, where participants work out project priorities regarding certain municipal services. These proposals then serve as a basis of information for elected representatives in their official decision-making process, so citizens themselves do not take decisions. The underlying logic of the procedure is that of a "communicative reformulation" of representative democracy, coupled from the outset with a strong process of administrative reform.

What have been the concrete outcomes in terms of participation and effectiveness? What broader results in relation to democracy and democratic innovations can be drawn from these two examples? After an overview of participatory budgets in Europe (section 2) and the empirical analysis of the two cases (sections 3 and 4), the conclusion (section 5) will highlight two broader challenges of top-down institutionalized forms of citizen engagement: the link between "small" and "big" issues as well as the relation between administrative and democratic reform.

Participatory Budgeting in Europe

In Porto Alegre, Participatory Budgeting was co-designed by members of the Workers' Party, local city administration and local social movements in a very particular local, national and historic context at the end of the 1980s (Avritzer

---

21 For a more nuanced perspective, see Roecke 2013. The different political contexts play only a marginal role in the present investigation. For more information on this aspect, see (Röcke 2013 ; Sintomer et al. 2008a)

2002). The Porto Alegre process involves a highly complex organizational structure involving different thematic and territorial assemblies and criteria of social justice that guide the making of decisions (in restricted and open deliberative forums). It has led to far-reaching results in terms of effective political mobilization of the poor population, increased legitimacy of the political/administrative system (reduction of clientelistic structures, modernization of local administration) and increased social justice (e.g. Abers 2000; Avritzer 2009; Gret & Sintomer 2005). The great success of the procedure has found a strong echo among different types of actors around the world (party or civil society activists, foundations or large institutions like the World Bank) and has led to a worldwide diffusion process. In 2010, around 1000 cases existed worldwide, more recently also in the US, Asia and Africa.

Figure 2.1 Participatory Budgeting Across the World (2010)

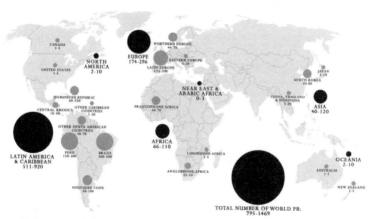

Source: Sintomer et al. (2010)

Everywhere where PB has been implemented in a new context, it shows very different procedural shapes (Sintomer et al. 2010, 2012; Wampler & Hartz-Karp 2012). In relation to Europe, the following criteria have been developed in order to determine the procedural specificity of a PB process (Sintomer et al. 2008a)[22]:

---

22 These criteria constitute a good starting point for comparative research, but can be legitimately changed in different research projects.

- it deals with financial and/or budgetary issues;
- the city level has to be involved, or a (decentralized) district with an elected body and and some power over administration;
- some power over administration;
- it has to be a repeated process;
- it must include some form of public deliberation within the framework of specific meetings/forums;
- there needs to be accountability on the output.

More than 10 years have past since the introduction of the first participatory budget institutions in Europe. The number of such institutions has grown considerably over the last few years, from only a few at the end of the 1990s to around 200 in 2009.

Figure 2.2 Number of PB Institutions in Several European Countries (1993-2005)

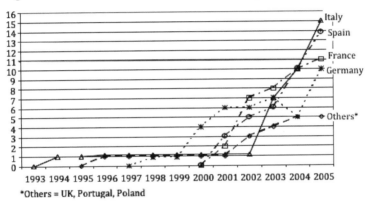

*Others = UK, Portugal, Poland

Source: Sintomer et. al. 2008a

Three broad trends have characterized this development (Röcke 2013):

1. a geographic and quantitative diffusion from France, Germany, UK, Italy, Portugal and Spain (the 'core countries'), where PB has been implemented since around the new millennium, to North (Sweden, Norway, Finland) and Eastern Europe (Poland, Bosnia, Albania) since the second half of the 2000;
2. an evolution in the type of actors supporting PB: from traditional left wing parties to conservative, liberal and green parties as well as to an increasing role of international organizations (especially in Eastern Europe);
3. a process of institutionalization (particularly in England/UK and Italy) characterized by the simultaneous great diffusion of cases and the de-radicalization of ideas and practices linked to PB (Röcke 2010; Sintomer & Allegretti 2009).

In Europe, the implementation of Participatory Budgeting is typically the result of an initiative taken by an individual, committed actor, for example a mayor, although many local, national and international diffusion networks have promoted the idea and practice of PB. The UK is so far the only country in which a "national strategy" for the introduction of this process has been developed by the (former) government (Communities and Local Government 2008). In general terms, the creation of a particular PB process is influenced by the combination of actor-related strategies and goals, the role of networks and "best practice" examples, contextual features (institutions, existing participatory practices, etc.) and ideas or "frames" of citizen participation (i.e. "participatory democracy") that actors refer to in order to justify and publicly present a political initiative (Röcke 2013). In order to identify some broad characteristics of PB processes in Europe, six ideal-type models have been developed (Sintomer et al. 2008a,b): "Porto Alegre adapted to Europe"; "Proximity Participation"; "Consultation on public finances"; "Public/private negotiation table"; "Community funds on local and city level"; "Participation of organized interests".[23]

The two examples discussed in this section of the chapter represent, respectively, a combination of "Proximity participation" with "Porto Alegre

---

23 The criteria used for the construction of these models are: the origins of the procedure (a link to existing structures or a completely new process); the organization form of meetings (thematic and/or territorial; restricted number of participants or open access; etc.); the type of discussions (content of discussions; project-based discussion or discussion about general orientations of public policy, etc.); and the role and nature of civil society (type of citizens that take part; role of citizens on the process rules, etc.).

adapted for Europe" (Poitou-Charentes) and with "Consultation on public finances" (Berlin Lichtenberg). The "proximity" model intends to create a dialogue between policy makers and citizens, confers participants with little procedural autonomy and usually lacks a formal body of rules. Meetings are most often organized at the neighborhood level and deal with small projects of micro-local interest, but can also consist of discussions about broader policy guidelines of a town; there is no ranking of projects by the participants themselves. In the model "consultation on public finances", citizen participation is part of an overall modernisation process of local bureaucracy. Here, too, participants have little procedural autonomy and there are rather informal rules for establishing priorities. Participants come together in one or several city-wide meetings and discuss (consultation, no decision-making) the overall budget priorities or the offering of services. The "Porto Alegre" model is the most far-reaching one in political and procedural terms. It consists of meetings at neighbourhood- and town level (election of delegates) and contains formalised procedural rules that specify the role and powers of citizens, who enjoy genuine procedural autonomy. Criteria of social justice exist in order to establish a list of citizens' priorities. Discussions focus on public investments and citizens.

It has to be underlined that a specific empirical case never overlaps completely with an ideal-type, but may come more or less close to one or be situated between two or more. Moreover, a specific position may change as soon as the procedural shape is modified – a process that recently took place in Poitou-Charentes. I shall start the empirical analysis with this case.

Poitou-Charentes: Participatory Democracy and/or Administrative Reform?

In France (like in most other southern European countries), the process of Participatory Budgeting has been introduced in reference to Porto Alegre. The Brazilian reference provided the idea to go beyond existing neighborhood councils and establish more comprehensive approaches to local citizen involvement. The first initiatives of Participatory Budgeting were set up by members of the French Communist Party in the Paris region in order to renew their political image and fight against their decreasing electoral support in France. From this perspective, PB was interesting as a novel mechanism with a certain radical touch, opposed to authoritarian socialism and representing a credible alternative to neo-liberal globalization. Somewhat later, members of the Socialist Party became interested in the topic of PB, which continued to develop in the country. Some of them, most notably Ségolène Royal, also tried to integrate PB into programmatic party discussions. Like other Socialist and Social Democratic parties in Europe, the Socialist Party has been struggling for years with a substantial crisis of identity and a lack of new ideas. It was also S. Royal – Socialist candidate for the 2007 Presidential elections and since 2004 President of the Poitou-Charentes Region – who selected the term participatory democracy in order to build her political program around this notion. This has played an important role for the dissemination of the concept in French public debates.

Whereas the initial enthusiasm seems somewhat in free fall today, one process is still working, and quite successfully: the "high school participatory budget" (*budget participatif des lycées*) in Poitou-Charentes. Launched by Ségolène Royal, it represents one of the most interesting cases in France. In June 2004, shortly after winning the regional elections, which allowed her to become President of the Poitou-Charentes Region, Ségolène Royal launched this project[24]. Her campaign had been carried out under the banner of "participatory democracy", with PB being one of three initiatives announced in the case of victory. Until 2011, the regional council allocated 10 million euros to the process per year, which represents roughly 10 per cent of the total budget line of 110 million euros for regional high schools. Two meetings form the core of this Participatory Budgeting process, which welcomes the whole high-school community: students, teachers, administrative and technical staff and parents.

During the first meeting, the procedural functioning is explained. Projects for improving the school are discussed in working groups and then presented to the general assembly. Thereafter, the regional technical services have the duty to evaluate the projects and estimate their costs. When further clarification is necessary, they meet with a group of volunteers from the school. During the second meeting, all projects are presented, discussed and finally voted upon (Everyone can cast ten votes). At the end of the meeting, participants fill out an evaluation form. Through the webpages and information sheets pinned up in every school, the high school community is informed about the results.

The results of the high school participatory budget in terms of *participation* and *effectiveness* are strong. First, participants decide upon concrete projects for the high schools, and the sums at stake can be considerable, reaching more than 250,000 euros per year and high school (Mazeaud 2011a). Furthermore, the influence of the participants goes beyond the projects voted for and implemented in the framework of the PB meetings. When they fit the regional priorities, the regional assembly also implements the schemes which did not receive funding within the PB process. In this way the participants have an indirect influence on the overall regional education policy (criterion of overall ef-

---

24 This section is based on different research projects and publications (Sintomer et al. 2008a; Röcke & Sintomer 2006; Röcke 2013).

fectiveness). Through this proceeding, the regional assembly has been able to introduce a stronger social agenda in the regional policy (favoring disadvantaged high schools), which is not an integral part of the participatory process due to lacking cooperation on the intra-school level (participants decide on projects for and within every single high school, but do not engage in a discussion about common allocation criteria concerning all schools). Second, participation rates have been increasing over the last years and the process can be said to be largely inclusive:

- 2005-06: 10,702 participants (7018 pupils)
- 2006-07: 14,043 participants (10,751 pupils)
- 2007-08: 15,399 participants (13,350 pupils)
- 2008-09: 17,658 participants (14,939 pupils)
- 2009-10: 23,000 participants (19,000 pupils)

These numbers are impressive. However, the human, organizational and financial resources for realizing the process are important; moreover, some school directors oblige students to take part in meetings that take place during regular school hours, which is certainly one reason why numbers have been increasing during the last years. In addition, the procedural power of participants is very limited, as they have no direct influence on the "rules of the game" (only indirectly through the evaluation forms and several extra evaluation meetings that members of the regional staff have organized).

To what degree the participatory budget process has had an impact on the overall functioning and the power hierarchies within the 93 high schools[25] – an aspect that can be summarized under the criterion of the overall *effectiveness* of the process – is difficult to evaluate (Röcke 2013: chap. 7). One important factor for explaining the success or failure within the institution is the degree of support by school directors and teachers. Some are convinced of it and try to inspire the regular functioning throughout the year by the participatory principles; others simply tolerate it or use it in a merely strategic sense for the funding of expensive projects (Mazeaud 2011a). In this case, however, they have to cope with the process during the meetings. For instance, they need to convince the majority of participants of the usefulness of their project in order to get enough votes for it.

---

25 For instance, the quality of the discussions and the relation between the different groups working in high schools in the "regular" meetings taking place all over the year (administrative council etc.).

As to the criteria of *"enlightened citizens"*, it appears from personal participant observation that the participants, who take part on a regular basis, develop not only considerable knowledge of the process, but also of the regional policy and programs. Many of these, but by far not all, are often already active members of the high school community (e.g. student or parent representatives). The structural problem lies in the fact that they stay no more than three years in the high schools. The BPL process can represent an initiation to political/voluntary activism in the school or beyond, but so far no research has shown to what extent students could indeed improve their democratic skills through the process. A further problem lies in the fact that the content of the curriculum is determined by the National Ministry of Education - the region has no means to integrate the topic into the school syllabus.

The *legitimacy* of the procedure is considerably high, although no statistical data exists on this issue. The serious organization of a process that has clear rules and results has convinced many of those who initially were rather skeptical or openly opposed to a procedure implemented in a top-down manner by the region (mainly directors, teachers and regional administrative staff). Moreover, the procedure has shown very strong results in a domain that was not in the focus of the organizers: the regional administration itself. The implementation of the high school PB has hit the regional administration like a bomb. Critical debate and the need for public justification during the participatory meetings replaced a system where the members of the educational community had to rely on the decisions taken by the school internal management. This enabled the regional staff responsible for the process to discover the real situation, needs and problems within the schools as well as the great differences that exist between them. In terms of administrative modernization, which also relates to the overall effectiveness of the procedure, four main results can be highlighted. This is, firstly, the creation of direct communication channels between service users and regional staff. Second, one can mention a better control of public finances, which is mainly a result of the fact that cost calculations have been made transparent. Third, concrete measures aimed at ameliorating the deficiencies discovered through the process have been developed (e.g., cultural or nutrition programs). Fourth, it seems that "participation" has become part of the professional culture within the administration, at least for an increasing number of servants. Initial criticism (as regards to extra workload) was reduced because the regional employees could learn from past experiences in the evaluation of projects. Moreover, new and politicized officers have been hired who supported the process from the outset (Mazeaud 2011a). And finally, the administrative structure was reorganized in order to strengthen its functioning.

This process of transformation is still under way, but has probably been much quicker than in other places. The most recent development constitutes the introduction of an additional level of participation, organized twice in 2011

(Mazeaud 2011b). It consisted of a regional meeting where representatives of every high school came together in order to develop and discuss criteria for the allocation of different amounts of money per institution depending on the overall level of needs. The selected criteria were the quality of buildings and equipment, the geographic localization (rural or urban), and social background of pupils (low versus medium or high). Every school received a certain number of points for these criteria and the corresponding amount: 30,000 euros, 66,000 euros, or 150,000 euros at the February meeting; 45,000 euros, 71,500 euros, or 90,000 euros at the November meeting.[26] This development constitutes a move away from the "proximity" towards the "Porto Alegre" model of PB presented above (section 2), but it needs to be seen if this type of more complex process will be organized again. In the last years Royal experienced some important political defeats at the national level that weakened her position and influence.[27] In addition, two people who had been crucial for the Participatory Budgeting process in the regional administration left in 2012. The future development is open.

Berlin-Lichtenberg: Between Budget Consultation and Administrative Modernization

The Lichtenberg process differs considerably from the French one. Berlin was the first city in Germany where civil society activists, influenced by the Porto Alegre model and a huge corruption scandal in the German capital, brought Participatory Budgeting on the political agenda – until then, German Participatory Budgeting institutions had been introduced by organizations and ideas linked to the New Public Management reform agenda and in relation to the city of Christchurch in New Zealand (that had won a prize for its broad reform program in the domain of local citizen participation and public administration in 1993). The context of the 1990s, characterized by a very strong crisis of municipal finances and increased emphasis on participatory instruments (partly in resonance to the civic movement in former East Germany that led to the collapse of GDR), plays an important role for the implementation of Participatory Budgeting in Germany. In this context, an important diffusion channel was the best practice network "cities of the future", created by different organizations

---

26 See http://bpl.poitou-charentes.fr.

27 2007 presidential elections against Sarkozy; 2008 PS party president elections against Martine Aubry; 2012 parliamentary elections against a dissident candidate in the department of Charentes-Maritime

involved in the introduction of the New Public Management agenda in the German context. The process criteria developed by these organizations – information, consultation, accountability – influenced the implementation of participatory budget institutions in Germany (Bertelsmann Stiftung et al. 2001; Bertelsmann Stiftung, Innenministerium des Landes Nordrhein-Westfalen 2004). Most, if not all, PB examples of the first period (roughly 1998 to 2004) share similar traits, which come close to the ideal-type "consultation of public finances". They are designed as purely consultative devices: civil servants provide information, citizens discuss and political representatives make the decision.

The Lichtenberg procedure launched a new period of PB, characterized by a much stronger emphasis on the actual *participation* of citizens and the possibilities of *deliberation*, both goals being pursued, amongst others, by new information technologies. In Berlin, civil society and Left-wing party activists managed to convince a member of the Federal Institute of Political Education, as well as the newly elected mayor of Lichtenberg, Christina Emmrich to support the process. The district mayor (belonging to the post-Communist "Left" party) managed to gain the support of the district council for the initiative and make it a central part of her new political project of developing the district into a "citizens' town" (*Bürgerkommune*), thus becoming the German *pendant* to Ségolène Royal's quest for a participatory democracy in French Poitou-Charentes[28]. Moreover, the PB initiative was integrated into a city-wide, administrative reform program aiming to increase the effectiveness and efficiency of public spending in a context of extreme financial squeeze (currently the debts rise to over 60 billion euros). The budgeting process in the district of Berlin Lichtenberg has been the first process in a big German city, although other large towns have since then followed (e.g. Cologne).

On September 24th 2005, the first meeting of the Participatory Budgeting in Lichtenberg took place (the following description of the process in widely based on Röcke 2013: chap.8, including direct citations). Representatives of the district Parliament signed a self-binding declaration about the non-partisan character of the procedure and their willingness to consider seriously the participants' proposals (Brangsch & Brangsch 2006: 70). A newspaper commented the event with the heading "Berlin becomes a citizen Republic", re-

---

28   The city of Berlin has a particular political and institutional structure: it is a city and a federal state. Therefore, its administration and government are based on two levels, the one of the districts and the one of the city (federal state) as a whole. The districts of the city are like municipalities, although with less powers and competences. Moreover, they cannot raise taxes, but receive all their funds from the city government; these add up to around three to four billion euros per year, which is about 20% of the city budget of 20 billion euros.

flecting the high political expectations linked to this new procedure and to the absolute majority of the "Left" party in the district (Sintomer et al. 2008a: 182).

The Lichtenberg participatory budget functions as a cycle all over the year. It involves municipal services which the district directly controls and delivers[29], adding up to a sum of about 30 million euros (roughly six percent of the overall district budget of about 555 million euros, in 2008)[30]. This money is not an additional sum to spend, but represents the overall "controllable" budget of the district. This is the reason why participants are not simply encouraged to outline proposals that imply additional costs, but also to make propositions whereby the district can save money, or which can be realized on a cost-neutral basis. Since 2008 (PB process 2010), the field of competences for citizens has been enlarged to include also the planning of construction investments in the district (involving four million euros in 2012 and 2013 respectively) as well as neighborhood projects provided by various voluntary associations and churches, even though financed by the district.

The participation cycle officially starts in May-June with a public central citizen assembly of around two hours organized in a public building[31]. It represents a kick-off meeting for the new round, as well as the final step of the previous one. All inhabitants are invited to attend and are welcomed by the district mayor. During the meeting, official representatives of the district executive and administration explain the core elements of the procedure and inform the participants about the state of decision about and implementation of proposals put forward during the previous year(s) (including projects that have been integrated in the official decision-making process and those that have not). Via a tracking number that is assigned to every scheme, participants can also control the current state of decision about single proposals via the internet.

---

29 All municipalities deliver "controllable" and non-controllable services. The district executive can only influence the first type of services. In Lichtenberg, these are public libraries, the music school, an adult education centre, cultural services of all municipal culture institutions, support of health, support of children and young people, voluntary services for elderly people, support of physical education, maintenance of green spaces and play grounds, planning of green spaces, support of local economy.

30 In this sum, costs for personnel are included, so that the actual sum of money to be spent is much smaller. Roughly 14% of the overall budget is spent for personnel (2008).

31 The following description is based on the 2010 process model, put down in the "Framework document for the participatory budget in Berlin Lichtenberg 2010" (Bezirksamt Lichtenberg von Berlin 2008). I attended the meetings of the cycle 2007-08, when the process included still a final voting meeting.

Starting from January, the residents of Lichtenberg can already make proposals for concrete schemes: by a letter or via the internet. The written proposals are presented at the neighborhood assemblies (September-October). Moreover, they are fed into the internet discussion; the participants of the internet platform can also put forward proposals of their own. In November, the internet participants establish a priority list (the written and their own proposals taken together) of 10 schemes. A second priority list is created at the decentralized meetings.

The decentralized meetings, organized in the 13 areas of the district, constitute a direct discussion platform among citizens, and between district policy makers and residents. Like the central kick-off meeting, they are well publicized in advance (internet, public institutions, flyers, etc.), child care is provided during every public meeting and a sign language interpreter is present. At the beginning of the occasion, the moderators present the written proposals put forward so far and propose, on this basis, the formation of thematic working/discussion groups. Participants are encouraged to present other topics, which might lead to the formation of other discussion groups. During the following group discussions, and usually moderated by a neighborhood manager or member of the local social-cultural centre, participants are encouraged to develop proposals and to comment on existing ones. Back at the open assembly, each group moderator presents the proposals. The last part of the meeting (there is no general discussion about the proposals of the working groups) contains the selection of priorities by participants. All project proposals are written down on sheets of paper, which are pinned up on several boards in the room. Every participant is given five points that he or she can distribute freely between the different projects. The official framework document (Bezirksamt Lichtenberg 2008: 12) is clear about the fact that this is not a voting process, but represents the "expression of opinion" through participants. In the end, all votes are counted and the results written down. Five projects with the highest score (and a minimum number of 25 points) pass to the next step.

During November-December, the five priorities of every district assembly, as well as the top10 from the internet vote, are sent to 50,000 randomly selected households. The participants of this survey also establish their priorities through the distribution of five points. In January, all three priority lists are given to the district council (BVV). Between February and April, the Parliamentary committees (public meetings) deal with these proposals and decide which ones to integrate in the budget plan. During the central citizen assembly of May-June, politicians publicly justify their choices (process of accountability); in the autumn the district council sets the budget plan for the next year. From January onwards, the district administration will begin implementing the projects. Projects implemented so far have been, for example, the protection and maintenance of park benches, the care for and new plantation of trees along street borders, and the acquisition of Vietnamese books and DVDs in two public libraries (there is a Vietnamese community in Lichtenberg). These are small-scale projects that reflect the priorities of the participants[32].

Participation has been increasing during the last years, but still covers less than 1 per cent of the population (numbers include participants at the local meetings, the internet dialogue and the household survey)[33]:

- 2007: 4,048 participants
- 2008: 4,140 participants
- 2009: 4,150 participants
- 2010: 5,794 participants
- 2011: 8,130 participants
- 2012: 7,989 participants
- 2013: 10,488 participants

Whereas the process involves more young people and members of minority groups, the overall participation is similar to other cases in Germany (Herzberg 2009). The organizers have increasingly made use of specific measures for increasing participation rates (see Röcke 2013: chapter 8). These are, for instance, the personal invitation of a randomly selected group (10 per cent) of the population as well as the organization of preparatory meetings to the neighborhood meetings, of which the number has been augmented from initially five to thirteen.

As to the question of *effective participation*, the role of the citizens is clearly limited in Berlin Lichtenberg (ibid.). Participants cannot take decisions (despite the newly introduced small sum for neighborhood projects) and the district Parliament remains the institution deciding autonomously "if, and if yes which" projects of the participatory budget process should receive funding (Bezirksamt Lichtenberg von Berlin (2009:1). In another document, it is clearly stated that "citizens suggest and discuss how the money should be used; politicians decide which suggestions will be included in the budget plan" (Bezirksamt Lichtenberg von Berlin 2008). The advantages of the process are described in terms of an "information gain" for citizens and elected representatives, of a "more efficient and effective use" of public resources that respect the "needs" of the population, and of a process that is based on a "public debate about needs and resources" and thereby enables greater "transparency of budg-

---

32 It is not possible to estimate the number of projects that have been realized through the PB process. Many answers in the official accountability documents specify the activities carried out by the district administration in the domain at stake (libraries, parks, etc.), but not to what extent this is related to, or even a result of, the participation procedure.

33 http://www.buergerhaushaltlichtenberg.de/site/pictures/2013_daten_%20 und_fakten_bueha2013_endfassung.pdf.

etary decisions" (Bezirksamt Lichtenberg 2008: 3-4). One key for understanding this orientation is related to the fact that the PB process involves all services the district is controlling – and not a limited percentage of the budget (10% of the total sum in the French case). Moreover, no political actor has so far had the will, or at least the possibility, to provide citizens with more direct or de facto decision-making competences. It is difficult or even impossible to measure the exact degree to which citizens' proposals have been transformed in official decisions by official representatives. In any case, the PB process in Lichtenberg (as in most German examples) does not bring in additional funds to the district, which is still confronted with a situation of financial squeeze; to put the priority on one aspect (e.g. libraries) implies less money for other areas (e.g. public music school)[34]. "Participatory Budgeting" in this case therefore means that the whole allocation process has been rendered more transparent and open to citizens' proposals, but not, as in Poitou-Charentes, that citizens do directly make decisions about (parts of) a budget.

The Lichtenberg process model was meant to include more moments of common *deliberation* than other German PB processes. Neither in the Internet forums, however, where comments are often not related to each other (Herzberg 2009), or in the public meetings I attended, there has been a real deliberation process. There was a lack of guidance and criteria that would enable participants to engage in a real discussion process about the value of each project in relation to the needs and problems in their local area or the whole district. Like in Poitou-Charentes, no figures are available as to the question of *citizens' enlightenment* and *perceived legitimacy*. It seems convincing that those participants who are really "part of the game" and come to various meetings will increase their knowledge about the process and about district politics. Whether this will enhance their broader democratic skills is an open question. Research in Europe has shown, for instance, that the introduction of PB institutions does not automatically lead to increased participation in local elections (Sintomer et al. 2008a). Compared to the high school PB, the legitimacy of the Berlin process is more fragile, because results are much more indirect as in the French case (consultation instead of direct decision-making). This is probably why the organizers have enlarged the field of activity to areas in which participants do have the possibility to decide upon small issues (the introduction of a small neighborhood fund). Moreover, there is a tendency to create stronger links to existing neighborhood structures, i.e. to

---

34 Due to the ongoing crisis of municipal finances in Germany, several recent examples of PB explicitly focus on PB as a process to provide legitimacy for difficult decisions: cost reductions. It is noteworthy that citizens are recognised as legitimate for making savings, but not for spending money.

"root" the procedure in local settings, which is why the process has come closer to the "proximity participation" model.

Overall, the procedure constitutes a platform for information exchange and debate between citizens and policy makers. It increased the transparency of public spending in the district and included the voice of ordinary citizens in the official budget process. The degree to which this really happens, however, depends on the willingness of elected politicians. In addition, civil servants can develop a better "standing" in society in that they can clarify their possibilities of action (Röcke 2013). After seven years of existence the procedure appears fairly established, but continues to be developed further. In 2012, the newly elected mayor (SPD) initiated an evaluation of the process together with citizens, politicians, civil servants and members of the Federal Institute of Political Education in order to cope with existing problems. In the meanwhile (April 2013), the process received a prize by the Theodor Heuss foundation, because it represents "new ways" for including ordinary citizens in the definition and spending of the local budget.[35] The conditions for deepening the participatory dimension (in comparison to the administrative reform aspect) of the process remain, however, quite important: continued strong political and administrative support to ensure a broad process of accountability; further emphasis on broad and inclusive participation (internet, meetings with small organizations and big open assemblies) and very clear communication about the concrete results of the PB procedure.

Conclusion

As the last two sections have shown, the processes of Berlin Lichtenberg and Poitou-Charentes represent quite different adaptations of the Brazilian PB model and different approaches to democratic innovation. In Lichtenberg, in the context of important financial squeeze and overall administrative reform, the overall *rationale* of the process is that of a "participative modernization" (participation is one vector of an overall administrative reform process) with the increasing importance of proximity participation (creating communication and participation links to neighborhood and community initiatives and programs). As has been shown, the priorities of participants have partly been considered by political representatives (partly not), which is why some of them "informed" the service offer in the district. There are, however, no clear rules

---

35 See: http://www.buergerhaushalt-lichtenberg.de/blog/der-buergerhaushalt-lichtenberg-erhaelt-die-theodor -heuss-medaille.

of how the citizens' priorities are fed into the official decision-making circle. It depends on the willingness and the priorities of politicians to use the information gathered in the different participatory meetings, the online discussion and questionnaires, although they need to publicly justify their choices. The deliberative quality of the meetings varies and depends largely on the way discussions are moderated. As to the question of the overall effectiveness, the scope of the procedure is limited to the discussion of "controllable" funds and does not include the overall political priorities in the district. The use of small-scale assemblies, district meetings, online forums and questionnaires allow politicians and civil servants to gain insights into peoples' priorities on the projects at stake, but the precise impact of these priorities is difficult, perhaps impossible, to evaluate.

In the Region of Poitou-Charentes, on the contrary, participants have a much more direct impact on decisions, i.e. participation is more effective. The voted first priorities of every meeting are considered by political representatives. In the past, politicians even went one step further and, at least partly, used the information and projects developed in the participatory meetings for the spending of (parts of) the overall budget. Here, the participatory process has clearly contributed to the identification of more general collective goals and their realization. Like in Berlin Lichtenberg, however, the influence of citizens on the procedural rules and the wider political agenda-setting of the district or region are limited and depend on the good-will of the organizers. Moreover, it needs to be seen in how far the regional level of participation that aims to strengthen the participatory as well as social dimensions of the process, will continue to exist.

Both instruments shed light on some broader challenges to democratic innovation, which are discussed briefly now in order to conclude these reflections. These challenges are the link between "small issues" and "big questions" and the relation between administrative and democratic reform. One core question of many participatory instruments is the meaningful articulation of small issues, for instance problems or needs in single neighborhoods (people are most easily mobilized on these questions[36]), and the wider political agenda-setting process. If participation is restricted to very local questions without any link to the broader political agenda, the risk is high that the participatory process becomes only a "legitimatory cloak" for a political system that remains at a great distance from the needs and priorities of local people. In Berlin Lichtenberg, for instance, the PB process not only remains distant to district wide concerns and decisions, but even more so in relation to the political

---

36 Notable exceptions in this regard have been national experiences with citizen assemblies, for instance on electoral reform (Lang 2007).

agenda of the federal state level and, for instance, its important privatization policies. In the middle– and long run, the privatization of formerly publicly owned services will reduce the influence of democratically elected bodies as well as of institutionalized forms of citizen engagement. This is why local participatory initiatives should somehow be linked to the overall political agenda-setting process.

Second, the link between administrative and political reform is important. In both cases discussed here, the role of administrative reform was a central piece in the implementation of the participatory approach, although the starting point was different. In Berlin, the existing process of administrative modernization was reinforced and complemented with a stronger emphasis on citizen participation; in Poitou-Charentes, the set-up of a participatory procedure led to an important reform activity in the regional administration. These examples suggest that a process of top-down democratic innovation will only have an effect on the wider political and administrative system if (parts of) the administrative structure is modernized in order to enable an informed, transparent and meaningful participatory process. This is why Sintomer, Herzberg and Röcke (2008a) put forward the hypotheses of an "elective affinity" that exists between citizen involvement and administrative modernization, which means that both procedures mutually reinforce each other.

The two cases discussed here, as many others, offer no answers to structural democratic problems (e.g. the increasing abstention of low-income groups from the political process), but they are one important part within a general strategy towards creating a more open, transparent and participatory public sphere (Röcke 2013).

References

Abers, R. (2000). *Inventing Local Democracy: Grassroots Politics In Brazil.* Boulder, London, Lynne Rienner Publishers.

Avritzer, L. (2002). *Democracy And The Public Space In Latin America.* Princeton, Oxford, Princeton University Press.

Avritzer, L. (2009). *Participatory Institutions In Democratic Brazil.* Baltimore, John Hopkins University Press.

Baquee, M.-H., H. Rey, Y. Sintomer, Eds. (2005). La Démocratie Participative, Un Nouveau Paradigme De L'action Publique ? Gestion De Proximité Et Démocratie Participative. Une Perspective Comparée. Paris, La Découverte.

Baiocchi, G. (2005). Militants And Citizens. The Politics Of Participatory Democracy In Porto Alegre. Stanford, Stanford University Press.

Bertelsmann-Stiftung, Hans-Böckler-Stiftung, Kgst., Eds. (2001). Der Bürgerhaushalt - Ein Handbuch Für Die Praxis. Gütersloh.

Bertelsmann-Stiftung And Landesregierung Nordrhein-Westfalen, Eds. (2004). Kommunaler Bürgerhaushalt. Ein Leitfaden Für Die Praxis. Gütersloh.

Bezirksamt Lichtenberg Von Berlin (2008a). Rahmenkonzeption Zum Bürgerhaushalt In Berlin-Lichtenberg Ab 2010. Berlin, Bezirksamt Lichtenberg Von Berlin.

Bezirksamt Lichtenberg Von Berlin (2009a). Drucksachen Der Bezirksverordnetenversammlung Lichtenberg Von Berlin, Dr/1201/Vi, 26.2.2009.

Brangsch, P. And L. Brangsch (2006). Weshalb? Wieso? Warum? Argumente Für Den Bürgerhaushalt. Berlin, Kommunalpolitisches Forum E.V., Berlin.

Communities And Local Government (2008). *Giving More People A Say In Local Spending. Participatory Budgeting: A National Strategy.* London, Communities And Local Government Publications.

Crouch, C. (2004). *Post-Democracy*, Oxford, Oxford University Press.

Fung, A. And E. O. Wright, Eds. (2003). Deepening Democracy - Institutional Innovations In Empowered Participatory Governance. London, New York, Verso Books.

Fung, A. (2011) Reinventing Democracy In Latin America (Review Essay), *In: Perspectives On Politics*, 9(4), P. 857-71.

Geissel, B. And K. Newton (Eds.) (2012). *Evaluating Democratic Innovations. Curing The Democratic Malaise?* London And New Yorck, Routledge.

Gret, M. And Y. Sintomer (2005). *The Porto Alegre Experiment*, London, New York, Zed Books.

Herzberg, C. (2009). Von Der Bürger- Zur Solidarkommune. Lokale Demokratie In Zeiten Der Globalisierung, Hamburg, Vsa.

Lang, A. (2007). But Is It For Real? The British Columbia Citizens' Assembly As A Model Of State-Sponsored Citizen Empowerment. *In: Politics & Society* 35(1), P. 35-69.

Manin, B. (1996). Les Principes Du Gouvernement Représentatif. Paris, Flammarion.

Mazeaud, A. (2011a). Le Budget Participatif Des Lycées: Un Instrument De Justice Sociale? *In :* Y. Sintomer And J. Talpin (Eds.) La Démocratie Participative Au-Delà De La Proximité. Le Poitou-Charentes Et L'échelle Régionale. Rennes, Presses Universitaires De Rennes, P. 57-74.

Mazeaud, A. (2011b). Un Saut D'échelle Vers La Justice Sociale, *In:* Territoires, Juin-Juillet 2011, P. 28-29.

Röcke, A. (2010). Le Développement Des Budgets Participatifs En Grande Bretagne. *In:* Généalogie Des Dynamiques Participatifs Contemporaines. M.-H. Bacque And Y. Sintomer (Eds.). Paris, Adels/Yves Michel.

Röcke, A. (2013, Forthcoming). Framing Citizen Participation. Participatory Budgeting In France, Germany And The United Kingdom. Basingstoke And New York, Palgrave Macmillan.

Röcke, A. And Y. Sintomer (2006). Il Bilancio Partecipativo Dei Licei Del Poitou-Charentes: Verso Una Democrazia Partecipativa?", *In:* Democrazia E Diritto, 44 (4), P. 57-70.

Rosanvallon, P. (2008). La Légitimité Démocratique. Impartialité, Réflexivité, Proximité. Paris, Seuil.

Sintomer, Y., C. Herzberg, A. Röcke. (2008a). Les Budgets Participatifs En Europe. Des Services Publics Au Service Du Public. Paris, La Découverte. [English Version Forthcoming]

Sintomer, Y., C. Herzberg & A. Röcke. (2008b). Participatory Budgeting In Europe: Potentials And Challenges", *In:* International Journal Of Urban And Regional Research, 32 (1), P. 164-178.

Sintomer, Y., Herzberg, C. & G. Allegretti (With The Collaboration Of A. Röcke) (2010). Learning From The South: Participatory Budgeting Worldwide – An Invitation To Global Cooperation (Bonn: Inwent Ggmbh, Service Agency Communities In One World), http://www.service-Eine-Welt.De/Images/Text_Material-2152.Img.

Sintomer, Y., Herzberg, C., Röcke, A. & G. Allegretti (2012). Transnational Models Of Citizen Participation: The Case Of Participatory Budgeting, *In: Journal Of Public Deliberation*, 8(2), Article 9, http://www.Publicdeliberation.Net/Jpd/Vol8/Iss2/Art9.

Sintomer, Y., Röcke, A. & J. Talpin (2013). Participatory Democracy or 'Proximity' Democracy? The 'High School Participatory Budget' in Poitou-Charentes, France *In:* Participatory Budgeting in Asia and Europe. Key Challenges of Participation. Y. Sintomer, R. Traub-Merz, J. Zhang (Eds.). Basingstoke And New Yorck, Palgrave Macmillan, P. 245-259.

Smith, G. (2009). Democratic Innovations: Designing Institutions For Citizen Participation. Cambridge, Cambridge University Press.

Tokal & Montero (Eds.) (2006) (Eds.). Political Disaffection In Contemporary Democracies. Social Capital, Institutions, And Politics. London And New York, Routledge.

Wampler And Hartz-Karp (Eds.) (2012). The Spread Of Participatory Budgeting Across The Globe: Adoption, Adaptation, And Impacts, *In:* Special Issue Of The *Journal Of Public Deliberation*, 8(2).

Weise, S. (2007). Bürgerhaushalt In Berlin. Das Bürgerhaushaltsprojekt Des Bezirkes Lichtenberg. Münster, Lit.

Participatory Instruments and Democratic Innovation
Evaluating Four Italian Cases of Participatory Budgeting

Antonio Putini

Introduction

The ordinary political landscape, with particular reference to so-called "consolidated democracy", has produced a series of phenomena, for example the mistrust of citizens towards their representatives, which emphasizes an alarming gap not only between the political and social characteristics that shape democracies, but also between descriptive and normative meanings of the same regimes.

In such democratic regimes, many scholars have pointed at an increasing qualitative crisis, which can be summarized as the emergence of a *post-democratic model* (Crouch 2005), the presence of *"rhetorical democracies"* (Canfora 2007) or *"the failing to keep their democratic promises"* (Bobbio 1995).

Considering this and the progressive degeneration of Western democratic regimes, several authors, such as Patenam (1970), Macpherson (1980), Barber (1984) and, more recently, Habermas (1996), Dryzek (1990), and Ackerman (1991) have expressed their theoretical schemes which are based on the concepts of participation and deliberation.

In such a climate, Participatory Budgeting can be seen as a democratic instrument able to provide new ways of involving citizens in the definition of the local political agenda and the ensuing of public policies. By starting a deliberative process focused on the main budgeting entries among representatives, citizens and local institutions, this instrument has been able to generate positive effects not only in the *governance* dimension, but also in our value system and inside the prescriptive meanings that constitute the concept of democracy.

Among the five dimensions presented in the introduction to evaluate a democratic innovation – participation, deliberation, effectiveness, enlightenment and legitimacy – our analysis focuses on the four first ones.

Participatory Budgeting

By analyzing numerous Latin American cases, scholars such as Allegretti (2001), Harnecker (1999), Avritzer (2006), de Sousa Santos (2003) and Abers

(2000) have confirmed many elements that point towards a positive solution of the malaises of contemporary democracy, above all in their local forms: by introducing such a democratic innovation, for example, local governments in South America have been able to strengthen their legitimacy, to start a more equal distribution of local resources so as to reduce the existent gap between the highest and lowest social classes, and to improve the civil and participative culture of their inhabitants.

In fact, among the so-called "deliberative arenas" (Bobbio, 2002: 5-29), Participatory Budgeting is the only form of extending the role of citizens' participation, and offering a real possibility of change to the normal decision-making process within local administration. This is because Participatory Budgeting (PB) is an inclusive method of deciding upon the use of the investments of a municipality's annual budget. We can generally define it as "*a mechanism that allows citizens to decide, or contribute in to deciding, how and in which way to allot public assets*" [my translation] (Cabannes 2007: 20).

According to Gensro and de Souza Santos, PB is "a direct democracy process through which people can debate and decide upon public budget and public policies. The citizen does not limit his/her participation to the vote, but goes even further all the way to the decision and the checking action of the public management (…) for these reasons PB connects together representative and direct forms of democracy" (Gensro, de Sousa Santos 2002: 115).

Leonard Avritzer (2006: 624) aptly summarizes the main characteristics of this policy-making instrument. According to him, the main aspects of PB are:

- the sovereignty which the majority gives to a body of public assemblies that act respecting universal principles of participation;
- the special mix of different elements, which combine participatory and direct rules with representative standards, such as the presence of city-councilmen and delegates, elected by and among citizens;
- the possibility, for the citizens who participate, to modify the annual code by which the instrument can take place;
- the chance for the population to change the normal distribution criteria of public goods, so as to reach a better allocation of the resources from an equity point of view.

From a procedural point of view, we can describe PB as "processes with which citizens, as individuals or civic organizations, can voluntarily and constantly contribute to the decision-making process of their local government throughout a series of public assemblies called with the presence of city-hall authorities" (Goldfrank 2006: 4).

Case Studies

Our field study concerns four cases of Participatory Budgeting carried out in four Italian municipalities: Grottammare, Modena, Novellara and Priverno. The first municipality is a small town (about 14 thousand inhabitants) located in the Marche region; it is known to be the first Italian experiment of Participatory Budgeting, started in 1994, even if its initial procedure was less structured than the ones developed in Porto Alegre during the same years[i]; Modena and Novellara are both located in the Emilia region: Modena is a medium-size city (180,000 inhabitants), while the population of Novellara is the same as that of Grottammare. These two municipalities are situated in a region characterized by high levels of participation, both political and social: the entire area is known as the "region of the red sub-culture", a territory in which the left wing – and in particular what remains of the Italian Communist Party (PCI) – still shows its heritage in terms of social customs, economic behaviours and political tradition. Priverno is a small town of about 14 thousand residents located in the South of the Lazio region, with a hybrid political past, swinging between Socialist interest and Christian Democrat heritage, merged together in the Berlusconi political era.

The selection of case studies was made after a first general survey in which we tried to trace a map of Italian Participatory Budgeting experiences by using several sources such as scientific reviews and studies, newspapers, web sites and direct participation in the main conferences and public meetings concerning this theme. The period of data collection ended in the second half of 2007.

After examining the available cases, we chose the ones listed above because of their heterogeneous context variables, which can be summarized as follows:

- Temporal duration of the experiment (which can affect the democratic innovation through its institutionalisation, i.e. by changing a temporary tool into a stable process) (Wampler 2007);
- Political majority (Grottammare is a case of electoral lists without any direct relationship with existing political parties; Priverno is a unique case with a right-wing coalition; Modena and Novellara are both expressions of the aforementioned "Red Sub-culture" political area, represented by the left-wing parties);

In this way, it has been possible to undertake a broad analysis, which we have tried to adapt to the specific evaluation framework of this book.

The analysis was carried out using three methods, which are usually connected with the qualitative approach of social sciences:

- Content analysis of documents and administrative data, elaborated by the four municipalities;

- Direct observation of eight Participatory Budget Assemblies;
- Interviews with Privileged Witnesses who took part in the participative cycle;

Documents and data enabled the reconstruction of the formal features of both the participatory budget itself (shaping, duration, number of participants, proposals, financial resources) and the general context in which it was implemented (economic texture, political context, social and demographic indicators, type of Civil Society).

Direct observation of assemblies has been particularly useful for an in-depth understanding of the practical execution of this instrument. In fact, due to direct observation, it has been possible to outline the effective deliberative setting of each meeting and to check its correspondence with what the interviewees have told us: the presence, and the role, of mediators; the way in which citizens took part in the assembly (just as a common audience, or with a real chance of taking the floor? What kinds of arguments were usually brought up, and were they attached to personal interest or to a more common interest?); the effective role of representatives and civil servants; the effective shape of the deliberating moment (e.g. just voting or with a real debating/discursive moment before reaching a resolution?).

Finally, the interviews became a tool for an in-depth investigation and analysis of the specific points of view of the process embraced by each category of the participants. As "Privileged Witnesses" were considered the members of those groups who play a seminal role in the procedure:

- the assemblies' spokespersons represent the city: they are the "voice" of the citizenry, not only by participating in the assemblies, but also by knowing the indirect moments of the process, such as those represented by the feasibility studies made during the meetings with politicians and civil servants);
- the Mayor or the councillor who promotes the initiative;
- the parties' representatives (belonging both to the government and to the opposition) might be the "wings" of this process, not only due to their will to take part in and to promote the PB that could allow a wider range of action and broader participation, but also because they are the final judges of the whole process as they must approve or reject the PB proposals;
- civil servants who deal particularly with this instrument (i.e. the employees of economic and financial offices: they are the

"technical" arm of the process, and thus represent also the technocratic power within the participative process)[37].

Evaluating Democratic Innovation

Participation

By developing this dimension and its indicators, Geissel defines the principle of participation according to two main "aims" that a democratic innovation should pursue: its *inclusiveness* and its *effectiveness* (*meaningful*). The participative dimension raises two simple questions: Who participates (every potential stakeholder and/or shareholder, or only the "traditional" active citizens)? and with what effects (binding or consultative)? In this respect, two out of four cases examined – Modena and Grottammare – have shown only a formal/consultative level of participation. This means that by analysing the contents of the Participatory Budget settlement and of the other administrative acts, we cannot find any rules regulating the number of proposals that must be inserted in the budget document. The implication is that citizens do not have a real decisional power to draw up the budget, and this can diminish the consideration of participants' preferences by political representatives in the municipal assembly.

However, we must add that during several years of PB implementation, Grottammare assumed the informal custom to approve one local proposal for each area in which the Participatory Budgeting takes place, as well as the three most voted city-level proposals.

In the other two cases, it is possible to talk about a co-decisional role of the participants: the administration has in fact the formal duty, expressed in the Participatory Budgeting settlement, to carry out the proposals that have received the largest number of votes (in the Novellara case) or to spend a certain amount of public money in the implementation of the most voted proposals (Priverno an average of 4.5% of the total amount assigned to investments).

Only in one case, Priverno, PB proposals assume a binding form – something representatives *must* take into account. However, this occurs only when

---

37 The interview patterns follow the following scheme: Reasons for the introduction of Participatory Budget; Role and expectations of the respondent; Limits/ difficulties of practice implementation; Change/Evolution of the practice; Effects of the practice on the political and social context;General opinions regarding Participatory Budget.

the assemblies reach 3% of the participation within the total population of the area where it took place.

The common ground of the examined cases is that, even when a specific and formally legalised co-decisional power exists, it suffers from the negative effect due to the presence of politicians and civil servants.

This presence is felt not only in the last phase of the budgeting process (when the definitive budget proposal has to be presented to the Council), but also in the intermediate participatory phases of the budgeting, for instance during the feasibility studies (by rejecting the most expensive proposals).

The negative effects of this presence limit the initial phase as well: during the first turn of PB Assemblies, politicians control proposals guiding the deliberation towards the most feasible ones.

Therefore, the role of representatives and administrators seems to go beyond what could be considered both as a rightful and proper act of mediation between representation and participation. This might be seen as an awareness of the real economic and legal limits of the administrative action. This evidence moves the focus from the nature of participation to the outcome. So the question is what type of proposals emerge, which ones are approved, and how many of them are implemented.

Inclusive Participation

If PB had been created to allow the participation of those who normally do not participate (inclusive dimension), the interviews with Privileged Witnesses and our own participation in the assemblies show that the majority of the participants are active citizens. Thus, the social categories for which the experiment was created (i.e. women, teens and immigrants, and in general all those who do not participate in politics) are still the categories with a lower level of participation in PB.

Our collected data do not contain any "strong" quantitative indicator referring to the social composition of the participants (such as economic class affiliation, the actual participants' occupation or the age composition of each assembly); in fact, the data collected by the participative offices of each municipality have proved not to be completely reliable (e.g. because neither do they take into account the effective number of participants – counting, instead, the total number of presences, without subtracting those who take part in more than one assembly – nor do they present any social data, except for gender composition).

Nevertheless, we gathered some indicators of this variable with the help of the interviews, and some other indirect tools: for example, among the assembly delegates who were interviewed, only 4 out of 16 were under the age of 30, and all four of these were deeply involved in local political affairs (they were members of a specific political party, or activists in a local Civil Society organization, or belonging to families who historically played an important role within the local political context).

Moreover, the only case in which we found massive participation of young citizens was in Novellara, during the first year of the Participatory Budget cycle, when a group of teenagers asked for a skate-park and then joined the second cycle of assemblies as the most numerous group. In this way their proposal was the most voted.

Despite the weak effect of inclusive participation in Novellara, the strategic use of the participative instrument can be seen in the action of the councillor to whom the teenagers had previously submitted the proposal.

Effective Participation: Impact of Procedures on Debates and Policies

The "strategic use" of Participatory Budgeting also surfaced during the analysis of the proposals: the same citizens often present proposals that are closely tied to personal or individual needs. It is very rare to find a proposal that ranges beyond subjective interests or the interests of small groups. By examining the municipal official reports, it is possible to demonstrate that the majority of the proposals consist of minor infrastructural works rather than major ones: during the Participatory Budget of 2007 in Grottammare, almost half of the proposals concerned interventions in the upkeep of roads and street signs, and the types of interventions were subdivided as follows: 82 notifications (minor interventions), 35 area-level proposals (medium interventions) and 11 city-level proposals (major interventions).

In Novellara, the number of small-range requests by participants during the participative process has also been constantly larger than that on a city-level. Comparing the first PB cycle with the second, a decreasing number of city-level proposals can be noted (minus 20% or only 20 proposals out of 95 concerned city-level issues), while the area-level proposals remained the same. Priverno is an exception both concerning the number of proposals and their allocation. In fact, the administrators not only decided the financial limits of the process, but also the allocations for the different municipal zones in which the participative cycle took place (the amount per zone ranged from 30 thousand to 90 thousand euros, depending on the number of inhabitants of each municipal area). In Modena, about 80 % of the proposals concerned minor interventions (78% in 2005; 79% in 2006).

This trend of minor interventions mostly concerning the neighbourhood area and public work sector, is even more evident in the testimonies of the Privileged Witnesses. In fact, both the citizens and politicians who were interviewed declared that, in the majority of times, the general level of the proposals was not focused on common, or public interests. Obviously, these kinds of requirements neither go in favour of a wide debate concerning the policies to be adopted by the municipality, nor do they show the capability of changing the trend of the actual political planning process.

If effective participation is seen as a tool to *"increase effective involvement"* (Geissel in this volume), i.e. reaching the possibility of modifying the agenda-setting options, our case-study analysis emphasizes how restricted these possibilities are.

Consideration of Participants' Preferences by Political Representatives and Implementation

In view of this indicator, our analysis proves that both implementation and political consideration are inversely proportionate to the relevance of the theme expressed by the citizenry's proposals: in the case of strongly relevant issues, citizens are usually completely excluded from the decisional process. Borrowing Arnstein's terminology concerning the measurement of participation, it seems that our case studies could be described as *"pseudo participation"* practices. The more a citizen's proposal may affect the general assets of the local government's political program, the less it plays a relevant part in the public policies production's strategy.

The Grottammare Participatory Budget has been the only case in which issues that had been excluded from the process have, in some cases, been given another chance of public debate. This has been done by creating a specific participative frame, in this way showing a first step towards a different political decision-making procedure. However, in this case, we also have to recall the role played by the duration, i.e. 16 years, of the participatory budget. This variable, together with the stable political will of Grottammare mayors and the ruling elected representatives, had led to an institutionalisation not only of this specific democratic innovation but, above all, of a new participative paradigm of local governance.

The same features are found in a sub-territorial case: the area of the historical centre of Modena. This zone has not only been the area with the best results in terms of proposals turned to practical interventions, but also the only one that continued to enlarge the scope of the topics to insert in the debate and to widen the political frames in which this participative practice has been adopted. The reason for this participative and deliberative achievement is to be found, once again, in the present political culture, according to which participative experiments not only are considered as simple procedures but, above all, as a real political and territorial management pattern.

The relationship between the function of participation and the relevance of the proposal can also be explained by looking at the number of participants in these processes: in the four cases that we have examined, the percentage ranges from 1% (Modena) to 4% (Grottammare) of the resident population, a percentage in line with what can be found in several other studies (see Allegretti 2001;

Baiocchi 2002; Cabannes 2005). Moreover, we must emphasize the fact that the actual percentage of participants is lower than the formal one, because – as mentioned before – all the reports counted the total number of participants in both cycles of the assemblies (the one for emerging proposals and the one for voting priorities), which means that it may be possible that those participating in the entire process have been counted twice. Even though the number of participants has to be lowered, it is still impossible to know what the real number was.

The principle of representation is used to justify the limits of effective participation within these practices: Local representatives used to believe that a low percentage of participants is a good reason not to allow the practice to obtain strong decisional power. Nevertheless, it must be pointed out that the same percentage of participants hides a larger number of needs and expectations: each participant is, in turn, a sort of informal representative of a particular social group (from the familiar one to the micro-territorial one). During the interviews we discovered that, in many cases, the person who participates in the assemblies is something of a spokesman for the needs of an entire building, or a representative of the interests of his/her neighbours. Participatory Budgets are not able to attract a high number of participants, but mostly this participative minority reflects a larger number of interested citizens who, for several reasons, cannot participate.

Deliberation

The analysis of the case studies has shown, once again, that deliberation is limited, and that the virtuous effects generally recognized to these practices have to be diminished. Even if in some cases (first of all those of Novellara and Modena) concrete efforts have been made to make the participative processes come as close to the ideal as possible, the results have not met the original expectations of the planners.

We shall start by examining what kind of discursive model has been used during the assemblies: participating directly in the assemblies, we noticed that the interaction was rarely fully dialogical, meaning that the argumentative assumptions of the interaction are fully inspired by the search for an agreement which goes beyond the initial positions of each participant. The majority of the debates show what is normally called a "strategic use of deliberation" (Elster 1998), which is the use of apparently common needs and arguments to reach individual or restricted aims.

We must also deal with the way in which assemblies are managed: although the presence of political representatives is generally considered by citizens as proof of the importance given to this instrument, many delegates have told us that the same presence has limited their own freedom of speech or the possibility to start a real dialogical debate because, on many occasions, politicians have tried to stop the debate, in order to exclude particular issues from it or to monopolize the assemblies by transforming them into some form of political campaign speech. So, the lack of fair mediators, instead of politically oriented representatives who act in the role of facilitator, is one among several indicators of a low qualitative deliberation profile.

The low quality of the deliberative dimension is also stressed by another indicator, that is the mechanism through which citizens are called to choose the annual priorities: not only does no criterion exist from a social and economic point of view, for both the previous territorial analysis and the citizens' needs[38], but the same proposals are chosen according to the simple majority voting model.

In this way, the largest group, or the spokesperson with the highest level of eloquence in the assembly, has the best chance of realizing its priorities in the absence of any dialogical mechanism or any coefficient able to balance the simple quantitative methods of voting.

On the other hand, some positive effects regarding the quality-of-deliberation variable have to be pointed out: first of all, the information and communication flow between the political structure (i.e. representatives, mayor) and the residents was quite sufficient. Every Participatory Budget was promoted with various kinds of advertising instruments (newspapers, radio, public announcements, flyers, web announcements on the municipal web site, etc.), which allowed citizens to know the date and the place of the assemblies, the theme of the meeting, the structure of the entire process and other general information.

If we go from this general level to one which is more specific and in depth, things appear to be more ambiguous: only in Grottammare have we found complete information concerning the financial resources and the annual budget composition, the activities planned to implement the several priorities resulting from the process and a punctual reporting action concerning the updates on the process in the implementation of the proposals. At the beginning of every assembly, the Mayor gives a presentation of the annual budget with its different thematic allocations, the annual variations of each section of the budget, the general program of the administration and the state of implementation of the past year's proposals. Moreover, in the institutional web site we found all the documents not only concerning the state of the works (realised, in execution or denied), but also the reasons for the rejection of each proposal that emerged during the assemblies. Noting this, we cannot forget what has been said about the participative dimension and the criteria of evaluation, but we want to stress

---

38 In Porto Alegre the proposals are listed and put in order following a multi-criteria scheme based on objective statistical indicators concerning, for instance, several infrastructural public services of each zone: sewage system, city bus, schools, public libraries, etc.

that after going beyond a certain level of participation and deliberation, the process becomes sufficiently transparent and its communication of information to the citizens appears suitable.

In all the other cases, this level does not seem completely overcome: the Municipality of Modena did not reach a high level of information flow concerning the outcomes during its biennial participative experience; this is caused by wrong management of the information flow regarding the proposals, in its turn caused by previous wrong management of the assemblies themselves (during the first year some areas did not produce a list of priorities –thus all the proposals coming in for evaluation were not prioritized and the evaluators themselves could not complete their task). Novellara provided a medium-level degree of information concerning the feasibility of the priorities and the motivation of their refusals, but it lacked in the statement of the interventions produced by the proposals during the following participative cycles. Lastly, Priverno provided only little information explaining the rejection of the proposals as well as the final allocation of PB funds.

Nevertheless, the essential question is not "what has been done?" but "how has it been done?"; Both citizens and civil servants (above all those who form the Participative Offices) agree that the feasibility analysis of each proposal is superficial, based more on political opportunity than on its effective implementation limits. No general criterion is used to evaluate the proposals and to allocate the financial resources[39].

Even in the cases of Novellara and Modena, in which representatives and officers are more willing to build a true participative and deliberative process, the same organizers admit that the innovative thrust that usually belongs to the deliberative character of Participatory Budgets is really missing. In spite of the numerous recommendations to the assemblies' mediators to improve the deliberative level of the arena (in the case of Modena, for instance), these tools were not put to use.

As usual, there are some cases in which these tools worked, but the fact that one of these was present in the same context in which the general level of deliberation was not so high, shows how important the political will can be in such practices. The President of the Centre District of Modena played an essential role as mediator of the assemblies, by possessing the ideal personal characteristics described by the experts of deliberative practices. She did not

---

39 Only in Priverno we found a sort of analytical criterion of allocation, consisting of the number of inhabitants of each zone: the higher their number, the larger the financial support directed to the area. The criterion considers only quantitative data, with no mention of qualitative criteria such as the presence and levels of basic services.

face the assemblies with an impartial and cold judgemental attitude, but with an "impartial but warm and sympathetic" approach (Bobbio 2002).

In addition to these considerations regarding the quality of deliberation, it should be noted that often the same places chosen to host the citizens' assemblies – which could be named the physical arena in which the deliberation should take place – were not the most appropriate, in particular for their political characteristics, which can have an inhibiting effect on participation. In fact, most of the times the assemblies took place in the buildings of the left-wing parties, or belonging to associations strictly connected to the political party whose members supported the initiative, or in other cases, in places which were commonly used by local committees, like the so-called "Comitati di Quartiere", a kind of organized communities which take care of the needs of the inhabitants in a restricted area.

Effectiveness

Regarding its efficacy, on the contrary, we must use a different approach: In spite of the temporal implementation difficulties, due to the chronic lack of monetary funds of many Italian local administrations, Participatory Budgeting appears so effective that in many cases it was perceived as a real preferential vehicle in comparison with other participative instruments (such as petitions). Not only citizens but also their representatives, both of the government and of the opposition, together with the administrative staff seem to agree with this perception. *Once a proposal passes the feasibility study and receives a certain number of preferences*, its chance to be transformed into a real intervention grows progressively if compared with that of the same proposal presented through some other channel of participation. The fear of not fulfilling the citizens' expectations once fostered through the introduction of this top-down participative instrument is so high that the priorities which are the product of the Participatory Budgeting find a preferential channel compared to the autonomous initiatives coming from a bottom-up process. This behaviour of the political level can be seen as a far-reaching result of both the so called "predictable reaction principle", theorized by Friedrich (1950) and of a strong mechanism of responsiveness. This responsiveness can be explained by two factors: the facility to individualize the political subject responsible for the bad functioning of the participative instrument (because most of the time the initial will as well as the political accountability of the instrument depends on a single political actor) and the public dimension which characterizes the mechanisms of interaction between citizens and public administration.

After this brief description of the real potentiality of a PB from an effectiveness point of view we must, however, keep in mind the meaning of the term as used in this book: the capacity of a political system to solve *"collective problems"* throughout the outcomes which can meet the needs of the citizens.

So, the question is: Are patched streets or the upkeep of parks collective needs? Perhaps according to one interpretation of the term "collective need", these examples can be included into the definition, but we are not sure that they could be presented as "normative" samples of a wider and higher meaning of collective goals.

Enlightened Citizens

Even if in a weak sense, and despite what we said regarding the participation's dimension, our survey has highlighted evidence that seems to confirm the role of potential citizen enlightenment played by democratic innovations in general and PB in particular. This can even be seen in our study, and is not as para-doxical as it might appear at first sight, where the so called "civic culture" has been historically weaker and the political culture has always been more ori-ented towards a parochial one, i.e. in the municipalities of Grottammare and Priverno.

In fact, Modena and Novellara belong to the "red sub-culture" regions where the Communist and Socialist culture, made up of participation, aiming towards equity and social justice, have always been stronger than in other Ital-ian regions, such as Grottammare and Priverno.

In the aforementioned two municipalities, the introduction of a democratic innovation, such as PB, has led to the creation of several organized local groups (six in Priverno and four in Grottammare). These consist of citizens who live in the same neighbourhood, and take part in the PB after participating in self-organized assemblies/meetings, in which they discuss the priorities of their micro-areas and establish a kind of agenda referring both to the PB and other actions that should be implemented in the municipality through the year.

Even if it is only a first step among several possibilities to measure the en-lightening of a social group towards a higher level of substantial democratisa-tion, and even if it certainly has not concerned the majority of people who took part in the process, it can be seen to happen on the actor level.

By creating these groups, part of the participants have had the opportunity to learn, for the first time, how their local institutions operate, and to be in close contact with their political representatives and the whole administration staff.

This proof comes from the areas with the lower levels of the so called "civic culture" and this fact may be explained using the concept of *"Stato Nas-cente"* (flourishing-state), introduced by Alberoni, wherever the practices have been introduced: it consists of a period of time in which a group of people, bound together by a common aim or a common hope – in our case throughout the implementation phase of a democratic innovation – join their efforts to create a new force (a movement) which acts towards a specific culture represented by specific institutions.

In our micro-sociological cases, the "Comitati di Quartiere" represent this group, connected by the hope given them by the introduction of a participative culture derived from the implementation of a Participatory Budget.

Obviously, whereas this original and particular state of action meets a consolidated participative culture – this is the case of Novellara and Modena – it cannot have the same outcome, because it is generally seen by citizens, as well as by the municipality's representatives and associations, as a kind of useless repetition of the several instruments actually operating, even if it really introduces some new tools (as the deliberative ones of the Participatory Budgeting).

Moreover, in these cases, a kind of institutionalisation of the social groups has highlighted the dynamics within Civil Society, with its "neo-feudalist" mechanisms, as I term them. In this way, each association has its "personal" fast track to communicate with the representatives and to participate in the political agenda-building and agenda-setting process: it does not mean that in these cases participation does not exist, only it takes other forms, closer to concepts like those of public/private negotiation or participation of organized interests (Sintomer/Allegretti 2009), and the real outcomes coming from the implementation of a democratic innovation are strongly reduced.

Final Remarks

After a description of the dimensions and the indicators with which the effects of the implementation of a PB democratic innovation within different Italian contexts have been evaluated, we shall finish this chapter with some general remarks related to the "prerequisites" rather than the effectiveness of these democratic innovations, in other words, the possible context variables affecting the level of effectiveness.

First of all, we want to stress how much the administrative capability of answering the citizens' proposals and priorities, lays upon the type of requests produced by the participative instruments themselves and on the importance not only of the *political will*, but also of the *financial resources available to the administration*, depending, in the Italian system, on the transfer of reducing funds from the central government. This is why, while trying to find an answer concerning the efficiency of PB, we have to not only analyze the political will, but above all, to check the availability of funds and the degree of financial autonomy of local administrations.

As we have pointed out, some kinds of deliberative and participative features can be found in our four case studies. However, these features change participation from a broad to a partial form as well as deliberation from a *dialogic* to a *strategic* level (Pellizzoni 2005).

Firstly, political representatives generally seem to support the introduction of a Participatory Budgeting experience (the introduction decree is voted, for instance, by a large majority, which often includes the support of the opposition parties) but, once the veil of appearance has been lifted, the participative practices have to face the opposition. This can be seen in the daily difficulties encountered by its original supporters, such as non-participation in the public assemblies and reluctance to inform about the instrument. In this sense, the possibility for instruments such as Participatory Budgeting is deeply connected to the political will of representatives.

A possible explanation for this apparently incoherent political behaviour can, however, be found in the pluralist analysis derived from Schumpeter (1973): a political system is built on competition and allows privileges. This explains how each political group, confronted with the proposal of starting a participative initiative, is forced to support such a purpose even if later they will try to underestimate and weaken its results. Another possibility is to accuse these initiatives of not respecting the real participative values, thus not only discrediting the instrument itself but also its promoters. This strategy is usually adopted by the opposition after a first period of implementation of the practice.

Secondly, the low quantitative level of participation among the citizens that usually does not reach two per cent, is connected to the low quality of deliberation, composed of strategic actions and personal interests. Both participative and deliberative dimensions present features that can be seen as the effects of a cultural system based upon individualistic and consumerist principles. The public dimension and its values are strongly underestimated within this cultural system, with the consequence of diminishing both the social trust in the political system and the confidence in the actors who represent it. Citizens are tired; they rather relax at home watching a television show than go out and participate in an assembly ending without any actual decisions being made. This is the common-citizen picture that sadly appears to those who still believe in this kind of practice. Their task, as that of the political promoter of similar initiatives, is to persuade those "citizens" of the virtuous effects of a constant and active participative role. As Almond and Verba (1963) have already proved, it is a civic culture issue expressed through the respect and preservation of the public good and the collective values.

The third phenomenon concerns the so-called bureaucratic apparatus: with the exception of the Grottammare case, the administrative staffs have refused to collaborate in tasks required in Participatory Budgeting. The attitude of the civil servants is generally negative: citizens' proposals are often judged as unfruitful repetitions or tasks adding to their already demanding every day work load. Moreover, according to some interviewees belonging to the administrative apparatus, the small dimensions of the cities add to the danger of public exposure, since the possibility of meeting a participant of the assembly to whom they have made a promise they did not maintain is very high. The hostile attitude of the bureaucratic system towards innovations involving changes in practices and logics of behaviour, as well as the trend to preserve a certain degree of autonomy towards external requests are common features used by scholars to describe this system (Eisenstadt 2002; Crozier et al. 1977). Nevertheless, as the Grottammare case study seems to show us, the limits produced by the "natural disposition" of bureaucratic systems towards new categories can be overcome by setting a fixed duration to the participative instrument.

Although we are conscious of the contrasting tendencies described, the deliberative and participative approaches, we also recognize the fundamental justness of both the Schumpeterian analysis and the theories which assume the essential and deeply individualistic nature of human beings (such as the free rider theory and the so-called rational choice theory) From a practical point of view, both participative and deliberative theories find their justification and their higher intent precisely in the effort of reintroducing those normative elements that are strongly tied to the concept of democracy itself, elements that descriptive theories seem to remove through an analysis of our contemporary society that is too cynical and realistic.

References

Abers, R. N. (2000). Inventing Local Democracy-grassroots Politics in Brazil. Colorado, Lynne Rienner Publishers.

Ackerman, B. & J.S Fishkin (2004). Deliberation Day. New Haven, Yale University Press.

Ackerman, B. (1991). We the People: Foundation. Cambridge (Ma). Harvard University Press.

Allegretti, G. (2001). Bilancio Partecipativo e gestione urbana: l'esperienza di Porto Alegre in Il Ruolo delle Assemblee Elettive. M. Carli. Torino, Giappichelli, vol. I.

Allegretti, G. & Herzeberg C. (2004). Between Efficiency and Local Democracy Growth, TNI New Politics Working Paper.

Almond, G.A. & S. Verba (1963). The Civic Culture. Boston, Little Brown & Co.

Arnstein, S.R. (1969). "A Ladder of Citizen Participation". Journal of the American Institute of Planners, 35 (4): 216-24.

Avritzer, L. (2006). "New Public Spheres in Brazil: Local Democracy and Deliberative Politics". International Journal of Urban and Regional Research 30 (3): 623-37.

Baiocchi , G. (2002). Synergizing Civil Society: State-Civil Society Regimes in Porto Alegre, Brazil. Political Power and Social Theory, vol. 15: 3 -86.

Barber, B. (1984). Strong Democracy. Berkley, University of California Press.

Bobbio, L. (ed.) (2004). A più voci. Amministrazioni pubbliche, imprese, associazioni e cittadini nei processi decisionali inclusivi. Napoli, ESI.

Bobbio, L. (2002). "Le arene deliberative". Rivista italiana di Politiche Pubbliche 3: 5-29.

Bobbio, N., (1984). Il futuro della Democrazia. Einaudi, Torino.

Bosetti, G. & S. Maffettone (2004). Democrazia Deliberativa: cos'è. Roma, Luiss University Press.

Cabannes, Y. (2005). Presupuesto Participativo y finanzas locales. RED URBAL. Alcaldìa de Porto Alegre, Brasil, 9: 24-35.

Canfora, L. (2007). Critica della retorica democratica. Bari, Laterza.

Cohen J. & C. Sabel (1997). "Directly-Deliberative Polyarchy". European Law Journal, 3 (4): 313-42.

Crouch, C. (2005). Postdemocrazia. Bari, Laterza.

Crozier, M., S. Huntington and J. Watanuki (1977). La crisi della democrazia. Milano, Angeli.

Dahl, R.A., (1961). Who Governs? Democracy and Power in an American City. New Haven, Yale University Press.

Dryzek, J. (1990). Discursive Democracy. Cambridge, Cambridge University Press.

Eisenstadt, S.N. (2002). Paradossi della Democrazia. Bologna, Il Mulino.

Elster, J. (ed.) (1998). Deliberative Democracy. Cambridge, Cambridge University Press.

Fishkin, J. &P. Laslett (ed.) (2003). Debating Deliberative Democracy. Oxford, Blackwell.

Fishkin, J. (1991). Democracy and Deliberation. New Directions for Democratic Reform. New Heaven, Yale University Press.

Friedrich, C. J. (1950), Constitutional Government and Democracy. Boston, Ginn & Company.

Gbikpi, B. (2005). "Dalla teoria partecipativa a quella deliberativa: quali possibili continuità?". Stato e Mercato 73 (1): 97-130.

Gensro, T. & U., de Souza, Santos. (2007). Il Bilancio Partecipativo. L'esperienza di Porto Alegre. Limbiate, La Ginestra.

Goldfrank, B. (2006). "Los processo de Presupuesto Partecipativo en America Latina: exitos, fracasso y cambio". Revista de Ciencia Politica 26 (2): 3-28.

Goldfrank, B. (2007). Lessons from Latin America's Experience with Participatory Budget. A. Shah (ed.) Participatory Budgeting. Washington D.C. The International Bank of Reconstruction and Development.

Habermas, J. (1996). Fatti e Norme. Guerrini e Associati, Milano.

Harnecker, M. (1999). "Delegating power to the people: Participatory Budget in Porto Alegre". www1.worldbank. org/wbiep/decentralization/laclib/harnecker.pdf.

Held, D. (1987). Modelli di democrazia. Bologna, Il Mulino.

Herzberg, C. & G. Allegretti (2004). El 'retorno de las carabelas'. Los presupuestos participativos de america Latina en el contexto europe. Madrid, FIM.

Lijphart, A. (1999). Patterns of Democracy: Government Forms and Performance in Thirty-Six Countries. New Haven and London, Yale University Press.

Macpherson, C.B. (1980). La vita e i tempi della democrazia liberale. Milano, Il Saggiatore.

Morlino, L. (1998). Democracy between Consolidation and Crisis: Parties, Groups, and Citizens in Southern Europe. Oxford, Oxford University Press.

Morlino, L. (2003). Democrazie e democratizzazioni. Bologna, Il Mulino.

Olson, M. (1963). The logic of Collective Action. Cambridge, Harvard University Press.

Patenam C., (1970). Participation and Democratic Theory. Cambridge, Cambridge University Press.

Pellizzoni L., (2005). La deliberazione pubblica. Roma, Meltemi.

Pellizzoni, L. (1999). "Reflexive Modernization and Beyond: Knowledge and value in the 'Politics of Environment and Technology'". Theory, Culture & Society 16 (4): 99-125.

Pont R., (ed.) (2005). La democrazia partecipativa. L'esperienza di Porto Alegre e i progetti di democrazia. Roma, Edizioni Alegre.

Rawls, J. (1993). Political Liberalism. New York, Columbia University Press.

Sartori, G. (2006). Democrazia cos'è. Milano, Bur.

Schumpeter, J.A. (1973). Capitalismo, socialismo e democrazia. Bologna, Il Mulino.

Sintomer Y. & G. Allegretti (2009). I bilanci partecipativi in Europa. Roma, EDIESSE.

Sousa Santos, B. de (2003). Democratizzare la democrazia. Firenze, Città Aperta.

Vitale, D. (2006). "Between Deliberative and Participatory Democracy". Philosophy & Social Criticism 32 (6): 739-66.

Wampler, B. (2007). "A Guide to Participatory Budgeting". Participatory Budgeting. A. Shah (ed.) Participatory Budgeting. Washington D.C., The International Bank for Reconstruction and Development.

Wampler, B. (2005). Does Participatory Democracy Actually Deepen Democracy? Lessons from Brazil. www.internationalbudget.org/themes/PB/ParticipatoryInstitutions.pdf.

Appendix

Both the Porto Alegre experiment and the four Italian ones analysed in this essay are built on a process in three phases: a first cycle of assemblies, in which citizens expose the proposal of each municipality area where the process is implemented; a second moment in which all the priorities are examined under the point of view of their feasibility; and, at last, a third meeting cycle, in which the proposals are discussed and voted.

Nevertheless, the Porto Alegre experiment presents some elements that make it appear more structured than the Italian ones, as, for instance, the presence of a permanent citizens' council (Participatory Budget Council) composed of assemblies delegates; the existence of a specific planning administrative cabinet (GAPLAN); the presence of citizens' commissions created with the aim of evaluating the outcomes reached by the municipality according to the approved priorities.

The 52 interviews are divided into several categories of key-witnesses, as in the table below:

Key-witness								
Categories		*Citizenry*	*Representatives*			*Civil Servant*		
Case Studies	N° BP Area	Spokes-person	Loc. Gov.	Municipal Council		Econ omic Dep.	Planning Departm.	Particip. Dep.
				Maj.	Opp.			
Modena	4	3	4	5	4	-	-	1
Novellara	4	3	2	1	3	1	1	1
Priverno	8	5	1	1	2	1	1	1
Grottammare	7	4	1	1	1	1	1	1
Tot.Interviews: 51		15	8	8	10	3	3	4

When Deliberation Happens
Evaluating Discursive Interactions among Ordinary Citizens in Participatory Budgeting Institutions

Julien Talpin

Introduction

While in the beginning mostly theoretical (Harbermas 1996; Gutman & Thompson 1996; Elster 1998), research on deliberative democracy has recently taken an empirical direction. Answering the calls for the empirical evaluation of appealing democratic theories, a wealth of participatory and deliberative experiences has been observed to test the grand theories. Deliberative polls (Fishkin 1997; Fishkin et al. 2002), citizen juries (Goodin & Niemeyer 2003; Sintomer 2007) and more broadly mini-publics (Goodin & Dryzek 2006; Fung 2008; Smith 2009) have been studied in depth, especially to assess their capacity to enlighten citizens' preferences. Existing research faces, however, two short-comings: little research has been carried out on deliberation in less artificial settings than mini-publics and, above all, the methodological approaches that have been used allow evaluating the impact of deliberation on individuals' preferences, but do not assess the quality of deliberation and more broadly, whether deliberation took place at all in these institutions (for a similar critique, see Ryfe 2005). Deliberation is at the centre of social science attention, but its very process is generally overlooked. While it is one of the central criteria for evaluating the democratic potential of a political innovation, as emphasized in the introduction of this volume, the quality of deliberation in participatory institutions has until now received little attention.

To answer these shortcomings, I offer a different methodological approach – which is nevertheless complementary to the other ones – to the study of deliberation: namely direct observation and ethnographic research. To understand the nature of the discursive interactions taking place in the public sphere one needs to observe them in detail, follow the voice and tone of lay citizens, hear the difficulties and breakdowns of interpersonal communication, and sometimes the emergence of deliberation. The direct observation of public meetings in participatory institutions makes it possible to gather a rich material of hundreds of discursive sequences and interactional situations, full of citizens' voices and discussions. Thus, the regularities in the practices of different actors can be discerned and compared to irregularities, moments of crisis and tensions.

Far from my initial hypothesis, deliberation was not the norm of the participatory institutions I studied. On the contrary, the direct observation of public meetings indicates that the norm of public interactions among ordinary citizens resembles much more a succession of monologues than a truly interactive deliberation. This is why social sciences dealing with communicational phenomena in the public sphere should try to understand *when* deliberation happens. Given its scarcity, we need to understand what the institutional, social and political conditions for the emergence of deliberation are. The aim of this chapter is therefore to evaluate one central criterion of the democratic potential of participatory innovations, namely the *quality of deliberation*. How can we explain that sometimes discursive interactions are highly fruitful and constructive, while at other times they end up being extremely confrontational, agonistic and defensive? How can we assess the emergence and vanishing of argumentative sequences in participatory arenas?

To answer these questions, I compare two experiences of Participatory Budgeting in Europe. Based on an ethnographic study conducted over two years, I analyse the discursive interactions in Participatory Budgeting (PB) assemblies in Municipio XI in Rome, Italy and in Morsang-sur-Orge in the periphery of Paris, France. Methodologically, my research is based on direct observation, from January 2005 to September 2006, of 120 PB public assemblies, of which each one contains dozens of discursive sequences[40]. By comparing several hundred discursive sequences among ordinary citizens in PB institutions I can discern the norms which regulate interactions and understand the nature of discursive interactions among ordinary citizens in PB institutions[41]. I also include questionnaires and interviews with participants, but the analysis of deliberation in practice first and foremost requires observation of how it happens in real time.

It might, however, appear surprising to study deliberation in institutions not especially designed for promoting the quality of discussion. Participatory Budgeting indeed aims at including ordinary citizens in cities' or regions' decision-making processes, and therefore tries to include as many participants as possible (especially to increase the legitimacy of such procedures). The focus on numbers might therefore make deliberation difficult, as small numbers have been highlighted as a favorable condition for the quality of deliberation (Smith 2009). In this respect this chapter sheds new light on the link between deliberative and participatory democracy: while the two bodies of literature increas-

---

40 By « discursive sequence » I mean a set of sentences logically linked together, i.e. dealing with the same issue and with participants answering each other.

41 I therefore follow an inductive analytical method, inspired by symbolic interactionist sociology. See Strauss & Corbin (eds.) 1997.

ingly develop in different directions (Mutz 2006), it can nevertheless be interesting to study how much deliberation there is in participatory institutions and, conversely, how much participation or inclusion there is in deliberative institutions. Within the framework of this volume, this chapter can help questioning the deliberative quality of democratic innovations based on the cooperation between interest groups and state actors.

First, I show that deliberation is scarce, as the discursive interactions in the public arenas that I studied vary considerably, thus showing a plurality of forms of communication in participatory institutions. Second, I present the diversity of the discursive forms observed and third, I investigate the favourable conditions for the emergence of deliberation. I thus analyse the role of procedures in the emergence of deliberation before stressing the social conditions fostering the expression of disagreement (mostly the importance of leaders and stakes), which is a crucial condition for the emergence of deliberation, albeit hard to reach.

Public Discussion in Two Participatory Budgeting Institutions in Europe

Participatory Budgeting (PB) started in 1989 in Porto Alegre in Brazil, and has since then been a tremendous success due to poor people participating and due to its decisive impact on the social and economic development of the city (Baiocchi 2005). The Porto Alegre PB has even been recognized as a good governance practice by the United Nations and the World Bank, and has spread all over the world. In 2008, there were about 100 PBs in Europe and more than 1,000 around the globe (Sintomer et al. 2008; Cabannes 2003). A participatory budget can be defined as the institutionalized inclusion of ordinary citizens in the budgeting cycle of a public administration. The creation of a PB therefore means regular organization of public assemblies at the neighbourhood, district or city level, which are open to all residents, and in which citizens participate by setting up projects which are then integrated into the municipal or regional budget. Part of the annual investment budget (between 2 and 20% in European cases) is thus decided more or less directly by the citizens (Talpin 2011). In this paper, two case studies are compared: Morsang-sur-Orge (France) and the 11th district of Rome (Italy). These cases were selected, because they appear to be among the most empowered in Europe in terms of the proportion of the budget directly decided by the citizens. A brief description of the two locations may be useful to provide the context of these experiences.

Morsang-sur-Orge is a typical suburban city of 20,000 inhabitants, situated about 20 km south of Paris. Since 1945, the municipality has been ruled by three successive Communist mayors. Despite its historical embeddedness, the

Communist Party almost lost the local elections in 1995, which steered the municipal administration to innovate. From the beginning, participatory democracy in Morsang has been seen as both a response to electoral decline and an answer to "the crisis of representative democracy". The municipal majority decided to create eight *Comités de Quartier* [Neighbourhood Councils], which allowed the institutionalization of participation, with public meetings organized every other month. The main innovation was to grant a financial portfolio of about 60,000 euros to each neighbourhood council, to finance local projects. Allocated 480,000 euros per year, neighbourhood councils decide on about 20% of the investment budget of the city (2.7 million euros in 2004). After its re-election in 2001, the municipality decided to go one step further and create city-wide *Ateliers Budgétaires* [Thematic Budget Workshops], focusing on the main areas of competence of the city, from urban planning to schooling policies and environmental issues. Workshops are held a few times a year, allowing residents to discuss and propose investment priorities to the Municipal Council on the different issue areas. In both cases, elected officials attend public meetings alongside city residents, which is a French peculiarity in comparison to the other European experiences (Talpin 2011). Discussion is moderated by public functionaries, but is nevertheless poorly proceduralized.

Since 2003, Municipio XI[42] in Rome has developed Participatory Budgeting, which is linked to the electoral success of a Left coalition deeply inspired by the anti-globalization movement and the Porto Alegre experience. The Roman PB is essentially based on neighbourhood assemblies organized regularly to decide on local projects to be financed by the Municipio's budget. Projects can be presented in the main areas of competence of the Municipio, from urban planning and environmental issues to youth and cultural policies. PB assemblies then follow a yearly cycle. The most important phase, generally between January and May, gathers *Grupi di Lavoro* [Working Groups] in each neighbourhood to develop projects and proposals in the different thematic areas. Proposals are discussed by the citizens, progressively refined and operationalized to make them applicable, and then analyzed by the representatives of the Municipality's technical services, who evaluate whether they fit the competences and financial capacities of the Municipio. At the end of the process, a final assembly open to all residents is organised, where the proposals are ranked by voting. In this view, collective discussion and aggregation procedures do not necessarily appear contradictive.

---

42 Municipio XI is one of Rome's 15 Districts, each one having a certain political and financial autonomy (on local matters). Municipio city council and mayor are elected directly.

Participatory budgets therefore offer the residents a formal mode of inclusion, since public meetings are indeed open to all. Participation remains fairly low, however: about 1,500 people in Rome and 500 in Morsang, i.e. between 0.5% and 2.5% of the total population of those cities. An over-representation of middle-class, educated and over fifty-year-old people can be discerned in open participation activities, though. Civic or political activists are also well represented in PBs. It should, however, be noted that gender does not appear as an exclusionary factor in PBs as, for example, 53% of the Roman PB participants are women. Even if the participation in the process does not mirror the population – which raises questions concerning the legitimacy of the decisions made by these institutions – it should be noted that it is nevertheless relatively diverse. We now turn to the assessment of the discursive interactions in PBs.

The Scarcity of Deliberation Among Ordinary Citizens

The regularities of the discursive sequences observed in the field allow for conclusions to be drawn about the conditions under which deliberation can emerge in real-life settings[43]. One of the main conclusions of this study is that deliberation among ordinary citizens is scarce in PB institutions. The observation for over two years of more than 120 public meetings showed that deliberation rarely happened. This does not mean that deliberation never occurred, but that each meeting gave rise to different types of discursive interaction, from bargaining, rhetoric, polemic and monologue to sharp argumentation.

A Strict Definition of Deliberation

While it can be contrasted with aggregation as a mode of collective decision – as mentioned in the introduction of this volume – deliberation is understood as the development of preferences by discussion. To specify the type and quality of the discursive exchanges at stake a more precise definition could also be provided. If the quality of the democratic process depends on its deliberative nature, the nature of deliberation itself is an important factor to take into ac-

---

43 While much research on deliberation in mini-publics is based on experimental or quasi-experimental protocols – such as deliberative polls or lab experiments – it also appears interesting to study deliberation in a « real-life » setting, as it is not clear, whether citizens' attitudes are transferable from the social science lab to the real life of power and politics.

count (Steiner et al. 2005). Therefore, I define deliberation as *a reasoned exchange of arguments preceding a collective decision.*[44] First, deliberation is a collective exchange of arguments, requiring that the pros and cons of a certain course of action are weighed. It does not necessarily exclude emotions, anecdotes or personal stories from the picture, but considers that they can nurture deliberation only in so far as they open up for a collective discussion nourished by contradictory interpretations of the moral or political meaning of otherwise personal and idiosyncratic stories or testimonies (Young 1996; Sanders 1997; Mansbridge 1999; Polletta 2005). Thus, a deliberation is a collective discussion in which certain types of propositions, or arguments, are voiced. Arguments, thus, are propositions backed up by reason rather than by threat, power or money. Deliberation is therefore analytically different from bargaining, in which threats or interests are mobilised and negotiated.

The aim of this collective exchange of arguments is to take a decision. The collective decision might not necessarily become a public policy, however; it might indeed be a consultative decision or one affecting the group internally, regarding its organisation, for instance.[45] Discussion is not just an end in itself – as in clubs or debating societies – it is aimed at affecting the wider world. Therefore, it is different from a conversation, in which reasoned exchanges of arguments can take place between different actors, but are not aimed at action.[46] The action-oriented feature of deliberation has two decisive effects. First, as a decision is at least indirectly at stake, deliberation has to be conclusive. Consequently, there are time constraints. This makes a discussion different from a conversation, which can always be stopped and continued later. Second, and more important, the fact that the discussion is aimed at taking a decision shapes the behaviour of the participants, who are, to some extent, bound by the arguments they voice. For both moral and pragmatic reasons – words might have an impact – participants will take a discussion more seriously than a conversation in which their words have little effect.

There is no doubt that given such an exigent definition, deliberation is scarce. It requires both institutional settings based on discursive decision-making (decisions are taken through discussion, rather than through aggrega-

---

44 For a relatively similar definition, see Manin 1987.

45 In this respect, what matters more than the policy impact of the collective discussion is that a decision be made, as in this case participants might feel accountable for the collective agreement.

46 My definition of a conversation is different from Gary Remer's (2000), for whom conversation is a collective discussion in which speakers and listeners constantly alternate (in contrast to the oratory mode, in which the roles of the speakers and the audience are fixed). I also disagree with Remer in considering conversations as a form of deliberation, as in that case deliberation is disconnected from decision.

tive means or authoritatively by a leader) and a certain competence of the actors, in order to reach a certain discursive quality. As summed up in Table 4.1, the two central features of deliberation are, however, analytically distinct. A collective discussion can be ruled by an exchange of arguments but not aimed at taking a decision; it will therefore be defined as a reasoned conversation. In contrast, non-argumentative conversations are coined casual conversations. On the contrary, a collective discussion aimed at taking a decision is not necessarily ruled by arguments.

While conversations have been left outside of this study, public discussions are at its core. What matters therefore is to evaluate under what conditions collective discussions aimed at taking decisions can become deliberations. Surprisingly, the theoretical and empirical literature on deliberation has remained, until now, naïvely optimistic about the possibility of deliberation to emerge. I argue that this stems both from an under-conceptualization of deliberation itself and from a lack of rigour in empirical research.

Table 4.1 Types of Discursive Modes

	No decision	**Decision**
Argumentation	Reasoned Conversation	Deliberation, Monologue
No Argumentation	Casual Conversation	Bargaining, Polemic

A Lack of Analysis of the Conditions of Emergence of Deliberation

According to one of the dominant approaches to deliberation, publicity is the crucial factor for the emergence of deliberation. Following a Kantian tradition taken up by Habermas, a large fraction of deliberative theorists sees publicity as the crucial social mechanism orienting people towards the common good. In certain public settings, self-interested arguments would merely be inexpressible. Thus, the force of publicity is attributed by Habermas (1984) to the presuppositions of language, by Elster (1994) to the strategic will to convince actors with unstable preferences and by Fearon (1998) to the submission to certain social norms.

Were it purely normative, one could buy the argument. However, a growing number of deliberative theorists try to enrich their approaches with the analysis of social science studies of past or present deliberative experiences. Leading researchers have thus studied the discursive sequences of constituent assemblies (Elster 1994), citizen juries (Goodin & Niemeyer 2003) or deliberative polls (Fishkin 1997; Fishkin et al. 2002). Designing quantitative studies based on pre/post surveys, their research above all aims at evaluating preference change through deliberation (Delli Carpini et al. 2004). The main problem with these approaches is the lack of analysis of the discursive sequences *per se*. They focus either on the external perspective – the procedural design – or on the micro-level of preference change, but not on the (social and discursive) process linking the two together. As Ryfe underlines, "In the process however, deliberation itself remains essentially unexamined." (Ryfe 2005: 54). Deliberative democrats are more interested in the effects of deliberation than in knowing whether deliberation took place *tout court*. The process of deliberation is therefore entirely overlooked.[47] Deliberative democrats do not enter the black box of deliberation and end up being unable to assess whether it is collective deliberation, information from documentation materials, or pure randomness that explains preference changes.[48] The only way they investigate this crucial question is by asking – in the final questionnaire – "what made you change your mind on this issue?". (Fishkin et al. 2002; Goodin & Niemeyer 2003). They do not therefore assess whether deliberation took place at all, and whether it was of rather good or bad quality.

Surprisingly, far from the rigour and conservatism of the theoretical analysis, they generally derive from their approach a rather minimalist definition of deliberation in their empirical studies, as Robert Goodin in his study of Australian citizen juries, who defines deliberation as: "Collective conversations among a group of equals aiming at reaching some joint view on some issues of common concern." (Goodin & Niemeyer 2003: 633) Any collective discussion would thus become a deliberation, independently of the type of propositions that is voiced. Deliberation would thus emerge automatically from public bodies adopting discursive decision-making procedures.

I argue, on the contrary, that any "collective conversation among a group of equals aiming at reaching some joint view on some issues of common concern" is not necessarily a deliberation. It can be bargaining, polemic or monological discursive sequences. Deliberation is a very specific form of discursive interaction, requiring a collective exchange of arguments and reasons (that can, however, be based on and backed up by personal experiences, testimonies, i.e. emotional narratives) in the aim of taking a collective decision. All the discursive sequences in public arenas are not deliberative. On the contrary, the few sociological studies dealing with the discursive interactions in

---

47 With some exceptions however, see Mansbridge 1980; Fung 2004.

48 See for instance Fishkin et al. 2002, 484: "Another question is how much of the information gains and changes in policy preferences came from the briefing materials, versus talking, reading and thinking about the issues in group discussions, versus the large group sessions with policy experts, versus large group sessions with politicians, etc."

non-experimental public institutions appear sceptical about the quality of collective discussion in these settings. Deliberation appears to be of rather low quality, or even non-existent (Bacqué & Sintomer 1999; Blondiaux 2000). This is the case especially when public arenas involve lay citizens, more than professional politicians, which is the focus of attention of most empirical research on deliberation.[49] As far as discussions among lay citizens are concerned, it seems as if large fringes of the participants try to avoid argumentation and justification of their viewpoints at any cost. Considering their opinions as private matters, prime markers of their identity, people seem not to be ready to justify them publicly, and even less to change them as an outcome of deliberation (Conover et al. 2002).

Even if actors participate in order to express themselves, discuss collectively and eventually take binding decisions, the result of the inter-action is not necessarily a deliberation. That requires interventions following each other, as well as people listening to and answering each other in a con-structive and argumentative manner, which seldom happens. The repeated observation of public meetings in PB institutions does not confirm that only disinterested arguments oriented towards the common good are expressible in public arenas. Personal testimonies, feelings, and private matters are regularly presented in these public settings. Participants can bargain, dispute, exchange impressions, and sometimes deliberate.

The three Discursive Modes of Participatory Institutions

This study does not indicate that certain types of arguments are inexpressible in certain public settings, but rather that personal interventions are evaluated differently by the audience – sanctioned, rewarded or ignored – given the norms regulating interactions in public. In many ways, these norms are often not powerful enough to impede people voicing arguments that appear inappropriate or incompatible with the discursive norms of the group. The norms regulating interactions in a certain social setting are not integrated immediately and automatically by the participants but have to be learned progressively (Talpin 2011); hence the existence of a plurality of discursive modes. I observed three different discursive modes in Participatory Budgeting institutions: (1) polemic; (2) bargaining and (3) argumentation. The distinction between the three stems primarily from the way claims were backed up and justified by different actors.

---

49 For an interesting empirical analysis of the quality of deliberation in parliaments, where actors have different skills than ordinary citizens, see Steiner et al. 2005.

Their differences do not derive from the actors' intentions, but from the words they use in public.

First, I saw – however very rarely – polemic sequences, participants using personal attacks to criticize others' positions. Far from fostering constructive deliberations, polemic sequences often led to discursive confusion. It mostly occurred in the French case, where citizens were opposed to elected officials, the former criticizing the latter. For example: A citizen's car had been stolen and in a public meeting he asked the mayor: "I got robbed, what can you do about it?"[50]; or, a group of teenagers asked for the creation of "premises, to meet in the neighbourhood". In both cases, participants were bashed, which in the second case ended with youngsters leaving the meeting obviously angry[51]. Sometimes participants also bashed each other, condemning each other's self-interested motives. An excerpt from a meeting of a *Comité de Quartier* in Morsang-sur-Orge illustrates this clearly:

"The meeting started with a discussion about the new urban planning project of the neighbourhood. At a certain point, however, Josiane – a woman in her late 60s – started to speak in a rather aggressive way of a completely different topic: "I'd like that the bus stop in front of my house be removed! I don't feel at home anymore since it's been put there. Would it be that complicated to move it 50 meters? What should I do for that? I'm fed up! I'm really fed up! You have to do something about it!" Jacky, member of the technical services of the municipality, answered rather harshly: "There's nothing to do about it! I'm sorry! It would require a lot of permits and official authorisations. And it doesn't depend on us anymore; it is a competence of the agglomeration community." The answer was not sufficient for Josiane however: "Ok, but this bus stop was not here when we bought the house! Otherwise ..." Given the increasing tension of the discussion, Francis, the participatory democracy official, intervened: "You know Madam, bus stops depend on a multiplicity of actors: the region, the agglomeration, the police, the firemen, etc. It's not to duck the question, but ... you know, the problem with bus stops, is that they are great as long as they are in front of other people's houses." The audience became more and more critical. Jokes started to burst forth: "It's always better in front of other houses, hum!"; "you should move out!"; "ok, we got your point, this is useless!" The discussion became a mess and finished in an atmosphere of disgrace for this woman."[52]

---

50 Observation notes, Robespierre neighbourhood council, Morsang-sur-Orge, 01.10.2005.

51 Observation notes, Wallon neighbourhood council, Morsang-sur-Orge, 21.11.2005.

52 Observation notes. Morsang-sur-Orge, 04.11.2005.

This excerpt illustrates how parochial arguments can be expressed publicly in Morsang-sur-Orge assemblies – the publicity of the interactions does not make them disappear, as argued by some deliberative democrats, but they are heavily sanctioned. In this case, the woman receives a double sanction, as she is both publicly ridiculed by the comments of the other participants – especially those of a local councillor, who is granted an important symbolic capital – and labelled "ball-breaker". (People who express parochial arguments are indeed generally labelled "ball-breakers", "pain in the neck", or "loud-mouths".)

The second discursive mode is bargaining, i.e. participants trying to foster their self-interest through public participation, to negotiate with the authorities in order to obtain what they want. The explicit use of self-interest to justify claims is rare, however, as it is both relatively non-functional (because inefficient) and socially disqualifying.[53] Most of the time, people try to offer at least a minimal public good justification of their claims, in keeping with the norms of civic engagement. Some empirical evidence of such argumentative sequences is provided below. However, argumentation does not always mean deliberation. An argument has to be answered (criticised or endorsed) to start a deliberation. Mostly, however, as will be seen below, Participatory Budgeting allows for the development of monological argumentative sequences: arguments are voiced but not answered. The rule of PB discursive interactions is not deliberation, but a succession of monological (argumentative) sequences not answering each other.

While ethnographic research allows to draw conclusions about the regularities of interaction patterns, these patterns also require to pay special attention to exceptional moments, when the routine is broken. In this respect, deliberation embodies a breakdown in the routine of PB discursive interactions. The task then is to evaluate how public discussion in PB assemblies can sometimes mean deliberative sequences and at some other times mere bargaining, polemic or monological sequences. When does deliberation happen? How can it be explained that in PBs the power of publicity did not always allow the emergence of deliberation? Why does it emerge more easily in certain contexts than in others?

---

53 Elster (1994) and Fearon (1998) both seem to be right concerning the filter of publicity pushing individuals to endorse public-spirited positions: the force of publicity comes both from actors' interests (the expression of self-interest is not very efficient to pursue one's interests in a public assembly) and social norms impeding the expression of self-interested claims.

Necessary Conditions for the Emergence of Deliberation

If deliberation in Participatory Budgeting is scarce, it can nevertheless emerge under certain specific social, political and institutional conditions. These conditions are worth investigating in depth in order to better understand the phenomenon of deliberation among lay citizens. I argue that the main conditions for the emergence of deliberation in non-experimental political settings are: (a) the procedural setting; (b) the emergence of disagreement; (c) the role played by discussion leaders; (d) the stakes of the discussion. These favourable conditions were more or less salient in the cases observed, but were nevertheless always present when deliberation happened. They also take different forms in the different cases as, for instance, conflict and disagreement are not framed similarly when they emerge between politicians and lay citizens, as among citizens themselves. Though these four conditions for the emergence of deliberation were established through observation of the discursive interactions, they are partly applicable to other participatory arenas, as well.

The Power of Procedures

One of the crucial prerequisites for the emergence of deliberation is the organization of the discussion. Deliberation does not emerge spontaneously from the interactions taking place in the public sphere. On the contrary, laissez-faire discussion is the best way to let powerful actors, those with the highest discursive skills and cultural capital, capture the floor. The focus on procedures is central in the deliberative democracy literature, in which good deliberation means a procedurally fair exchange of arguments. Fair deliberative procedures especially imply publicity and formal inclusiveness, everyone being able to participate, and the exclusion of internal constraints, everyone being allowed to have his/her say (Cohen 1989). In practice, the organization of the discussion around fair procedures includes different elements, however: scenography and size of the groups, limits framing public interventions (mutual respect, time limits, list of speakers, etc.), selection and style of the facilitators.

Besides spatial organisation, the size of the discussion groups is a crucial factor for deliberation. This issue is dealt with in a different manner from one case to another. In a small city like Morsang-sur-Orge, the idea to split assemblies has never been raised. *Comités de quartier* and *Ateliers Budgétaires* never gather more than 30 people, so the organizers never had the impression that affluence impeded deliberation. The awareness of the importance and difficulty of public communication pushed the organisers of the Roman PB to design it in such a way as to foster the quality of discussion. Discussion assemblies were therefore often split into smaller working groups – by thematic area – gathering four to ten people. The experience of the Montagnola neighbourhood assembly is quite telling in this respect:

The first two meetings of the year had been chaotic. The 30 participants had indeed refused to split into working groups, against the facilitators' advice. It resulted in a discursive messiness, people not listening to each other, speaking over each other, moving from one topic to the other. At the third meeting participants decided to split into three working groups, gathering between 6 and 8 people respectively. Discussion dynamics thus changed drastically. I followed one of the working groups, where the discussion was calm and constructive, the facilitator sometimes asking "not all at the same time" or "one after the other". A speaking protocol was organized, proposals were written down, and those cutting others short systematically sanctioned. Deliberation therefore emerged, based on the collective evaluation of arguments and proposals. In a few months, due to the imitation of some basic discussion rules, citizens had learnt to deliberate. The improved organization of the debate allowed participants to move away from agonistic and sometimes aggressive exchanges, to a much more cooperative and constructive atmosphere.[54]

Group size, therefore, makes a significant difference for the quality of deliberation. Not only do smaller groups make discussion more constructive, they also increase the nu3mber of speakers during the meetings. The smaller the size of the group, the higher the speaking rate (number of speakers per session): 79% in Rome, 68% in Morsang-sur-Orge (and 40% in Seville, the third case which was studied, but which is not accounted for in the present chapter)[55]. Apparently, then, there is a clear trade-off between quantitative inclusion and deliberative quality. While a higher number of participants increase the legitimacy of a democratic innovation, it reduces its capacity to foster deliberation. The speaking rate might indeed be an important factor in the emergence of deliberation, as it increases the diversity of the viewpoints expressed, and can therefore foster the expression of disagreement.

---

54 Observation notes. Montagnola neighbouhood. Rome, January-May 2006.

55 In Rome, only speakers in the working groups were counted, as the other meetings – to elect delegates or vote – were not aimed at collective discussion. Thus, 340 of the 430 participants to the Roman working groups I observed spoke up at least once.

The Difficulty and Necessity to Express Disagreement in Public Discussion

As stated earlier, deliberation is scarce. In public arenas, most of the people voice arguments, diagnose problems and evoke possible solutions in a mono-logical way. Personal interventions do not answer each other and seldom result in a constructive exchange of arguments and counter-arguments in search of a common good. Deliberation relies on3 argumentation, but it also requires an *exchange* of arguments.

Most of the time, it was the absence of conflict, dissent or disagreement that impeded the emergence of deliberation. It can appear trivial, but when everybody agrees from the beginning or when people do not care or bother to express disagreement, deliberation cannot emerge. Most of the empirical literature on deliberation has stressed, until now, the importance of heterogeneity or diversity for deliberation. Deliberation usually does not occur among like-minded people. Mutz and Martin (2001), for instance, have shown that a more heterogeneous social network prompts a more deliberative frame of mind. Huckfeldt, too, has shown that heterogeneous discussion networks create more reflexive political choices (Huckfeld et al. 2004). Heterogeneity and diversity of views are, however, necessary but not sufficient conditions for the emergence of a deliberation; what matters is the discursive expression of diversity. Indeed, for many social, situational and pragmatic reasons heterogeneous groups might remain fully consensual, not expressing any disagreement.[56]

I thus assisted, over my ethnographic study, to very sophisticated delibera-tions, but only when some disagreement was voiced. An excerpt from a discus-sion that took place in the Garbatella neighbourhood assembly in Rome is quite telling:

Participants decided to split into working groups at the beginning of the meeting, and I followed the one dealing with urban and environmental issues. It was composed of 6 people, 3 women and 3 men. The discussion was immediately organised by Elena, the youngest participant, but an experienced activist in a social centre and a housing rights association. She proposed to start with a short introduction by each participant and then asked each of them to voice their priorities in terms of urbanism for the 2005 PB.
Maurizio, a man in his early 50's, member of the environmentalist organization Legambiente as he introduced himself immediately, was the first one to speak: "Per-sonally, what I want, is to fight against the influence of cars in the city. It's unbearable and dramatic for the environment [...] I want to make two proposals: the creation of a

---

56 I here use a minimal definition of disagreement, understood as the expression of a counter-argument during a collective discussion.

cycle path and the creation of a "Zone 30" – limiting cars' speed – in the centre of the neighbourhood." His intervention spurred some strong reactions. Franco, a man in his 70's, immediately voiced a counter-argument: "It's not a problem of urbanism or roads ... it's not a technical problem, it's a problem of culture. Culture is to know what are one's rights and duties. [...] It's really nice to change the rules, but where are the policemen to make them respected?"

Maurizio answered these criticisms by reformulating his argument. He found an ally in Stefano, a man in his early 30's, and a regular participant in the PB process: "I think speed bumps would be enough. And it doesn't cost that much. [...] If we were a civilised and educated people everything would be easy of course, all these discussions would be useless ... but we're far from it. [...] That's why we need speed bumps." He therefore answered Franco's cultural arguments, to justify a technical solution from both a political ("we cannot change people's culture") and financial perspective ("it doesn't cost that much.")[57]

In this case, a deliberative sequence emerged: a problem was identified and framed as an environmental issue. Solutions were then proposed: the limitation of the use of cars, by the creation of a cycling path and a "zone 30". The procedural organisation of the discussion was probably good enough to allow for the emergence of a constructive discourse. The small size of the group, and the facilitator organizing the turn-taking, played a crucial role. As one participant was speaking after the other, people listened to each other. The procedural and situational conditions of the discussion therefore made the expression of disagreement possible. The expression of disagreement – by Franco in this case – pushed Maurizio (and Stefano) to offer a more comprehensive justification of his proposal, and thus to argue.

Even if disagreement is important for the emergence of deliberation, it is scarce, because the public expression of disagreement is a difficult move. Mostly, people consider their opinions and preferences as private matters, which do not need to be discussed, justified and eventually modified after discussion with strangers. In most public arenas, there seems to be a strong cultural force pushing people to respect the opinions of others, and therefore refuse to contradict or convince them. This might be linked to group dynamics – and what Goffman (1959) calls the "principle of unanimity" – especially when participation is organized at the neighbourhood level. Diana Mutz (2006) explains convincingly how difficult it might be for individuals embedded in cross-cutting social networks to express their views or simply talk about politics, as people are afraid of jeopardizing their social relationships. Despite all these difficulties, sometimes disagreement is voiced, allowing for the emer-

---

57   Observation notes, Garbatella working group, Rome, 17.02.2005

gence of deliberation. How can some people be ready to argue, or exchange views in a collective and public discussion, considering the risks in terms of reputation and social integration? What are the social and situational conditions for the emergence of disagreement in public arenas? Two factors appeared crucial here: the role of leaders and the stakes of the discussion.

The Role of Leaders and the Stakes of the Discussion

Some actors play a more important role than others in the expression of divergent views and the emergence of conflict within the group. Actors must indeed be confident enough about their ideas and standpoints to voice them explicitly and to be ready to argue with others. In this respect, activists and political party militants had a decisive influence on the quality of PB discussions. Holding strong preferences, they had the cultural and political resources necessary for the expression of dissent. Belonging to a group or a collective also fosters the expression of dissent, as it allows sharing the risks of expressing divergent views with others (party members for instance).

In the case of Garbatella, as seen above, politicized actors like Elena, Stefano and Maurizio played a crucial role throughout the discussion, both in the way the discussion was organized and in the expression of counter-arguments. One of the clearest signs of the importance of leaders and politicized actors is the vacuum created by their absence. Maurizio, Elena and Stefano were indeed absent from the following meeting of Garbatella's working group, which ended up being of mediocre discursive quality. Proposals followed each other without justification or counter-arguments, as no disagreement was expressed. While it is often assumed that activists are anti-deliberative agents, preferring direct action to cooperative discussion (Young 2001), in Rome deliberation could not happen without the commitment of local militants.

Given the presence of the elected representatives at the public meetings in Morsang-sur-Orge dissent and conflict generally emerged between citizens and members of the municipal majority. Here, the role of leader and dissenter is played by the elected officials themselves. There is therefore a gap between the participatory practices of Rome and Morsang-sur-Orge. While Roman activists can act as a countervailing power against the municipality (Fung & Wright, eds. 2003), in Morsang-sur-Orge the whole process is dominated by elected officials. If leaders are crucial in the emergence of disagreement and deliberation, the type of leader necessarily frames the nature of the deliberative interactions.

Then, discussions in PB institutions are not ends in themselves; they aim at taking binding decisions about the attribution of part of the municipal budget (up to 10 million euros in Rome). Even if these participatory institutions can be considered little empowered – the proportion of the municipal budget "decided" by the residents being relatively modest – the mere fact of having to take decisions changes the dynamic of the discussion. The crucial difference made by the stakes of the discussion is that they lower the cost of dissent, or better, make it worth expressing (Sunstein 2003, 23-25; Ryfe 2005). Stakes push people to express their views – not to keep them private –, if they want (as their presence in the assembly indicates) to make a difference concerning the final decisions. The importance of the stakes can be illustrated by comparing cases of decision-free discussions with discussions aimed at affecting public policies.

Decision-free discussions take place when participants talk about issues out of the realm of the local government competences. Arguments can be voiced, but disagreement is generally silenced, as no decision has to be taken. An excerpt from a *Comité de quartier* discussion on the issue of a new law about French kindergartens (the PSU law, "Prestation de Service Unique"[58]) illustrates this quite clearly:

"Francis, a town councillor started to evoke the reform: "The aim of this law is to liberalize the kindergarten system. Parents will be able to let their children for only a few hours a day, and not for the full day as it used to be." Participants reacted straight off. Isabelle, obviously surprised, was the first one to speak: "That's terrible! That's terrible for the future of our kids! Ok, it's more convenient for the parents, but what about the kids?" Francis answered: "I think this is the true question: what is the priority, parents or kids? I guess the law tries to take into account the complexity of modern life, with flexible schedules, part-time jobs, precariousness etc." Isabelle went on with the same line of argument: "Parents want kids, but then they throw them to the kindergarten and that's it. It's really terrible for the future of these kids, it's gonna destabilize them, disturb them ... It is terrible!"[59]

This excerpt could lead us to think that deliberation without disagreement is possible. Arguments were voiced and the discussion reached a certain level of generality. But the arguments all went in the same direction, everybody agreeing on the damageable character of the law. It was not, however, as if consensus was magically created from the beginning, but rather that disagreement was not expressed publicly. A juxtaposition of similar arguments does not make a deliberation, but a collective plea. Once the discussion about the PSU was over, my neighbours started to talk in an aside and one of them said: "But me, personally, I don't think that this PSU idea is so stupid. I'm for performance and efficiency." This argument would have clashed with those expressed publicly by the other participants, as they rest on different ideological grounds.

---

58   The PSU has been set up by law n.78/203 of January 2005.
59   Neighbourhood council Langevin, Morsang-sur-Orge, 21.01.2005.

This participant did not, however, dare express his counter-argument publicly. He probably did not feel competent enough to do so, but above all, he certainly tried to avoid a useless conflict. For disagreement to be expressed it has first to exist latently, but its expression has to be seen as worthwhile by the actors. In this case, no decision had to be taken; the debate was an end in itself. Expressing dissent was therefore not worthwhile for the participants, who would have had to accept the discursive and social costs (especially in terms of reputation) of a dissonant argument. It is indeed socially and pragmatically risky for individuals to engage in adversary conversations and to put their opinions on the table. Stakes make the expression of disagreement worthwhile by adding a value and an interest to argumentation. This conclusion is rather dull for the prospect of a deliberative participatory democracy, as most experiences of public participation are consultative. Even in relatively empowered cases like participatory budgets, disagreement and deliberation are exceptional, and only an addition of favourable conditions can make deliberation happen.

Conclusion

The results of this study may appear disappointing as to the democratic potential of Participatory Budgeting institutions. While granting direct decision-making power to citizens – which is rare among democratic innovations – their deliberative quality remains fairly low. Most of the time, discussions among ordinary citizens take the form of polemic or dispute, or simply of monologue, little disagreement appearing as regards non-contentious public policy proposals. Aware of the difficulties of deliberation in the public sphere, deliberative democrats have increasingly opted for insulating deliberation from real-world settings, thus developing experimental and artificial deliberative arenas such as mini-publics. While deliberation in such settings can be of high quality, their impact on the wider world remains fairly limited (Chambers 2009). The question for deliberative democrats then is how to infuse deliberation – or improve its quality – in the public sphere and among ordinary citizens in order to foster democracy more broadly.

The results indicate some steps forward for further research. It requires a deep procedural organization of the discussion – small groups, systematic facilitation, etc. – and the emergence of disagreement. While the former is relatively easy to achieve, the latter is much more uncommon in contemporary societies, where individuals tend to avoid conflict. Disagreement therefore has to be stimulated. This can be achieved artificially, through specific facilitation techniques, as sometimes employed in mini-publics. Some situational factors might nevertheless allow for a more « spontaneous » emergence of disagreement, such as the presence of individuals with strong preferences – like activists – and high stakes in the discussion being favourable conditions. The last point has to be stressed: while it is often assumed that citizens entering deliberation should get rid of their self-interests and orient towards the common good, it is only if they are interested in deliberation that they might be ready to enter into discursive disagreements and therefore allow deliberation to happen. The stakes of the discussion and therefore the level of empowerment of democratic innovations nurture their deliberative quality. Power and deliberation go therefore together.

References

Bacqué M.-H., & Sintomer Y. (1999), "L'espace public dans les quartiers populaires d'habitat social", in Neveu C. (Ed.) *Espace public et engagement politique, Enjeux et logiques de la citoyenneté locale,* Paris: L'Harmattan.

Baiocchi G. (2005), *Militants and Citizens: the Politics of Participatory Democracy in Porto Alegre*, Princeton: Princeton University Press.

Blondiaux L. (2000), "La démocratie par le bas. Prise de parole et délibération dans les conseils de quartier du vingtième arrondissement de Paris", *Hermès*, 26-27: 323-338.

Cabannes Y. (2006), "Participatory budgeting: a significative contribution to participatory democracy", *Environment and Urbanization*, 16, 1 27-46.

Chambers, S. (2009), "Rhetoric and the Public Sphere: Has Deliberative Democracy Abandoned Mass Democracy?", *Political Theory*, 37/3: 323-350

Cohen J. (1989), "Deliberation and democratic legitimacy", *in* Hamlin A., Pettit P. (eds.), *The Good Polity:Normative Analysis of the State*, Oxford: Basil Blackwell, 17-34.

Conover P., Searing D. & Crewe I. (2002), "The Deliberative potential of Political Discussion", *British Journal of Political Science* 32: 21-62.

Delli Carpini, M.X., Lomax Cook F. & Jacobs L.R. (2004), "Public Deliberation, Discursive Participation, and Citizen Engagement: A Review of the Empirical Literature", *Annual Review of Political Science,* 7: 315-344.

Elster J. (1987), "The Market and the Forum", in Bohman J. & Rehg W. (Eds.) *Deliberative Democracy. Essays on Reason and Politics,* Cambridge: MIT Press: 3-34

Elster J. (1994), "Argumenter et négocier dans deux assemblées constituantes", *Revue Française de Science Politique*, 44, 2 p. 187-256.

Elster J. (1998) (Ed.), *Deliberative Democracy*, Cambridge: Cambridge University Press.

Fearon J. (1998), "Deliberation as Discussion", in Elster J. (Ed.), *Deliberative Democracy*, Cambridge: Cambridge University Press: 44-68.

Fishkin (1997), *The Voice of the People. Public Opinion and Democracy*, Yale: Yale University Press.

Fishkin J., Luskin R.& Jowell R. (2002), "Considered Opinions: Deliberative Polling in Britain", *British Journal of Political Science*, 32: 455-87.

Fung A. (2004), *Empowered Participation, Reinventing Urban Democracy*, Princeton: Princeton University Press.

Fung A. (2008), "Minipublics: Deliberative Designs and their Consequences", *in* Rosenberg S. W. (Ed.), *Can the people govern? Deliberation, Participation and Democracy*. New York: Palgrave Macmillan: 159-183.

Fung A. & Wright E.O. (2003) (Eds.), *Deepening Democracy, Institutional Innovations in Empowered Participatory Governance*, London: Verso.

Goffman E. (1959), *The Presentation of the Self in Everyday Life*, New York: Doubleday Anchor Books.

Goodin R. & Niemeyer S. (2003), "When Does Deliberation Begin? Internal Reflection versus Public Discussion in Deliberative Democracy", *Political Studies*, 51: 627-649.

Goodin R. & Dryzek J. (2006), "Deliberative Impacts: The macro-political uptake of mini-publics", *Politics & Society*, 34, 2: 219-244.

Gutmann A. & Thompson D. (1996), *Democracy and Disagreement*, Harvard: Belknap Press.

Habermas J. (1984), *The Theory of Communicative Action*, vol. 1, Boston: Beacon Press.

Habermas J. (1996), Between Facts and Norms: *Contributions to a Discourse Theory of Law and Democracy*, Cambridge: The MIT Press.

Huckfeldt R., Johnston P.& Sprague J. (2004), *Political Disagreement: The Survival of Diverse Opinions within Communication Networks*, New York: Cambridge University Press.

Manin B. (1987), "On Legitimacy and Political Deliberation", *Political Theory*, 15: 338-368.

Mansbridge J. (1980), *Beyond Adversary Democracy*, New York: Basic Books.

Mansbridge J. (1999), "Everyday Talk in the Deliberative System", in Macedo, S. (Ed.) *Deliberative Politics: Essays on Democracy and Disagreement*, Oxford: Oxford University Press p.211-140.

Mutz D. & Martin P. (2001),"Facilitating communication across lines of political difference", *American Political Science Review*, 95, 1: 97-114.

Mutz, D. (2006), *Hearing the Other Side: Deliberative vs. Participatory Democracy*, New York: Cambridge University Press.

Polletta F. (2005), *It Was Like a Fever. Story Telling in Protest and Politics*, Chicago: Chicago University Press.

Remer G. (2000), "Two Models of Deliberation: Oratory and Conversation in Ratifying the Constitution", *The Journal of Political Philosophy*, 8, 1:68-90.

Ryfe D. (2005), "Does Deliberative Democracy Work ?", *Annual Review of Political Science*, 8: 49-71.

Sanders L. (1997), "Against Deliberation", *Political Theory*, 25, 3: 347-376.

Sintomer Y. (2007), *Le pouvoir au peuple. Tirage au sort, jurys citoyens et démocratie participative*, Paris, La découverte.

Sintomer Y., Herzberg C. & Röcke A. (2008) "Participatory budgeting in Europe: potentials and challenges", *International Journal of Urban and Regional Research*, 32, 1: 164-178.

Smith G. (2009), *Democratic Innovations: Designing Institutions for Citizen Participation*, Cambridge: Cambridge University Press.

Steiner J., Bachtiger A., Sporndli M. & Steenbergen M. (2005), *Deliberative Politics in Action. Crossnational Study of Parliamentary Debates,* Cambridge: Cambridge University Press.

Strauss, A. & Corbin, J. (Eds.), (1997), *Grounded Theory in Practice*, Thousand Oaks: Sage.

Sunstein, C. (2003), *Why Societies Need Dissent*, Cambridge: Harvard University Press.

Talpin J. (2011), *Schools of Democracy. How Ordinary Citizens (sometimes) Become Competent in Participatory Budgeting Institutions*, Colchester: ECPR Press.

Young I.M. (1996), "Communication and the Other: Beyond Deliberative Democracy", in Benhabib S. (Ed.) *Democracy and Difference. Contesting the Boundaries of the Political,* Princeton: Princeton University Press: 120-136

Young I.M. (2001), "Activist Challenges to Deliberative Democracy", *Political Theory,* 29, 5: 670-690

The Biased Inclusiveness of Local Democratic Innovations: Vehicles or Obstacles for Political Equality?

Clemente Navarro/Joan Font

Introduction[60]

"If democratic innovations simply replicate and reinforce the differential rates of participation witnessed in most other forms of political participation, then their legitimacy will be cast into doubt. After all, one of the attractions of democratic innovations is their potential to tackle the "unresolved dilemma" of unequal participation." (Smith 2009: 163)

The search for political equality has been one of the driving forces behind the development of new participatory instruments that have been mostly used at the local level. The appearance of these participatory mechanisms has often been associated with rising levels of abstention or other "democratic malaises" (see the Introduction to this volume for further discussion). These symptoms have produced a substantial concern to find complementary vehicles for participation that would incorporate those who fail to vote in elections or feel alienated from traditional vehicles for participation. At the very least, almost all participatory processes have incorporated some concern regarding their capacity to adequately represent different interests and population sectors and, many of them, have given equality a very central role. In fact, the main priority for some of these processes has even been building more equal political communities.

However, the empirical results of many of these processes point in a very different direction. Except in a limited number of cases where this concern for political equality has been strongly incorporated into the basic institutional design of the participatory mechanism, most experiences have resulted in quite unequal participatory patterns among different social groups. In fact, even if

---

60 This paper has been developed as part of project CSO2010-08968, funded by the Spanish Ministry of Science. Previous versions were presented at the ECPR Potsdam general sessions, at the UPF Research Seminar of the Political Science Department and in the ECPR Münster Joint Sessions. In the three presentations we benefited from generous comments from other participants. We also thank the book editors for their interesting comments on previous versions of the text.

some of the most well publicized experiences have been able to achieve more egalitarian outcomes, our claim in this paper is that, at least in the Spanish case, they very often result in very unequal participatory patterns. Evaluations that have reached more optimistic conclusions have been based on case studies that represent "best practices", but it is quite likely that less well known more common experiences achieve worse performances in the equality domain. Our data comes from a representative sample of the general population and, as a result, allows us to reach conclusions that capture general trends, as both more successful and less successful participatory experiences are included.

We claim that this negative inclusiveness outcome is the result of three complementary mechanisms. First, the development of participatory devices that require more intense citizen intervention provokes a larger role for social and educational resources, contributing to more limited participation from resource-poor social sectors. Second, since Hirschman (1970), we know the importance of lack of satisfaction as a driving force to explain participation of members of any kind of societal institution. The very unequal social distribution of satisfaction with policy results will result in a second mechanism fuelling unequal participatory outcomes. Third, and most important, the most frequent mobilization processes used in these experiences centrally involve the associational networks most deeply connected with the local policy-making process. As a result, the involvement in associational networks and particularly in political associations will have a strong effect on the final likelihood of individual participation. However, participation biases will not be independent of the institutional design of the participatory experience: organisational choices will have effects on who is called to participate and, as a result, on the final level of participation bias.

We consider as local participation processes all those one-shot experiences (such as a citizen jury or an electronic survey) or permanent mechanisms (e.g. an environmental council) which have been developed at the local level to capture citizen preferences regarding local policies[61]. Basically, these mechanisms correspond to types 2 (procedures of deliberation) and 3 (new forms of cooperation) as defined in the introduction, since local referenda (type 1) have been quite scarce in the Spanish context. In this paper we will use the concepts of inclusive participation and political equality as interchangeable, meaning the equal representation of different social sectors in participatory processes.

---

61 Through the paper we will use the words participatory processes, experiences or mechanisms as synonymous.

We will develop our argument and examine the empirical evidence behind it in the next five sections. In the first one, we will provide a basic descriptive overview of the experiences of local participation developed in Spain in recent decades and the (limited) role that political equality has played among them. We will continue by discussing the comparative importance that political equality has played in the normative and empirical discussion about local participation and explain the three causal mechanisms which, according to our interpretation, are generally responsible for the unequal outcomes of participatory processes. This section also presents the main hypotheses to be tested in this paper. The next section will discuss the empirical data to be used in our analysis and present its main methodological characteristics as well as describe and justify the operationalizations chosen. The following section will present the empirical data, first analyzing the individual impact of each of the independent variables and then providing a joint analysis of the effect of all of them. In the last part of this empirical section we will also test our hypotheses on a subset of the sample that will allow us to control for the effect of institutional designs on the level of participatory bias. The final section will summarize the findings and discuss its main implications.

Spanish Local Participation and Political Equality

In Spain, the first processes of citizen participation in local government took place shortly after the first democratic local councils were elected in 1979. However, even if participation was on the agenda of most parties' platforms, local councils faced a crucial lack of basic services and citizen participation ended up not being a priority in the first decade of democratic local government. The initial instruments developed during the 1980s were basically oriented towards the participation of the associational sector, through advisory councils organized for each policy or neighborhood (Navarro 2004; Blakeley 2005). This created a strong relationship between local governments and the more politically oriented associational sector: they were more often invited to participate in participatory instruments than non-political associations (Navarro & Juaristi 2006), they generated more intense processes of cooperation and resistance in their relation with local governments (Font, San Martín & Schneider 2006), and they promoted more political activism (contact and protest) among their members (Anduiza, Bonet & Morales 2006).

During the second half of the 1990s, Spanish local governments experienced the same shift towards citizen-based participatory processes that also occurred in other countries (Lowndes et al. 2001). New forms of participation using new technologies, adopting citizen-based instruments such as juries or strategic participatory processes, were developed in some municipalities.

Mechanisms relying basically on associations continued to be the central pillar of local participation, but they were more often accompanied by these new devices, more oriented towards the individual citizen (Font 2002). This has not been without controversy and has often provoked a quite reluctant attitude from the associational realm, unwilling to share their role in local governance with individual citizens, fearing this move has been specifically planned to dilute their power[62].

One of the main arguments to justify this shift has been precisely to avoid "those who participate always being the same people" and who do not accurately represent the interests of the general population. However, the argument has been framed as basically a question of "representativeness" and of adequately representing plural interests in local policies, rather than as an issue of social or political equality. In fact, a comparative study focusing on one of the major networks of European and Latin American participatory cities points to a rather different emphasis in the different legitimization discourses in the two geographic contexts: whereas in Latin America, the search for more equal societies has been the most important reason to develop participatory processes in 19 percent of the cases, this was not the case among the Spanish and European experiences, where none of them considered equality the most important goal[63]. The fact that many experiences are primarily addressed to the associational sector and that only a few of those which aim to mobilize individual citizens make specific efforts to guarantee adequate representation, or to forcefully mobilize among the underprivileged, is also an important symptom of the limited role that equality plays in the Spanish local participation arena.

The move towards more participatory local polities has been primarily a locally driven process in the Spanish case. Unlike the French "politique de la ville" or the efforts made by the British government to push their municipalities to open new channels for citizen participation, in the Spanish case the supra-local contribution has been very limited[64]. As a result, Spanish municipali-

---

62 See Ganuza (2010) for the Spanish case or Hendricks (2002) for a similar argument in Australia.

63 The research considered all the experiences incorporated in the OIDP (International Observatory for Participatory Democracy, a network formed by several hundred municipalities belonging mostly to Latin American and Southern European countries, funded by the European Union) database, which included 26 Latin American experiences and 32 European ones (Font, Teixidor & Herrera 2004).

64 In the last decade, a few regional governments (Andalucía, Aragon, Canarias, Catalonia and Valencia) have started to work in this direction, with interesting programs being developed in some of them. New legislation was approved at the Spanish national level in the last decade, but no resources or important incentives were given to fully implement it.

ties do not have a shared model for local participation, but rather extremely different offers of participatory instruments. In any case, their development has been especially intense in medium-size cities. With almost no exceptions instruments have been put in place in all of them[65], while the reality has been much more diverse in very large cities and much less formalised in small municipalities.

There is no complete picture or map of all the Spanish local participatory projects; however, it is clear that these instruments are extremely unevenly distributed, with quite interesting experiences being developed in some cities (Sintomer, Herzberg & Röcke 2008) and no efforts at all in others. In most cases, the influence of these processes on policy-making has been rather limited, but the range of issues being discussed has become more relevant, moving from very peripheral concerns to the tackling of central issues within areas such as urban planning, local budgets or mobility (Font & Galais 2011).

Theory and Hypothesis

While inclusiveness has not been very important in practice, it has been more so in the comparative analyses of participatory processes carried out by social scientists. In fact, one of the first serious evaluations of the performance of participation mechanisms already highlighted that political equality was one of their major potential weaknesses (Mansbridge 1983). The relative importance accorded to this criterion, as well as the precise idea used to capture it changes from one author to another, but most of the important contributions have continued to incorporate this issue in one way or another (Fung & Wright 2001; Smith 2009)[66]. As a result, some of the most clearly academically driven experiences, such as Deliberative Opinion Polls (DOP) have incorporated random selections of participants trying to guarantee effective egalitarian participation (Fishkin 1991).

Concern about the risks of unequal participation has also been widely expressed. Fiorina's (1999) case study is probably the most well known text developing the idea of the perils of domination by extreme voices, but the inherent tension between extension and intensity of preferences has often been

---

65 Navarro, Font and Cuesta (2009) have examined the opportunities for participation in each of the 51 cities ranging from 100,000 to 400,000 inhabitants. Only one of them offered no instrument at all for local participation.

66 See the Introduction to this volume for a more detailed discussion of the central role of inclusiveness.

highlighted: precisely because these mechanisms normally involve higher costs than voting, they will result in less extensive and very often more biased representation. The promises of deliberation could be achieved at the expense of more unequal participation. Even if this unequal participation did not occur, the importance of arguments and the social distribution of sophistication and language skills would still involve the risk of certain participants dominating, and the outcomes would likely reflect the previously existing inequalities (Przeworski 1998).

The majority of the existing empirical evidence points in this direction. Quite different mechanisms like public hearings (Hampton 1999), citizen assemblies (Lang 2007), experiences with electronic democracy (Carman 2009) or traditional consultation committees (Sintomer & Demaillard 2007) end up offering quite biased pools of participants. The only exceptions to this rule are experiences that have incorporated a very clear concern for equality[67] in their methodological design or that have made special efforts to mobilize in a particularly intense way sectors which traditionally participate less (Abers 1998).

What are the mechanisms explaining these biased participatory outcomes? Participation in local processes is just a partially peculiar form of participation. In fact, the potential explanatory factors to understand who attends public hearings, citizen assemblies, etc., or who does not are quite similar to those that would help us understand the decision to protest or to vote. To start with, as in any other participation activity, the decision cannot be fully understood if we do not consider factors related to both the existing institutional opportunities to participate and to the personal circumstances of individual citizens. Regarding the latter, we will address the two sets of factors that most commonly explain individual participation: resources and attitudes.

If resources matter for relatively low cost activities like voting, it is likely that they play a more important role when participatory activities are more time – and skill – consuming (Verba et al. 1995), as often happens in many participation activities. Thus, we expect that traditional resources which help overcome those participation costs will have an effect on who participates in local participation experiences.

Several attitudinal factors have been shown to be important to explain participation. Among them, lack of satisfaction has been considered crucial, at least since Hirschman (1970). However, the role of satisfaction may be even more central when institutionally created processes are involved: while local government voters and/or individuals who are satisfied with local policies have

---

67 In addition to the aforementioned DOPs, citizen juries and other instruments that use selection by lot, also tend to reach participants who represent quite adequately their constituencies (Font & Blanco 2007; Sintomer 2007)

much less of a need to have their voices heard, the existence of an institutionally created scenario where dissatisfied voters can voice their discontent represents a crucial opportunity for them[68].

Finally, mobilization has also been considered a crucial force behind participation (Rosenstone & Hansen 1993; Verba et al. 1995). Associational membership provides information, helps develop civic skills and places citizens in social networks that will be targeted for mobilization. As a result, associational membership (especially in the case of political associations) has been considered to fuel political activism (Welzel, Ingelhart & Deutsch 2005; Van der Meer & Van Ingen 2009). Moreover, in Spain the earliest instruments of participation in municipalities were oriented towards local associations, especially towards the more politically oriented among them (Navarro, 1999).

Even if all these mechanisms contribute to unequal effective participation, we claim that this third set of factors will be especially important. The three causal mechanisms that help us understand the mobilization role of associations are reinforced by the strategic role that the Spanish model of local participation gives to political associations. The result is what we refer to as a "double asking effect", where associational members are mobilized by local governments through their strategic place in social networks and as the main target population of their diffusion activities, but also by their own associations which need their involvement in the local participatory processes to see their own proposals supported. As a result, regardless of social and attitudinal traits, the mobilization capacities of participatory instruments are especially modulated by previous mobilization through associational membership.

However, these likely effects are, in turn, strongly modulated by institutional choices. The different procedures used to select or to mobilize the participants will be likely to have effects on the final pool of participants. As mentioned, the call for participation may privilege reaching a more egalitarian outcome either through random selection or through targeted mobilization addressed to incorporate usual non-participants. Or, it may be considered more important to have a process open to anyone willing to participate or to have the most powerful and relevant stakeholders involved[69]. These choices will make

---

68 On the role of satisfaction with specific policies or public services, see also Kriesi and Westholm (2006).

69 These mechanisms would include most of the new forms of cooperation between interest groups and state actors included in the third group of participation processes discussed in the introduction to this volume. Both kinds of participatory mechanisms included here, those making a general mobilization call and accepting any participant, as well as those involving only associations are among the most common types of existing local participation mechanisms in many European countries, and certainly in the Spanish case (Font and Galais, 2011).

an important difference in the resulting level of participatory bias, with processes mostly addressed to the associational world resulting in more biased participation, while those experiences which focus on all the citizenry and make specific mobilization efforts towards them resulting in a more limited participatory bias (Font and Blanco, 2007). Table 5.1 summarizes the main hypotheses presented up to now that are going to be tested in this paper.

Data, Variables and Operationalizations

To test the aforementioned hypotheses we use a survey conducted by CIS[70] among the Spanish adult population in 2006. The survey had three main peculiar characteristics. The first one was to limit the universe to the cities where these instruments have been most fully developed: those with 100,000 to 400,000 inhabitants. Thus, the survey includes 3994 interviews carried out in 51 cities and is representative of the adult population living in Spanish cities of that medium size[71]. In large cities and small towns there are very different socio-political contexts regarding opportunities for political participation and the existence of participatory instruments (few formalized ones in small towns), as well as costs to use them (high in large cities). As a consequence, the sampling was limited to more homogeneous cities to control potential size effects. Nevertheless, these cities are heterogeneous enough to include different local socio-political contexts (e.g. local government ideology, existing participatory devices, etc.).

Secondly, to be able to more fully explore the effects of more participatory contexts, the survey included oversampling of five cities which had been quite actively using participatory methods. 2494 interviews were carried out in those five cities and the rest of the interviews (1500) were carried out in the remaining cities in our universe (those with 100,000 to 400,000 inhabitants). Using the appropriate weights, the 3994 cases can be analyzed as a sample of the total Spanish population living in cities of that size.

.

---

70 CIS is the public survey institution devoted to conducting social and political surveys used by both policy makers as well as the academic community. Occasionally, CIS conducts surveys in cooperation with research institutions, as in this specific survey developed jointly with the Pablo Olavide University.

71 See full sampling details at www.cis.es, survey number 2661 (2006), as well as in Navarro, Font and Cuesta (2009).

Table 5.1 Main Hypotheses

Hypothesis 1	**Biased inclusiveness**	*Inclusiveness in participatory instruments is biased due to social, attitudinal and mobilization factors*
	Hypothesis 1.1	*Social bias: participation in participatory devices depends on social resources (skills, time, experiences, etc.)*
	Hypothesis 1.2	*Attitudinal bias: participatory instruments attract particularly those more dissatisfied with local government action*
	Hypothesis 1.3	*Mobilization bias: previous mobilization through associations promotes use of participatory instruments*
Hypothesis 2	**The double-asking effect**	*Mobilization bias is the strongest bias: participatory instruments mobilize especially those citizens who are already politically active in associations*
Hypothesis 3	**Institutional design matters**	*Participatory mechanisms which make a specific effort to mobilize individual citizens will result in more limited participation bias*

Thirdly, the survey covers a wide range of issues related to local governance, but focusing more on specific behaviors and perceptions, and less on general vague attitudes towards enhanced participation. Specifically, a question was included about participation in different kinds of participatory devices during the last year (2005).

Our main dependent variable measures participation in local participatory instruments, considering six different participatory instruments. They represent the main types existing in Spanish municipalities: Neighborhood Councils, Policy Councils (both especially addressed to associations), Local Agenda 21 and Local Ombudsman (both oriented towards different publics), Participatory Budgets and Citizen Juries (both more innovative and citizen oriented). The variable has been elaborated distinguishing between interviewees who have been active in at least one of them (5 percent of the total sample) and those who have not participated in any of them[72].

In the final part of the paper we will be interested to see, whether different participatory experiences result in different participatory outcomes. With that goal in mind, we will concentrate on two cities which used the same two kinds of instruments, (Getafe and Córdoba[73]), but instruments which are quite different from each other (Participatory Budgeting and consultation councils). In 2006, both cities had a Participatory Budgeting process that aimed to intensely incorporate individual citizens (Ganuza, 2010). Simultaneously, they also had consultation councils in which neighborhood associations played quite a central role and whose participants were fundamentally mobilized through associational networks.

Our first hypothesis claims that inclusiveness in participatory instruments is biased due to social, attitudinal and mobilization factors. We will test it in the next section through bivariate analysis, using differences in percentages. A simple subtraction is made of those that participate in the group that are expected to be more active minus those in the category expected to be less active. Differences equal to zero means that no bias is present in the use of participatory instruments, whereas a positive difference shows a bias according to our hypothesis, and a negative difference a bias against our hypothesis. This provides a very simple system to show the existence of biases and their magnitude (Navarro, 2008). With this goal in mind, all our independent variables will be reduced to two-category variables that have been delimited in accordance with the classic literature on political participation.

Five variables have been used to measure social bias: gender, age, education, social class and children living in the household. The first one differentiates between female and male to catch the classic gender gap in political participation. The second one captures the difference between young citizens and other age groups, since age could mean more experience and skills facilitating participation. The differences between people with a degree and those who have attained a lower level of formal education are our third variable. Social class differentiates between classic 'blue collar' and 'white collar' occupa-

---

72 We combine different mechanisms, but the small number of participants does not allow distinguishing among them: the main issue is to know if people have participated in, at least, one of them. 50 of the 51 municipalities included in the sample had a minimum of one participatory mechanism and some of them had a quite rich and diverse participatory offer.

73 Each of them constitutes an independent representative sample of adult citizens. We use the aggregated data of the two cities, which include 1000 interviews.

tions[74]. The last social variable distinguishes the households where a child under six years of age is living. The assumption is that this implies less amount of free time to participate, especially among middle-aged women (Parry, Moiser & Day 1992).

Attitudinal bias has been measured using two components of local government legitimacy: the 'input dimension', measured by the degree of political trust in local government, and the 'output dimension', measured by the degree of satisfaction with local services (Vetter & Kersting 2003). The first one implies a general sentiment of trust in local public authorities as representatives of public interests, whereas the second one is a more concrete evaluative measure of attitude about their actions through service delivery[75]. These attitudes have been originally measured using a 10-point scale in the questionnaire, and variables for the next section have been dichotomized using the middle point of this scale[76].Voting behavior in the last local elections has also been included: according to the 'home team thesis', those who voted for the governing party ("winners") will show higher levels of trust in local government than those who did not ("losers") (Norris, 1999). Thus, 'losers' could use participatory mechanisms to channel their discontent, as a space to exercise opposition against local government. The difference between 'winners' and 'losers' (all those not voting for the governing party) is used to measure this potential bias.

Mobilization bias is measured by associational membership, including in two separate variables membership in political and non-political associations[77]. In both cases we simply distinguish between members (who will be targeted by the double asking effect) and non-members. Finally, political involvement (measured as an ordinal variable about political discussion of local issues) is

---

74   'Blue collar' includes 'unskilled workers', 'skilled workers' and 'self-employed'. 'White collar' includes middle-class (service workers, lower level professionals and managers) and upper class (employers, high level professionals & managers).

75   The bivariate correlation among them is moderate (0.467). Dissatisfaction has been proven as a good predictor of contact with local government (Navarro and Ramírez 2006) and the use of participatory instruments (Navarro, Font & Cuesta 2009). For these reasons we have preferred to use these variables separately.

76   Questions in the survey ask about 'trust' and 'satisfaction'. Thus, we have reversed the direction of answers to replicate our theoretical statement in the empirical analysis. The first five points of the original 10-point scales have been grouped together and coded equal to 1 (distrust and dissatisfaction), and the other values have been coded equal to 0 (trust and satisfaction).

77   The survey asked about membership in 14 different types of associations. We followed Navarro and Juaristi (2006) in distinguishing between political and non-political associations.

included in our analyses as a control variable[78]. This is a traditional measure of attitude explaining political participation as a result of psychological involvement.

Table 5.2 The Source of Bias in Participatory Instruments: Social, Attitudinal and Mobilization Factors

Bias	Variable	Negative effect	Positive effect
Social	Gender	Female	Male
	Age	Young (< 30)	Adult (> 30)
	Education	Below university	University
	Class	Working	Upper+Middle
	Child (> 7 years)	Yes	No
Attitudinal	Distrust	Trust (10-6)	Distrust (5-1)
	Dissatisfaction	Satisfaction (10-6)	Dissatisfaction
	Opposition (vote)	Winners (governing party)	Losers (others)
Mobilization	Political association	No member	Member
	Non-political association	No member	Member
Political involvement	Discussion about local issues (frequency)	Never/seldom	Often/Very often

To test the relative effect of each of these variables, the second part of the next section will use different logistic regressions models: a model for each kind of bias (social, attitudinal, and mobilization), as well as a model including all independent variables. Political involvement is included as a control variable in all of them. Differences in explained variance among models are used as an indicator to compare their relative impact in the use of participatory instruments (our dependent variable). In these analyses the aforementioned variables are included, using their original measurements standardized on a continuum scale (0,1). Local electoral behavior is included using 'winners' as reference category against 'losers' (voting for other parties), and other answers (did not vote,

---

78 We know from all previous research (Verba et al 1995; Anduiza et al, 2006) that this is a variable powerfully associated with the probability of participating in any kind of political activity. As a result, we include it to avoid attributing its explanatory power to another factor.

no answer), offering the possibility to know the mobilization impact due to a clear oppositional attitude against the governing party ('losers')[79].

Results

In this section we discuss the empirical analyses and their most important results; first a bivariate analysis to show the bias associated with single variables followed by a second multivariate analysis to show the relative effect of different sources of bias. Finally, a third analysis follows a similar logic, but compares only the participants on consultation councils and Participatory Budgeting in the aggregated Córdoba and Getafe local samples.

Biased Inclusiveness: Social, Attitudinal and Mobilization.

The use of participatory instruments reveals different sources of bias, similar to those found for other forms of political participation: greater socio-economic resources, dissatisfaction and mobilization promote participation in local mechanisms as our hypothesis 1 suggested (Figure 5.3; See the Annex for the full details of the data).

Two of the four variables capturing the role of social bias are significant: gender and age[80]. Difference between winners and losers is not a clear source of participatory bias, whereas other oppositional attitudes toward local authorities foster an unequal use of participatory devices. In fact, a 'dissatisfaction bias' promotes participation among those who feel distrust of local government, as well as those dissatisfied with local services. The mobilization variables reveal a stronger percentage difference: associational membership means a higher probability of using participatory instruments (around ten times higher than non-members), and this effect is more noticeable for political associations.

---

79 In fact, this variable captures some of our attitudinal hypothesis (lack of trust against governing party), as well as of our idea regarding mobilization (being more intensely mobilized by opposition parties to use participation mechanisms as a platform to oppose local government policies). However, we include it as an attitudinal factor to make a more rigorous test of our hypothesis 2 (mobilization is the most important source of bias).

80 Confidence intervals have been computed using this formula: (P1-P2) +/- (Z*SP1-P2). Difference is not significant when zero is included in the confidence interval. In addition, Chi2 tests have been computed showing the same results. Original Figures have been included in Annex I.

This effect is even stronger than psychological involvement in local issues (political involvement).

These basic bivariate analyses reveal that the inclusiveness of participatory opportunities supplied by local governments is limited and shows diverse and significant biases in the involvement of different social sectors. Stronger previous involvement in political activities, greater individual resources, and negative attitudes towards local government are clearly associated with the likelihood to participate.

Figure 5.1 The Impact of Social, Dissatisfaction and Mobilization Biases Difference in %

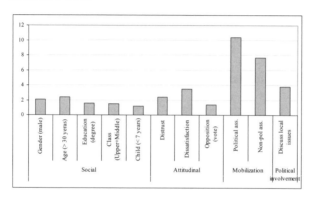

Source: survey CIS 2661 (2006).

On 'Participative Self-Selection': the Double-Asking Effect of Political Association.

The logistic regression models in Table 5.3 indicate that the mobilization bias associated with membership in associations is the most important factor in explaining who participates in local participation processes. Besides the classic gender gap effect, positive political involvement, and dissatisfaction with local services, previous mobilization through associational membership explains the use of participatory instruments. Specifically, membership in political associations has a stronger effect than membership in non-political associations. In fact, the model including only the mobilization bias explains more variance (9 percent) than the models including social or attitudinal bias (around 4 percent).

Thus, regardless of socio-demographic factors or attitudinal orientations, a 'double asking effect' appears as the strongest explanatory factor. As indicated above, political associations play an important role regarding participatory instruments in Spanish municipalities. They are more often invited than non-political associations to participate in participatory instruments, providing more information and opportunities to be mobilized by participatory initiatives among their members. From this point of view, the privileged invitation process made by municipalities regarding these associations also implies a privileged invitation process regarding their members. As a result, membership in associations, and particularly in political associations, is an important source of bias regarding municipal opportunities for participation.

However, these results also show that dissatisfaction with municipal services is an important factor explaining inclusiveness in participatory instruments. This effect is significant in the attitudinal bias model, as well as in the combined model, while the effect of distrust of local government disappears in the second one: participatory mechanisms appear as a space to channel discontent regarding the actions of local government. More than a general sentiment about local authorities, participation is explained by an evaluative judgment of local services. Participation is, thus, also based on political discontent about municipal outputs.

To summarize, the results presented in this paper reveal the biased inclusiveness of local participatory instruments. Our analysis shows that this participation is quite biased towards men, dissatisfied citizens, more psychologically involved individuals and, above all, members of associations. These biases resemble the basic traits that explain more traditional modes of political participation and reproduce the inequalities that are found in them. Our hypothesis 1 is confirmed since the three kinds of bias matter in understanding who participates and who does not in local experiences.

However, the mobilization bias is particularly strong and has a much larger effect in this realm (hypothesis 2). Our argument is that part of this effect is due to the classic mobilization argument (Rosenstone and Hansen 1993; Verba et al. 1995): associational members receive information, develop skills and are strategically placed in mobilizing networks. In the specific world of local participation this effect is probably reinforced by the double asking effect. Since associations in general and political associations in particular are the main target and agent of participatory policies, they receive two complementary calls to participate: one from the local government (which reaches them more than other people because of diffusion strategies and because of their strategic placement in social networks) and one from their own association, which is intensely entrenched and often has strong preferences regarding local policy-making efforts.

Table 5.3 The Role of Social, Attitudinal and Mobilization Bias

		Model 1 (social bias)		Model 2 (attitudinal bias)		Model 3 (mobilization bias)		Model 4 (combined)	
		B	Exp (B)	B	Exp (B)	B	Exp (B)	B	Exp (B)
Political involvement	Discuss local issues	**1.278**	**3,591**	**1.210**	**3.355**	**0.943**	**2.568**	**0.795**	**2.214**
Social bias	Gender (male)	**0.429**	**-1.535**					**0,433**	**1.542**
	Age	0.684	-1.981					0.726	2.067
	Education	**0.199**	**-1.22**					0.041	1.041
	Child (< 6 years old)	0.195	-1.216					0.121	1.129
Attitudinal bias	Distrust local government			**0.047**	1.406			0.055	1.057
	Dissatisfaction local services			**0.100**	1.105			**0.102**	**1.107**
Mobilization bias	Political association					1.075	2.931	**0.984**	**2.674**
	Non-political association					0.660	1.935	**0.570**	**1.768**
Cte		**-4.682**	**-0.009**	**-4.327**	**0.013**	**-3.946**	**0.019**	**-5.245**	**0.005**
Pseudo-R2 (Nagelkarke)		**0.04**		**0.036**		**0.09**		**0.099**	

⧠

Significant coefficients in bold (p<0.05)
All independent variables have been standardized to 0-1
Reference categories: Class: unskilled workers
Vote: 'winners' (support governing party)

Does Institutional Design Matter in Explaining Participatory Bias?

Do these results change if we focus on a specific participatory instrument? To make a meaningful comparison we need to look at similar local contexts using the same kinds of participatory instruments. To do this we have selected two cities (Córdoba and Getafe) that share very similar institutional designs, as they both have meaningful and long since established consultation councils, as well as a Participatory Budgeting process that was in place in the years previous to the survey. Additionally, in both processes of Participatory Budgeting an effort had been made to incorporate individual citizens giving them a central role in deliberations and voting processes[81]. Both processes had attracted a substantial number of participants, but larger for consultation councils since they have been in place for decades and our question did not have a specific time frame.

Table 5.4 shows that once we look at specific cities and instruments not all social biases always work in the same direction and have the same intensity (e.g. women participate more than men in the consultation councils of these two cities). However, the most important difference between the two instruments appears in the intensity of the associational bias, which exists in both cases but is considerably larger in the case of the consultation councils.

T 5.4 Instiutional Design and Inclusiviness of Participatory Instruments:

Social, Attitudinal and Mobilization Bias - Differences in % and Chi2

Bias		Difference in percentages		Chi2	
		Consultation councils	Participatory budget	Consultation councils	Participatory budget
Social	Gender (male)	-2.5	0.8	2.491	0.57
	Age (> 30) (1)	**6.1**	**3.2**	**10.72**	**6.44**
	Education (degree)	-0.4	-0.8	0.36	0.357
	Class (Upper)	0.0	0.8	0.001	0.525
	Child (> 7 years)	1.3	-0.1	3.46	0.001
Attitudinal	Distrust	1.4	-1.1	0.626	0.891
	Dissatisfaction	-1.8	-1.1	2.265	0.754
	Opposition (vote)	1.9	1.9	4.787	2.293
Mobilization	Political ass.	**14.4**	**5.8**	**57.366**	**19.747**
	Non-pol. Ass.	**13.4**	**5.5**	**43.354**	**15.198**
Political involvement	Discus local issues	**5.9**	**2.9**	**12.708**	**6.439**

Significant differences and Chi2 values in bold (p<0.05).

⬜

The regression analysis provides a more accurate picture of the importance of each of the variables (Table 5.5. and Figure 5.2)[82]. The results reveal that these

---

81 This is not the case in all Participatory Budgeting processes that often give a much more central role to associations. For example, we could not include Albacete in our comparison, because its participatory budget is mostly associationally based. More details about these cases in Sintomer et al. (2008).

82 Annex III provides the details of each of the different models, following the logic of Table 5.3. Annex II provides all the details for each of the variables and

two specific mechanisms continue to show the same kinds of bias in the recruitment of their participants, but their intensity is quite different, especially regarding the role of the associational bias, which is much larger in the case of the consultation council and does not reach statistical significance for any of the two variables in the case of Participatory Budgeting. The mobilization bias continues to have the most powerful effect in consultation councils (as it does for the whole sample), but plays a more limited role (slightly smaller than social bias) in the case of Participatory Budgeting, where age and education are the two variables that show a significant effect. In sum, inclusiveness seems to be less biased for participatory budgets than for consultation councils (using Pseudo R2). And the greatest difference is for the mobilization bias (Figure 5.2). Resources and political attitudes promote a similar degree of bias in participatory budgets and consultation councils; whereas mobilization bias is reduced in the first one. Thus, institutional design matters: the centrally targeted populations (associational members vs. individual citizens), is the 'crucial difference' between consultation councils and participatory budgets (at least in the cities analyzed) promoting the reduction of the 'double asking effect'. This result shows that the intensity of the mobilization bias is not a necessary result of any participatory process, but a result of the specific institutional designs of participatory mechanisms.

---

participation instruments in these two cities, following the model provided for the full sample in Annex I.

Table 5.5 Institutional Design and the Role of Social, Attitudinal and Mobilization Bias - Logistic Regressions

		Consultation councils		Participatory budget	
		B	Exp(B)	B	Exp(B)
Political involvement	Discuss local issues	**1.190**	**3.288**	0.945	2.572
Social	Gender (male)	0.278	1.321	-0.563	0.569
	Age	3.464	31.929	**3.225**	**25.163**
	Education	0.757	2.131	**1.652**	**5.215**
	Upper	-0.384	0.681	-0.611	0.543
	Middle	-0.207	0.813	-0.192	0.825
	Self employed	0.242	1.274	0.484	1.622
	Skilled workers	0.000	1.000	0.000	1.000
	Child < 7 years old	-0.395	0.673	0.443	1.557
Attitudinal	Distrust local government	-0.076	0.927	-0.034	0.967
	Dissatisfaction local services	**0.166**	**1.181**	-0.009	0.991
	Vote: others	0.126	1.135	-0.454	0.635
	Vote: losers	0.332	1.394	0.240	1.271
Mobilization	Political association	**1.239**	**3.453**	0.848	2.335
	Non-political association	**0.804**	**2.234**	0.733	2.081
Cte		**-6.615**	**0.001**	**-6.300**	**0.002**
Pseudo-R2 (Nagelkarke)		0.237		0.172	

Significant coefficients in bold (p<0.05)

All independent variables have been standardized to 0-1

Figure 5.2 The Impact of Instiutional Design Bias - Differences

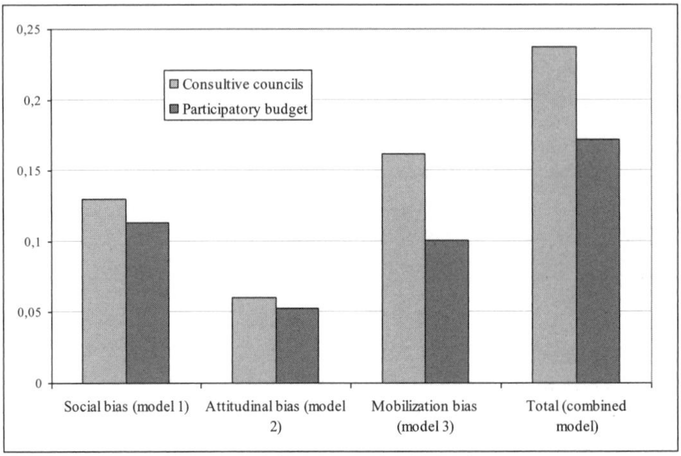

☐ Consultive councils	
■ Participatory budget	

Social bias (model 1)   Attitudinal bias (model 2)   Mobilization bias (model 3)   Total (combined model)

Conclusion

The overrepresentation of certain social sectors among participants has been documented in previous research about local participation. However, most of this research was based on evaluations of single experiences. Previous results help us understand what kinds of mechanisms are more likely to produce egalitarian participation rates, but do not tell us what is the overall participation effect of the existence of this set of mechanisms. From this perspective, the possibility of analyzing this issue with a representative sample of the population provides greater credence to the claim that, taken together, these instruments basically produce greater opportunities for participation for some and not more egalitarian opportunities for participation for all. As a result, if we had to judge these instruments from the point of view of their inclusiveness, the conclusion would be that they are not able to produce more egalitarian participation. On the other hand, equality cannot be the only criterion to evaluate their performance. If the goal was to produce more opportunities to participate for those interested in doing so, as Budge (1996) argued, then they probably perform this role quite adequately.

We have shown that this outcome is the result of the combination of three causal mechanisms: the role played by social resources that make things easier for some citizens to participate than others, the distribution of attitudes that attract those with greater need to make their messages heard and the mobilization networks used to recruit participants that result in the domination of associational members.

Is this a necessary result or is it related to the specific features of the existing participatory mechanisms in the Spanish case? Each of the three causal mechanisms requires a different answer to this question. Even if less costly mechanisms were used (e.g. surveys), the bias in resources that appears even in low-cost election outcomes is not likely to disappear. The importance of dissatisfaction as a mobilizing mechanism would also remain whatever kind of participatory experiences are being promoted. These two sources of bias are very likely to remain, except in mechanisms that use some kind of random selection of participants, which at this point constitute a very small minority of the existing ones.

On the other hand, these instruments are the clearest expression of the idea that their institutional design is crucial to achieve one set or another of participants. We have seen this when we have compared the bias introduced by two kinds of more common instruments: consultation councils and Participatory Budgeting. This comparison reveals that the role of the third causal mechanism of bias, associational recruitment networks, changes quite significantly when an effort is made to attract individual citizens, inequalities between associational members and the rest of citizens significantly diminishing. The lesson is that institutional design matters and it has significant effects on who is mobilized. As a consequence, the role of mobilization bias could probably be diminished in the context of a participatory model that would not give associations such a clear central role. However, only comparative research incorporating greater diversity in the participatory models being analyzed will permit us to answer this question adequately.

References

Abers, Rebeca. (1998) *Grass roots politics in Brazil*, London, Lynne Rienner.

Anduiza, Eva; Bonet, Eduard and Morales, Laura (2006): 'La participación en las asociaciones: niveles, perfiles y efectos', in Montero, Jose Ramón, Font, Joan and Torcal, Mariano (eds.): *Ciudadanos, asociaciones y participación en España*, Madrid, CIS, pp. 261-280.

Blakeley, Georgina (2005): 'Local governance and local democracy: the Barcelona model', *Local Government Studies*, vol. 31, no. 2.

Budge, Ian (1996): *The new challenge of direct democracy,* London: Polity Press.

Carman, Christopher (2009): "Barriers are barriers: participation bias in public petition systems", Paper presented at the ECPR General Conference, Potsdam.

Fiorina, Morris (1999): "The dark side of civic engagement", in Skocpol, T and Fiorina, M: *Civic engagement in American democracy*, Brookings Institution, Washington, 1999

Fishkin, James (1991): *Democracy and deliberation,* New Hampshire: Yale University Press.

Font, Joan (2002): 'Local participation in Spain: Beyond associative democracy', in Joan Font (ed*): Public participation and local governance*, Barcelona: ICPS.

Font, Joan & Blanco, Ismael (2007): "Procedural legitimacy and political trust: The case of citizen juries in Spain", *European Journal of Political Research*, 46: 557-589.

Font, Joan, San Martín, Jose & Schneider, Cecilia (2006): 'Asociaciones y democracia: contribuciones y causalidades', in Montero, Jose Ramón, Font, Joan and Torcal, Mariano (eds.): Ciudadanos, asociaciones y participación en España, Madrid, CIS, pp. 241-260.

Font, Joan & Galais, Carolina (2011): 'The qualities of local participation: the explanatory role of ideology, external support and civil society as organiser', *International Journal of Urban and Regional Research, 35(5): 949-968.*

Font, Joan; Teixidor, Anna; Herrera, Felipe (2004): Democracias participativas: Análisis de las experiencias del Observatorio Internacional de la Democracia Participativa, Barcelona, OIDP.

Fung, Archon & Wright, Erik Olin (2001): "Deepening democracy: innovations in empowered participatory governance", *Politics& Society*: 73-103

Ganuza, Ernesto (2010): "Les origines des budgets participatifs", in Bacqué, Marie Hélène & Yves Sintomer (eds) : *La démocratie participative inachevée*, Paris : Editions Yves Michel.

Hampton, G (1999): "Environmental equity and public participation", *Policy Science:* 163-174.

Hendricks, Carolyn (2002): "Institutions of deliberative democratic processes and interest groups: roles, tensions and incentives", *Australian Journal of Public Administration*, 61 (1): 64-75.

Hirschman; Albert O (1970): *Exit, voice and loyalty*, Harvard University Press.

Kriesi, Hans Peter & Westholm, Anders (2006): "Small-scale democracy: the determinants of action", in Van Deth, Jan; Montero, José Ramón and Westholm, Anders (eds): *Citizenship and involvement in European democracies*, London: Routledge.

Lang, Amy (2007): "But is it for real? The British Columbia Citizens' Assembly as a model of state-sponsored citizen empowerment", *Politics & Society*, 35 (1): 35-69.

Lowndes, V.; Prattchett, L. & Stoker, G. (2001): 'Trends in Public Participation: Part 1 – Local Government Perspectives', *Public Administration*, 79(1): 205-222.

Mansbridge, Jane (1983): *Beyond adversary democracy*, Chicago: Chicago University Press.

Navarro, Clemente (1999): *El Sesgo Participativo*, Madrid: CSIC.

Navarro, Clemente (2004): "Participatory democracy and political opportunism: municipal experience in Italy and Spain (1960–93)", *International Journal of Urban and Regional Research*, 28 (4): 819-838.

Navarro, Clemente (2008): 'Los rendimientos de los mecanismos de participación: propuesta de sistema de evaluación y aplicación al caso de los Presupuestos Participativos' *Revista del CLAD. Reforma y Democracia*, 40: 81-102.

Navarro, Clemente & Ramírez, María (2006): 'Servicios municipales y ciudadanía: 'exit, voice and loyalty' en una ciudad española', in *Ciudad y Territorio. Estudios Territoriales*, 147: 113-125.

Navarro, Clemente & Juaristi, Patxi (2006): 'Funciones, actividades y facilitación pública de las asociaciones', in Montero, Jose Ramón, Font, Joan and Torcal, Mariano (eds.): *Ciudadanos, asociaciones y participación en España*, Madrid: CIS, pp. 223-240.

Navarro, Clemente; Font, Joan & Cuesta, Maria (2009): ¿*Municipios participativos?: Participación y ciudadana en ciudades medias españolas,* Madrid: CIS.

Norris, Pippa (1999): 'Institutional Explanations for Political Support', in Norris, P. (ed.): *Critical Citizens. Global Support for Democratic Governance,* Oxford:Oxford University Press, pp. 217-235.

Parry, Geraint; Moiser, M & Day, N (1992): *Political participation and democracy in Britain,* Cambridge: Cambridge University Press.

Przeworski, Adam (1998): "Deliberation and ideological domination", in Jon Elster (ed): *Deliberative democracy,* Cambridge: Cambridge University Press.

Röcke, Anja (2009): *Democratic innovations through ideas? Participatory budgeting and frames of ideas in France, Great Britain and Germany,* Thesis defended at the European University Institute.

Rosenstone, Steven & Hansen, Marc (1993): *Mobilization, participation and democracy in America,* New York: Macmillan Press.

Sintomer, Yves (2007): *Le pouvoir au people,* Paris: La découverte.

Sintomer, Yves & Demaillard, Jacques (2007): "The limits to local participation and deliberation in the French 'politique de la ville'", *European Journal of Political Research,* 46: 503-530.

Sintomer, Yves, Herzberg, Carsten & Röcke, Anja (2008): "Participatory budgeting in Europe: potentials and challenges", *International Journal of Urban and Regional Research,* 32,1:164-178.

Smith, Graham (2009): *Democratic Innovations,* Cambridge: Cambridge University Press.

Verba, S.; Schlozman, K.L. & Brady, H.E. (1995): *Voice and equality. Civic voluntarism in American Politics*, Cambdridge, Cambridge University Press.

Van Der Meet, Tom & Van Ingen, Erik (2009): "Schools of democracy? Disentangling the relationship between civic participation and political action in 17 European countries", *European Journal of Political Research,* 48(2): 281-308.

Vetter, Angelika & Kersting, Norbert (2003): 'Democracy versus efficiency? Comparing local government reforms across Europe, in Kersting, Norbert and Vetter, Angelika (eds.): *Reforming Local Government in Europe. Closing the Gap between Democracy and Efficiency*, Opladen, Leske+Budrich, pp. 11-28.

Welzel, Christian; Inglehart, Ronald & Deutsch, Franziska (2005): "Social Capital, Voluntary Associations and Collective Action: Which Aspects of Social Capital Have the Greatest 'Civic' Payoff?", *Journal of Civic Society,* 1(2): 121-146.

117

Annex I

			Participation (%)			Total		Chi2	
			No	Yes	%	n	Value	Sigf.
Social	Gender	Male	95,9	4,1	100	2081	8,971	0,003
		Female	93,8	6,2	100	1913		
	Age	<30	96,8	3,2	100	835	7,509	0,006
		>30	94,4	5,6	100	3156		
	Education	<University	95,2	4,8	100	3199	3,778	0,052
		>University	93,6	6,4	100	791		
	Class	Working	95,7	4,3	100	1770	4,404	0,036
		Upper+middle	94,2	5,8	100	2128		
	Child > 7 years	No	95,1	4,9	100	3485	1,228	0,225
		Yes	93,9	6,1	100	509		
Attitudinal	Distrust local government	No (6-10)	95,4	4,6	100	2733	7,91	0,005
		Yes (1-5)	93,0	7,0	100	1005		
	Dissatisfaction local services	No (6-10)	95,8	4,2	100	2953	18,623	0,000
		Yes (1-5)	92,3	7,7	100	990		
	Electoral behavior	'Winners'	94,0	6,0	100	914	1,600	0,206
		'Losers'	92,6	7,4	100	1214		
Mobilization	Political associations	No member	96,6	3,4	100	3363	117,711	0,000
		Member	86,2	13,8	100	631		
	Non-political association	No member	96,3	3,7	100	3275	72,647	0,000
		Member	88,6	11,4	100	719		
Political involvement	Discuss local issues	Never/seldom	97,0	3,0	100	1794	29,56	0,000

Annex II

Consultation Councils

			Participation? (%)		Total		Chi2	
			No	Yes	%	n	Value	Sigf.
Social	Gender	Male	94,7	5,3	100	511	2,491	0,115
		Female	92,2	7,8	100	477		
	Age	< 30	98,2	1,8	100	226	10,72	0,001
		> 30	92,1	7,9	100	762		
	Education	< Degree	93,4	6,6	100	807	0,36	0,849
		Degree	93,8	6,2	100	178		
	Class	Working	93,5	6,5	100	463	0,001	0,996
		Upper+middle	93,5	6,5	100	510		
	Child < 7 years	No	92,9	7,1	100	849	3,46	0,063
		Yes	97,1	2,9	100	139		
Attitudinal	Distrust local	No (6-10)	93,8	6,2	100	690	0,626	0,423
	government	Yes (1-5)	92,4	7,6	100	275		
	Dissatisfaction	No (6-10)	94,2	5,8	100	741	2,265	0,132
	local services	Yes (1-5)	91,4	8,6	100	233		
	Electoral	Winners'	94,5	5,5	100	732	4,787	0,029
	behavior	Losers'	90,6	9,4	100	256		
Mobilization	Political	No	96,6	3,4	100	774	57,366	0
	associations	Yes	82,2	17,8	100	214		
	Non-political	No member	95,9	4,1	100	811	43,354	0
	associations	Member	82,5	17,5	100	177		
Political involvement	Discuss local	Never/seldom	97,2	2,8	100	351	12,708	0
	issues	Often/very often	91,2	8,8	100	615		

(1) Less than 5 cases in participatory category

Participatory Budgets

			Participation? (%)		Total		Chi2	
			No	Yes	%	n	Value	Sigf.
Social	Gender	Male	96,7	3,3	100	513	0,57	0,449
		Female	97,5	2,5	100	479		
	Age	< 30	99,6	0,4	100	228	6,44	0,011
		> 30	96,3	3,7	100	764		
	Education	< Degree	96,9	3,1	100	811	0,357	0,549
		Degree	97,8	2,2	100	178		
	Class	Working	97,4	2,6	100	469	0,525	0,468
		Upper+middle	96,7	3,3	100	508		
	Child < 7 years	No	97,1	2,9	100	853	0,001	0,972
		Yes	97,1	2,9	100	139		
Attitudinal	Distrust local	No (6-10)	96,7	3,3	100	693	0,891	0,345
	government	Yes (1-5)	97,8	2,2	100	276		
	Dissatisfaction	No (6-10)	96,8	3,2	100	743	0,754	0,385
	local services	Yes (1-5)	97,9	2,1	100	235		
	Electoral	Winners'	97,6	2,4	100	736	2,293	0,129
	behavior	Losers'	95,7	4,3	100	256		
Mobilization	Political	No	98,3	1,7	100	777	19,747	0
	associations	Yes	92,6	7,4	100	215		
	Non-political	No member	98,0	2,0	100	817	15,198	0
	associations	Member	92,6	7,4	100	175		
Political involvement	Discuss local	Never/seldom	98,9	1,1	100	350	6,439	0,011
	Issues	Often/very often	96,0	4,0	100	620		

(1) Less than 5 cases in participatory category

Annex III

Consultation Councils

		Model 1 (social bias)		Model 2 (attitudinal bias)		Model 3 (mobilization bias)		Model 4 (combined)	
		B	Exp(B)	B	Exp(B)	B	Exp(B)	B	Exp(B)
Political involvement	Discuss local issues	**1,273**	**3,570**	**1,213**	**3,365**	**1,027**	**2,792**	**1,190**	**3,288**
Social	Gender (male)	0,339	1,404					0,278	1,321
	Age	3,687	39,936					3,464	31,929
	Education	**1,369**	**3,932**					0,757	2,131
	Upper	-0,359	0,698					-0,384	0,681
	Middle	-0,066	0,936					-0,207	0,813
	Self employed	0,004	1,004					0,242	1,274
	Skilled workers	0,000	1,000					0,000	1,000
	Child < 7 years old	-0,557	0,573					-0,395	0,673
Attitudinal	Distrust local government			-0,062	0,940			-0,076	0,927
	Dissatisfaction local Services			0,136	1,145			**0,166**	**1,181**
	Vote: others			-0,324	0,723			0,126	1,135
	Vote: losers			0,255	1,291			0,332	1,394
Mobilization	Political association					**1,319**	**3,738**	**1,239**	**3,453**
	Non-pol. association					0,837	2,309	**0,804**	**2,234**
Cte		**-5,801**	**0,003**	**-3,846**	**0,021**	**-4,164**	**0,016**	**-6,615**	**0,001**
Pseudo-R2 (Nagelkarke)		0,130		0,060		0,162		0,237	

Significant coefficients in bold (p<0,005)

All independent variables have been standardized to 0-1

Participatory Budgets

		Model 1 (social bias)		Model 2 (attitudinal bias)		Model 3 (mobilization bias)		Model 4 (combined)	
		B	Exp(B)	B	Exp(B)	B	Exp(B)	B	Exp(B)
Political involvement	Discuss local issues	**1,238**	**3,448**	**1,157**	**3,179**	**1,116**	**3,051**	*0,945*	*2,572*
Social	Gender (male)	-0,499	0,607					-0,563	0,569
	Age	**3,814**	**45,343**					**3,225**	**25,163**
	Education	**2,086**	**8,053**					**1,652**	**5,215**
	Upper	-0,496	0,609					-0,611	0,543
	Middle	-0,048	0,953					-0,192	0,825
	Self employed	0,313	1,367					0,484	1,622
	Skilled workers	0,000	1,000					0,000	1,000
	Child < 7 years old	0,284	1,329					0,443	1,557
Attitudinal	Distrust local government			-0,060	0,942			-0,034	0,967
	Dissatisfaction local Services			0,003	1,003			-0,009	0,991
	Vote: others			-0,800	0,450			-0,454	0,635
	Vote: losers			0,211	1,234			0,240	1,271
Mobilization	Political association					**1,087**	**2,965**	*0,848*	*2,335*
	Non-pol. association					0,704	2,022	0,733	2,081
Cte		**-6,782**	**0,001**	**-3,881**	**0,021**	**-4,937**	**0,007**	**-6,300**	**0,002**
Pseudo-R2 (Nagelkarke)		0,113		0,053		0,101		0,172	

Significant coefficients in bold (p<0,005)

All independent variables have been standardized to 0-1

⬚

Improving the Quality of Democracy:
The case of Deliberative Poll held in 2007 in Turin.

Irena Fiket/Vincenzo Memoli

Introduction

We can say with certainty that globally, democracy health has improved over the last 30 years, particularly when we consider the increased number of countries characterized by democratic consolidation. At the same time, numerous studies agree that democracy is in crisis.

There are myriad reasons why many scholars see democracy in decline: the dwindling commitment to democratic institutions; the progressive disillusionment with electoral politics; declining participation; declining interest towards democratic institutions; the gradual detachment from the public sphere (Scharpf 1999; McNamara 2002) and declined public support for democracy (Norris 1999; Bellucci and Memoli 2012). These problems have consequently renovated scholars' interest in public deliberation; they see it as the remedy for the deterioration of democracy (Witte 1980; Wright 1992; Williams and Metheny 1995; Rossi 1997; Shapiro 1999). A number of scholars have identified the root of the problem within the inherent limits of a representative democracy that is unable to meet the needs of the public (Köchler 1987; Rosenthal 1998). In fact, approaches that stress stronger citizen involvement in decision- making through different forms of democratic innovations come with problems that seem difficult to manage using the traditional instruments of representative democracy. That is why many of these approaches propose a model of participatory and deliberative democracy based on a broad involvement of citizens in decisionmaking (Benhabib 1996; Habermas 1996; Cohen 1997). Citizens can be brought back into the public sphere by becoming engaged in thoughtful deliberation that aims at solving common problems, making policy makers more accountable, and producing legitimate policy outcomes that can meet the expectations of the polity. As was already highlighted by the editors, the list of democratic innovations that are based on deliberative democracy theory is a long one. They differ from one another, but they all share a common set of characteristics that distinguish them from other forms of participation experienced in the past, and obviously, from the ordinary processes of policy-making

(Bobbio 2002). Deliberative Polling[83] is one of those innovative processes. Even though the Deliberative Poll (DP) had already been implemented within the "real" world of policy making, it was mainly implemented as a social science quasi-experiment. More precisely, Deliberative Poll is a deliberative setting created by James Fishkin in 1988 for studying processes of deliberation and opinion formation which aim to show that people could become better citizens if they are given the opportunity to engage in meaningful deliberation on public issues (Fishkin 1997, Hansen and Andersen 2004). DP brings together a statistical microcosm of citizens in an environment which should enhance discussions, increase knowledge, motivate citizens and help them to form their opinions towards public issues in a more rational way (Fishkin 1997).

In our study, we will evaluate the case of Deliberative Polling that took place in Turin in 2007 in order to understand, whether the Deliberative Poll could satisfy the democratic criteria outlined in the volume's framework.

Many empirical studies have explored the effects of deliberation using the deliberative poll, confirming that participation in deliberation produces different "democratic" effects: political sophistication, political interest, internal political efficacy, political trust, political "respect", political empathy, "sociotropism" and more positive attitudes toward the political system (Luskin and Fishkin, 2002, Fishkin 2009, Mansbridge, 2010). Although the main idea on which deliberative experiments are based is that discussion and deliberation have a positive effect both on the health of democracy and the citizens involved in the deliberations, the main focus of empirical research remains primarily concerned with understanding the effects of deliberation on citizens' opinions about the issue at hand.

This chapter will follow the analytical framework outlined by the editors. In order to explore the effects of deliberative poll on the quality of democracy, it will cover all of the evaluation areas outlined by the framework except the one on effectiveness. Additionally, using previous analyses of Deliberative Poll outputs, this study will analyse the perceived legitimacy of the process through different phases of DP. The results from previous DPs have already offered some support for the idea that deliberation makes citizens more supportive of the democratic system (Luskin and Fishkin, 2002). The novelty of our research is the use of the indicator of citizens' assessment of how well democracy works – an indicator already used in quality of democracy studies – and to assess how it changes through different experimental phases of DP. In this way, we hope to understand not only whether the citizens would become more supportive of the political system, we also hope to learn which phase has the strongest effect on this support. We expect that during the phase in which citizens interact with

---

83   For more information on the Deliberative Poll, see Fishkin (2009)

politicians they will develop a better understanding of the political process and thus, increase their satisfaction with democracy.

First, we will briefly describe the Deliberative Polling experiment that took place in Turin.

The Deliberative Poll in Turin

The Deliberative Poll (DP) held in Turin on March 24th and 25th 2007 was organized by the University of Siena[84]. A random sample of 1.690 people from the Turin area participated in a 20 minute interview using the CATI software[85]. From the sample of 1,690 people, 463 citizens were initially selected as potential participants. While the initial goal was to recruit 200 people, only 175 were present during both days of the event. Despite the fact that the standard DP design is based on a representative sample of population (Fishkin 2009, Mansbridge 2010), the organizers decided to slightly oversample the population of Val di Susa, part of the Turin province (bringing the original 10 percent to 20 percent of the sample), because of the importance that one of the issues chosen for the experiment has on their lives. Their opinions represented those of the minority, but were characterised by a greater intensity than the opinions of the other participants. Thus, an adequate representation for the Val di Susa population was guaranteed in the Turin experiment.

Two issues were discussed in Turin: the right for immigrants from non-European countries to vote in local elections (RVI from now on) and the construction of a railway for the high-speed train running from Turin to Lyon (HST from now on). The HST is a highly controversial issue; a public debate over the construction of the HST lasted for more than ten years and was characterized by some very difficult moments. The major protests against the construction of the HST occurred in October-December 2005. The opinions among both the elite and the mass toward the issue were quite divided. On one side, there were the proponents of the project (The Italian Government, the

---

84 It was part of the IntUne project (Integrated and United? A Quest for Citizenship in an Ever Closer Europe), financed by the European Union within the 6th Framework Programme on the theme of Citizenship. IntUne is a four-year project coordinated by the University of Siena and was launched in September 2005. The IntUne project involves 29 European institutions and more than 100 scholars across Eastern and Western Europe.

85 The recruitment was organized by TNS INFRATEST, a survey firm of the TNS Opinion/EOS Gallup group and partner of the INTUNE Project.

Railways, the Piedmont Region, and the City of Turin) and on the other, the residents of the Val di Susa[86] and the social groups that supported "the cause" of the residents of Val di Susa. When the Deliberative Polling was held in Turin, the construction of the HST was still blocked and the opposing parties were still looking for a solution.

Data from the initial telephone interviews (conducted before the deliberation) confirm the strong polarization of the public's preferences toward the HST issue: 46% of the residents of Val di Susa were very opposed to the construction of an HST, while the percentage of those very favourable to its construction was very high among participants who are not from Val di Susa. At the same time, the HST is an issue on which information was abundant, but was often distorted. For this reason, a great effort was made to ensure the accuracy and balance of information provided to the participants in all phases of the deliberative process.

In the case of the other issue, the right for immigrants to vote in local elections (RVI), the situation was very different. It appeared that there was a consensus among major political and social actors, and the public was also mostly favourable to the recognition of this right. The only exception among political actors was represented by the Lega Nord, a right-wing political party distinguished by a strong anti-immigrant rhetoric. Until now, the Lega Nord remained the only political force that openly opposes the recognition of this right for immigrants. Still, the question of recognition is not as simple as it seems: in 2005, when the city council of Turin passed a resolution that extended the vote at the local level to all legal non-EU immigrants residing in the municipality for at least six years, the decision met with numerous objections.

The complexity of the issues led the organizers to dedicate considerable attention to the drafting of the informative (briefing) material. The briefing material is a very important element in the DP experiment, because it provides balanced information and includes all the arguments on the issue. Ideally, it should first be prepared by experts in the specific area and then controlled by the stakeholders committee which should represent all positions and interests on the issue involved in the public debate. In the Turin case, the inclusion of all positions was guaranteed for both issues. While in the case of the RVI, the drafting process was quite simple, for the HST issue, a further step was carried out in order to ensure the quality of the material. After the first draft was written by experts, all members of the committee were personally interviewed. The interviews were integrated into a briefing document that was rechecked by the

---

86 A part of the Turin province where the high speed train (HST) is planned to pass through.

stakeholder and scientific committee. The final version of the briefing material was then sent to participants two weeks before the event.

The effects of the Deliberative Poll are assessed by comparing the data collected by questionnaires. Unlike the standard design suggested by James Fishkin and Robert Luskin (Fishkin 2009) where participants complete the questionnaires at the moment of recruitment and at the end of the event, the Turin DP used three extra questionnaires in order to assess the effect of the different deliberative stages on the participants' attitudes. The first questionnaire was filled out at the arrival, the second, after the first group discussion, and the third, before the first plenary session. With the exception of the initial (T0) and final questionnaire (T4) which were submitted to all participants, all of the questionnaires were submitted to different groups in different stages according to a research design showed in Table 6.1. Macrogroup A, comprising 41 participants, received the questionnaire upon their arrival. Macrogroup B, made up of 47 participants, received the questionnaire after the group discussion and before the plenary. Macrogroup C, composed of 87 participants, received the questionnaire after the plenary session. At the end of the two days, Macrogroup D filled out the final questionnaire (T4) together with all other Macrogroups. While the ideal method for assessing the impact of different deliberative stages on participants' opinions and preferences would have been to ask the entire sample of participants to fill out the questionnaires, it was decided against; the two days of deliberation were already taxing on the participants and the activity would have been too time-consuming.

Deliberation in Deliberative Polling

Any discussion of deliberation should start from a clear conceptual definition of deliberation, but unfortunately, such a definition is still lacking (Macedo 1999; Burkhalter, Gastil, & Kelshaw 2002; Thompson 2008). For this reason, when scholars talk about deliberative quality, they often refer to different phenomena. This problem does not occur only when we compare theoretical and empirical research of deliberation; it even occurs within these two areas. A variety of studies using empirical research have applied different research designs, different measurements and different definitions of deliberation (Neblo 2007).

The Deliberative Poll structures the process in a way that should guarantee preconditions for a high-quality deliberation. It is based on the participation of a sample of the population that should represent the plurality of opinions necessary for reflection on the different positions on the issue. The expression of those opinions is further guaranteed by professional moderators who ensure a highly respectful environment and balanced participation. A balanced panel of experts and politicians within the plenary sessions further ensures the exposure to different opinions and preferences. So, what deliberation should actually look like is inherent in the institutional setting of DP (Siu, 2008)

In the following section, we will briefly describe the phases of DP which aim to guarantee a high quality deliberation.

Table 6.1 Experimental Design

	First Issue (Right to vote)			Second Issue (High Speed Train)	
Groups	**T1** Arrival	**T2** After group discussion	**T3** After Plenary		**T4** Final Questionnaire
Macrogroup A	X				X
Macrogroup B		X			X
Macrogroup C			X		X
Macrogroup D					X

Before the event, DP empowers the participants with knowledge by providing them with briefing materials. It foresees that participants should gather in small group discussions and initiate deliberation from equal starting positions in terms of their factual knowledge. Of course, there are no guarantees for such equality in the real world.

It is only after the input of factual information that the "deliberative" aspect of DP can take place. In the Turin experiment (following the standard design of DP suggested by Fishkin and Luskin), the deliberative piece was implemented in two stages: first, the participants gathered in small discussion groups with the assistance of a professional moderator; then, they met again in plenary sessions. The 175 participants were randomly divided into 19 groups which assembled at the round tables. Each table was assisted by a professional moderator[87]. At the end of the discussion, they formulated questions for the experts and politicians. Subsequently, they met in a plenary assembly to hear the answers from the experts and politicians. Over the two days, there were five small group sessions (each lasting 75 minutes[88]); five plenary sessions, including three with the experts (lasting 75 minutes) and two final plenary

---

87 TNS entrusted the recruitment and training of moderators to the company Avventura Urbana, who also handled some organizational aspects of the event.

88 The last small group session, held immediately before the final session, lasted only 30 minutes.

sessions with politicians (each lasting 45 minutes). Because of the complexity of the HST issue, the small group sessions and plenary sessions with experts were repeated so as to give participants the opportunity to discuss the issue in-depth. The RVI issue was discussed in a single plenary session with experts, preceded by two small group sessions.[89] The experiment ended with two consecutive plenary sessions with politicians dedicated to both issues.

Luskin and Fishkin (2002) contend that after deliberating in such a struc-tured setting, citizens learn how to become better "citizens". However, Delib-erative Poll ignores an important aspect of social reality – the fact that it is not predictable. Even though we regulate the setting of deliberation, we cannot be sure that the entire process of deliberation as we foresee it will really take place. From empirical research on DP, we know a great deal about the benefits of participation in a process, but we have little insight into the way in which deliberation in DP is actually performed.

Empirical research on DP does not measure to what extent the conditions that are necessary for deliberation are met. Furthermore, it was already under-lined by Ryfe (2005) that so far, the empirical research on deliberation has been less interested in the deliberation phenomenon itself than in measuring its effects.

A micro-analytic approach of process analysis is needed in order to assess whether all the criteria of deliberation are properly achieved. In our case, we considered the necessity of post-evaluation of Deliberative Polling after what happened in Turin during the plenary sessions on the right to vote for non-EU immigrants. While at the plenary sessions for the HST issue, cross-cutting in-formation and opinions were represented by experts and politicians, for the RVI plenary session, not a single expert or politician who was against recogni-tion of voting rights for immigrants actually attended the event, even though many had confirmed their participation. In addition, since indirect measures such as questionnaires cannot assess whether deliberation actually occurred, the research needs to collect insights on the process of discussion that occurs within small groups. Some direct measures could provide us with significant insights in the process of deliberation, (Bächtiger and Hangartner, 2010).

As we saw, some problems may arise when the research on deliberative arenas of citizens are based only on the data collected through questionnaires. Researchers who are not direct observers are unable to view the entire picture of what happens during the process. For this reason, we would suggest the in-clusion of analyses of the process itself as a part of the research on deliberative potentials of different arenas. In order to open the *black box* of the deliberation

---

89 In fact, the first of the small group sessions was devoted mainly to the presentation of the experiment and participants.

process, it is necessary to use recordings or other methods which allow for the analysis of discussions. One example of analysis of the deliberation process which might be applied together with the questionnaire is represented by Discourse Quality Index- DQI (Steenbergen et al. 2003; Steiner et al. 2004)[90].

Inclusive and Effective Participation

Deliberative Polling attempts to satisfy the criterion of inclusion of all of those influenced by the decision by applying the method of random sampling in the selection of participants. Hence, by giving all members of the same population the same possibility of being selected to participate, the instrument of DP meets the principles of substantive inclusion and equality - the fundamental principles of deliberative democracy. While the number of participants may vary, at least 100 participants must be included in the experiment. This criterion is important because when the sample is too small, it is impossible to claim representativeness.

By applying random sampling, DP avoids the self-selection often encountered in deliberative arenas where other methods of selection are adopted (Mansbridge 2010). Therefore, it avoids the risk of building an arena made up of homogeneous groups of citizens. The heterogeneity of participants is a necessary condition for learning and understanding that there are different visions of the same problem, different preferences, and different needs (Mutz 2002). Therefore, it should be made sure that the sample of participants is representative of the plurality that exists within a polity.

The main response provided by Fishkin and Luskin to this question is to see how representative the sample of participants is when comparing participants to those who, although contacted, did not accept the invitation to participate.

The main differences between participants and non-participants of the Deliberative Poll held in Turin are as follows: the sample of participants is slightly better educated and older than non-participants; it takes part in religious services less regularly than non-participants; it is more interested in politics and reads newspapers more than non-participants; it is more leftist; it is more pro-European; and it feels more politically effective. Similar socio-demographic differences were also observed in other Deliberative Polls (Luskin, Fishkin and Jowell 2002, Hansen and Andresen 2004, Fishkin 2009) and in

---

90   In the Europolis project, a Europe-wide DP (www.europolis-project.eu/) , both
     methods of analysis are being applied together for the first time: analysis of the
     data collected by questionnaires and analysis of the deliberation process using DQI.

other socio-political surveys. As was the case in other Deliberative Polls, there were only a few significant differences. Most importantly, between the two samples there were no differences concerning the attitudes towards the issues under deliberation.[91] Given that, the data confirmed that in statistical terms the sample of participants tends to be highly representative.

Although the method of random sampling can guarantee that the sample and the deliberative process would not be distorted by self-selection, the question of inclusiveness cannot be restricted to statistical representation. If deliberative democracy aims to "give voice" to minorities – those usually excluded from the public sphere - it follows that the arguments which should prevail in deliberation are those which are best justified in terms of universal justice and not those of the powerful majority (Young 2000). Therefore, the direct application of random sampling is not the best way to select the citizens for every social context. For this reason, the scientific committee decided to oversample the population of Val di Susa.

In fact, the argument that led the committee to oversample the population of Val di Susa stems from the demand of the deliberative democracy model for the equality and inclusion of voices of minorities, a model of democracy particularly suited to safeguard the interests of minorities (Benhabib 2005). Although they represent the minority of the Turin population, the population of Val di Susa would have been affected by the decision more than others. For this reason, the effort was made to represent them properly.

The problem of inclusiveness of minorities becomes even more evident if we think about how the principle of the inclusiveness is applied within each small group. The small groups include smaller numbers of citizens (from 10 to 20), so they should be composed in a way that at least partially ensures the representation of a variety of views on the issue. If the participants who represent the minority opinion find themselves in an arena that is completely hostile towards their opinion, there is little chance that they will freely express their opinion.

At the same time, one can ask why the principle of oversampling the minority has not been applied in the case of the VRT issue where those openly against the voting rights for immigrants, as verified in initial interviews, were not over-represented. The answer is that there are no easy solutions for the problem of "absolute" inclusiveness; selection criteria need to be discussed from case to case, taking into consideration the specific context of each social reality (Parkinson, 2006). What we should bear in mind is that the question regarding the composition of deliberative arenas is not only whether or not the

---

91 For detailed discussion of representativity of participants in Deliberative Poll in Turin, see: Isernia, Bobbio, Fiket, Manca, Podesta' (2008).

participants are statistically representative, but whether or not they represent all the voices that should be heard.

In response to such a complex problem, DP chooses a neutrality that derives from scientific design and random sampling, and it is making further efforts to assure the inclusion of all voices. The design prescribes that the experts and politicians who participate in plenary sessions are balanced in terms of their opinions on issues (pro and con). For the HST issue, experts and politicians who advocated different opinions were present at plenary sessions. In the case of the RVI issue, no single expert or politician argued against the recognition of the right to vote for immigrants. Despite having confirmed their attendance at plenary sessions, the representatives of this position did not attend the event, and left organizers little possibility of compensating for their absence in some way. In any case, even if this position had been represented at the plenary session, it would still have been difficult for participants who were against the recognition of voting rights for immigrants to sustain their positions in a totally hostile environment, where most of the participants were openly in favour of RVI.

Drawing from the Turin case, what we can conclude here is that even if Deliberative Polling starts from a scientific neutrality that derives from random sampling, guarantees heterogeneity and representativeness of participants, and avoids the problems that occur in arenas where other selection methods are used, it still cannot be considered the best practice for selection in all cases. The deliberative process should be a setting conducive to dialogue which includes those who are excluded from the public sphere or donot have enough power to make their voice heard. Therefore, the problems related to the selection of the participants cannot be resolved with pre-packaged formulas that do not account for the specific characteristics of the polity and the issue.

Is DP conducive to effective participation in decision- making processes? In practice, only a few DP processes have directly influenced the politics or policy (Fishkin2009), although more than 30 Deliberative Polls have been conducted in different parts of the world (Farrar et al. 2010). But it is not the process of DP that should be blamed for this minimal impact. It has been argued that even in the cases when the deliberative process was designed to influence decision-making, the impact of citizens' deliberation on policies remains somewhat limited (Sintomer and Maillard 2007). This result is probably due to the reluctance of politicians to "share" their power of decision-making (Font and Blanco 2007).

The University of Siena organized the DP in Turin without any preconceptions for directly influencing decision-making. It was designed as a practice aiming to analyse the process of deliberation and opinion formation. Still, DP could be implemented as an additional arena for political participation (Hansen and Andersen 2004). This added potential of DP was already confirmed in the case of a Chinese local DP where the results of citizens' deliberation were submitted to the Local People's Congress which ratified them (Fishkin 2009).

When we discuss effective participation, it is worth mentioning one significant difference between DP and some other methods of citizen involvement, such as Citizens' Juries (Coote and Lenhaglan 1997) and *Consensus Conferences* (Callon, Lascoumes and Barthe 2001). DP does not aim to reach consensus; it simply aims to consult the informed public. The outputs of deliberation are significantly different in these two processes: consensus is the output in citizens' juries, for example, and individual opinions and preferences is the output in DP. Of course, consensus as an output of deliberation is much easier to take into account in the decision- making process. Among the deliberative theorists, there is no agreement that consensus is a desirable goal of deliberation (Gutmann and Thompson 2004 Thompson, 2008)[92]. Empiricists suggest that consensus-reaching methods run the risk of creating a social pressure that may distort the process and manipulate participants, such as the domination of a more advantaged strata of society or even conformity (Fishkin 1997, 2009; Mansbridge, 2010). Sunstein (2002) finds that in Citizens' Juries, the pressure to reach consensual decisions often leads to polarization, but in the case of DP, for which participants are not required to reach a collective decision, polarization does not occur (Fishkin & Luskin 2005: 293).

In fact, DP expressly guarantees the secrecy of citizens' opinions expressed in confidential questionnaires. This additional dimension provides another reason, when we take into consideration the criteria of effective participation, for why the Deliberative Poll should be considered as a valuable democratic innovation.

Legitimacy

One of the most emphasised benefits of deliberative democracy is that it increases legitimacy (Habermas 1996; Young 2000; Dryzek 2000). Still, it is well known that the concept of legitimacy is elusive and is particularly difficult to define and operationalise. Some deliberative democracy scholars have even argued that legitimacy is not an empirical question because it is inherent in the process (Thompson 2008). Still, as underlined by Mutz (2008), empirical research must study some observable manifestation of legitimacy, such as the perceived legitimacy of the process.

---

92 See Neblo (2007) for a more positive view of the role of consensus in deliberation

Although we are aware of these problems in defining an operationalising legitimacy, in our work we will follow the specific definition of legitimacy outlined in the volume's framework. Further, we will explore the perceived legitimacy of the process of Deliberative Polling using the "satisfaction with democracy" indicator[93], one of the most used indicators of perceived legitimacy, employed in numerous surveys over an extended period of time. We hypothesised that the 'satisfaction with democracy' of the participants will increase after they have participated in the Deliberative Poll. Perhaps they would, in turn, better understand democratic procedures (Grönlund et al. 2010) and would develop more trust in and satisfaction with the workings of a democracy.

In our analyses we use the participants' *satisfaction with democracy* at the end of the experiment as dependent variable. By using a polynomial regression to estimate the effect that different phases of participation in deliberative processes (phase after phase) have on the level of the participants' satisfaction with democracy at the end of the deliberative process, we find a clear (cor)relation between the variables considered. The participants become more satisfied with how democracy works in practice after participating in the deliberative poll. Furthermore, the effect of the phases of participation on the level of *"satisfaction with democracy"* is very strong in terms of explained variance, as illustrated in Figure 6.1.

At the initial phase (T0-telephone interview answered by all participants), the percentage of citizens who were satisfied with democracy was 33.7 while in the last phase (T4-questionnaire compiled by all the participants at the end of the event), the percentage of citizens who were satisfied with democracy was 59.8. The trend increases during the different phases with a different percentage score, on an average of 2.6%. The only phase where the increase was very low is in phase T2. During this specific phase, the participants attended an initial small group session where the main activity was the presentation of the experiment and the participants. In phase T4, after the participants' first interaction with politicians (the first plenary after which the perceived legitimacy was measured was only with experts), the trend sharply increased, probably due to their understanding of the complexity of the decision-making process.

These results confirmed our expectations: not only did the participants' satisfaction with how democracy works increase after deliberation, but the increase is undoubtedly higher after the direct interaction with decision makers.

---

93 The question used is 'On the whole, how satisfied are you with the way democracy works in (country)'? The answer modalities are: very satisfied, fairly satisfied, not very satisfied, not at all satisfied.

Figure 6.1 Satisfaction with Democracy through Experimental Phases

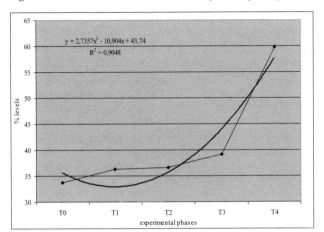

Enlightened Citizens and Democratic Education

The hypothesis of the transformation of citizens into enlightened citizens after participating in deliberation is the most explored hypothesis within the empirical research that uses the Deliberative Poll method. As already observed in other DP experiments (Fishkin 1997, Luskin, Fishkin and Jowell 2002; Hansen and Andersen 2004; Andersen and Hansen 2007; Isernia et al. 2008), the most effective change was the increase in the participants' level of knowledge about the issues. Furthermore, a comparison of the participants' opinions, measured through questionnaires given before and after the Turin Deliberative Poll, revealed many statistically significant changes regarding both issues. While in the initial interview, only 22% of the participants had responded that "The municipality has already approved the voting rights for immigrants, but this right has been revoked by the central government", by the end this group had grown to 65%. Initially, only 24% of the respondents knew in which year protests occurred against the HST in Val di Susa, while at the end 70% did. In order to illustrate how well informed a participant was, a summary index was built which assigns the number of correct answers to questions with a corresponding estimated level of knowledge.[94] At the time of recruitment, 21% of the participants were well informed about the right to vote (they had answered at least three of the four questions correctly). At the end of the experiment, 67% of them were highly informed about this issue. In terms of the HST issue, those who were highly informed (that is, those who gave a correct answer to at least two of three questions) rose from 12% to 61% among participants in the province of Turin and from 41% to 82% among participants from Val di Susa.

When it came to general attitudes and policy preferences, the changes were minor. For the RVI issue, there were statistically significant changes in 9 out of 22 items, the equivalent to 19.2%. No significant change in opinion was noted towards RVI in local or national elections, though opinions did become more favourable to the recognition of citizenship after five years of residence. The large majority of statistically significant changes pointed towards a greater understanding and acceptance of the immigrants and their needs. This increase can probably be attributed to the lack of opposing arguments both within the participants sample and during the penuries. In particular, the number of participants who disagreed with the statement that "immigrants increase the crime rate" and the number of those who would like "to make it easier for foreigners to acquire Italian nationality by allowing them to become Italian citizens after 5 years of residence in Italy", slightly increased.

On the other hand, the changes in the case of the HST were numerous and more conspicuous. From a total of 13 items related to the HST we observed statistically significant changes on 8 items. The percentage of those who were supporters of the HST dropped from 68% to 59%, while the opponents rose from 21% to 26% and the number who were indifferent (neither favourable, nor against) increased to 27% from 22%. One of the most important changes that occurred was that the polarisation on the HST issue had diminished. The number of supporters of the construction of the HST who were from the city of Turin or the surrounding areas fell from 75% to 66%. More precisely, the percentage of those who were "very favourable" fell from 52 to 35, those who were "somewhat favourable" rose from 24% to 31% and those who were un-

---

94 The questions on the RVI concerned the following: the voting conditions in Turin; the situation of local voting in Turin during the time; years of residence needed to obtain the right to vote and the percentage of immigrants in the municipality that could benefit from the recognition of RVI. Questions that measured the information level on the HST concerned: what year protests were held against the HST in Val di Susa; the type of HST transportation in Val di Susa (only for goods, only for passengers or both) and the stage of completion of the work at that time.

certain rose slightly from 8% to 12%. We observed something similar in the case of the participants of Val di Susa, where the participants who were "very contrary" decreased from 50% to 45% and those who were "quite contrary" rose from 5% to 18%. In both groups, the positions did not change radically, but they did fluctuate in terms of intensity.

When comparing changes which occurred in the Turin case with other DPs, such as the DP held in Britain in 1994, where Luskin et al. (2002) observed significant and intense changes in more than 50% of the items related to the topic of discussion, we notice that a minor number of changes were recorded in our case study. There are two possible explanations for why there were few differences registered in the Turin DP. First of all, we should take into account the highly controversial issue of the HST issue and second, the fact that participants were more highly informed about both issues at the beginning of the Turin experiment than they have been at other DPs. In fact, it has been already highlighted by Fishkin that, "Deliberative Polling® is especially suitable for issues where the public may have little knowledge or information, or where the public may have failed to confront the trade-offs applying to public policy."[95]

Even though policy preferences did not change very much, if we look carefully at the changes, we will realise that some other important changes seem to have occurred, especially regarding the HST. There was an increase in sympathy for the no-HST social movement and for the reasons for protest against it. The distance between the population of Val di Susa and that of Turin decreased at the end of the two days, in terms of their attitudes towards the no-HST movement which in the end grew in popularity among the participants, from 36% to 45%. The changes were always in the same direction - closer to the rationale of the Val di Susa population. At the end of the two-day experiment, the number of participants who agreed with the statements - "The costs needed to build HST prevail over the benefits", "The HST would cause irreparable damage to the territory of Val di Susa", increased, as did those who did not share the view that "The HST is an important opportunity for economic development for Piedmont" and that "Those who oppose the HST are opposed to progress". An understanding of the reasons for the protest and an estimation of the costs and benefits had increased, thus giving greater legitimacy to the argument of the counterparts. The idea that anyone who opposes the HST is contrary to progress was prevalent before participating in the Deliberative Poll. After participation, the percentage of those who shared this view dropped in both groups. In short, the no-HST arguments acquired greater legitimacy during the deliberation.

---

[95]   http://cdd.stanford.edu/polls/docs/summary/

Conclusions

Following the analytical framework outlined by the editors, we have illustrated the case of Deliberative Polling held in Turin in March 2007 and then discussed some of its results, trying to highlight both the benefits and the problems of the DP method.

First, we showed that participation in DP could be seen as a sort of school for better citizenship, in which the public debate plays a vital role. Actually, the two days of discussion undoubtedly served to "enlighten" and "educate" the citizens in democratic cohabitation. In each of the two cases, the experiment raised the level of information among the participants. In terms of the HST issue, the participants of the Deliberative Poll acquired two types of information: factual information and an awareness of the legitimacy of different points of view towards the issue. In the case of the RVI issue, participants gained factual knowledge but probably did not grasp the underlying reasons behind the opinions of those who oppose the RVI because they were not systematically exposed to different opinions.

This brings us to the discussion of deliberation in the DP setting. Although the DP design requires a systematic effort to guarantee the conditions for balanced deliberation, in our case we observed some problems related to the realisation of those conditions. That led us to suggest that the research needs to assess whether the conditions necessary for deliberation are actually fulfilled. As supported by our research, analyses of the process may actually be highly significant in explaining the results of deliberative experiments. Still, we are aware that the social reality is not predictable and that no matter what kinds of measures are taken in order to guarantee that the process of deliberation will take place, we cannot be certain that this will actually happen. In fact, we cannot expect to control all of the variables within a social science experiment as we could do with a natural experiment. The politicians who were against RVI decided not to come to plenary sessions, and there is not much we could have done to change that.

As regards the criterion of inclusive participation, we show that it was filled in the DP experiment held in Turin, as it had been in other DPs (Fishkin 2009). The sample of participants was highly representative of the population, both demographically and attitudinally. In general terms, a representative sample is desirable because it ensures external equality and increases the likelihood that all of the different voices can be heard. The novelty introduced in Turin was to oversample the population of Val di Susa, in order to give them a "voice" that counts in discussions. This decision was taken after long consultation of the scientific committee and experts on the issue. Even here, we highlight the possible problems that could arise with selection methods in all deliberative arenas. In an ideal world, the selection of the participants should not be resolved with pre-packaged formulas that do not take into account the specific characteristics of the polity and the issue. Still, if the social context is not well known by the organizers of arenas, the Deliberative Poll should be considered as one of the best methods to involve citizens, due to its scientific rigidity.

Participants selected through random sampling, random distribution of participants in small groups where they discuss "controlled" by moderators, and balanced representation of issues in plenary sessions are all guarantees of the neutrality of a DP experiment.

Furthermore, we discussed the effective participation criterion even if we had no empirical data available to analyse it, as the Turin case was mainly implemented in order to explore the opinion formation and deliberation. Still, due to the benefits of eliminating the need for consensus in DP, we argue that the DP could serve as a democratic innovation able to assure effective participation of the citizens, as has already happened with some other DPs.

In the end, as a novelty within the research that uses the Deliberative Polling method, in our work we analysed the effects of different phases of experiment on perceived legitimacy. We used participants' satisfaction with democracy as an indicator of perceived legitimacy. Following the assumption that after participating in deliberation within the DP setting, citizens should become more aware of the complexity of public issues and the democratic procedures that aim to deal with them, we tested the assumption against the empirical data from the Turin case.

We confirmed that after participating in the DP, citizens become more satisfied with how democracy works. Having analysed the effects of different phases of DP on participants' satisfaction with democracy, we find that the phase having the strongest effect is the one in which the participants interact with politicians in plenary sessions. In fact, it is only during the plenary sessions that participants had a possibility to hear the reasons and rationales for the politicians' positions on the issues. Thus, this phase allowed the participants to better understand politicians and their tasks.

In our contribution, we tried to analyse the benefits of Deliberative Polling without undermining the critical aspects and problems related to its realisation within a real world setting. However, taking into account all of the results and considerations we exposed, we can conclude that in many ways, the Deliberative Poll could be considered as a "gold standard" (Mansbridge 2010) for processes of citizens' involvement and that it is surely a satisfying model of democratic innovation according to the evaluative criteria outlined by the editors.

References

Andersen, Viebke N. & Hansen, Kasper M. (2007): "How Deliberation Makes Better Citizens: The Danish Deliberative Poll on the Euro". *European Journal of Political Research* 46 (4), 531–556.

Bächtiger, André & Hangartner, Dominic (2010): "When Deliberative Theory Meets Empirical Political Science: Theoretical and Methodological Challenges in Political Deliberation". *Political Studies* 58 (4), 609-629.

Bellucci, Paolo & Memoli, Vincenzo (2012): "The determinants of democratic support in Europe", in Pedro C. Magalhaes, David Sanders and Gabor Toka (eds.), *Citizens and the European Polity: Mass Attitudes Towards the European and National Polities (Citizenship, Identity and European Integration)*, Oxford: Oxford University Press

Benhabib, Seyla (1996): "The Democratic Moment and the problem of Difference". Benhabib, Seyla *Democracy and Difference: Contesting the Boundaries of the Political*. Princeton: Princeton University Press, 3-18.

Benhabib, Seyla (2005): *La rivendicazione dell'identità culturale*, tr.it. Il Mulino, Bologna.

Burkhalter, Stephanie, Gastil, John & Kelshaw, Todd (2002): "A conceptual definition andtheoretical model of public deliberation in small face-to-face groups", *Communication Theory*, n. 12, 398-422.

Bobbio, Luigi (2002): "Le arene deliberative" , *Rivista Italiana di Politiche Pubbliche,* 3, 5-29.

Callon, Michel, Lascoumes, Pierre & Barthe, Yannick (2001): *Agir dans un monde incertain. Essai sur la democratie technique*, Paris, Seuil.

Cohen, Joshua (1997): "Deliberation and democratic legitimacy", Bohman, James & Rehg William: *Deliberative Democracy: Essays on Reason and Politics*, MIT Press, 67-92.

Coote, Anna & Lenhaglan, Jo (1997), *Citizens' Juries: From Theory to Practice*, London: IPPR.

Dalton, Russel J. (2004): *Democratic Challenges, Democratic Choices: The Erosion of Political Support in Advanced Industrial Democracies*, Oxford: Oxford University Press

Dryzek, John S. (2000): *Deliberative Democracy and Beyond*. Oxford: Oxford University Press.

Farrar, Cynthia, Fishkin, James S., Green, Donald P., List, Christian, Luskin, Robert C. & Paluck, Elizabeth L. (2010): "Disaggregating Deliberation's Effects: An Experiment within a Deliberative Poll". *British Journal of Political Science* 40, 333–347.

Fishkin, James S. (1997): *The Voice of the People: Public Opinion and Democracy*, New Haven:Yale University Press.

Fishkin, James S. & Luskin, Robert (2005): "Experimenting with a Democratic Ideal: Deliberative Polling and Public Opinion", *Acta Politica* 40, 284–298.

Fishkin, James S. (2009): *When the people speak: deliberative democracy and public consultation*. Oxford: Oxford University Press.

Grönlund K, Setälä, M. & Herne, K. (2010): "Deliberation and civic virtue: lessons from citizen deliberation experiment", *European Political Science Review* (2010), 2: 95-117

Gutmann, Amy & Thompson, Dennis F. (2004): *Why Deliberative Democracy*. Princeton and Oxford:Princeton University Press.

Habermas, Jürgen (1996): *Between facts and norms: contribution to a discourse theory of law and democracy*. Cambridge: MIT Press.

Hansen, Kasper M & Andersen, Vibeke N. (2004): ""Deliberative Democracy and the Deliberative Poll on the Euro. *Scandinavian Political Studies* 27 (3), 261-286.

Isernia, P., Bobbio, L., Fiket, I., Manca, A. & Podestà, N. (2008): "La democrazia in un ambiente ostile, un quasi-esperimento deliberativo sul caso della Tav e del diritto al voto a Torino". *Stato e Mercato*, 84, 443-473.

Köchler, Hans (1987): *The Crisis of Representative Democracy*. Frankfurt /Berne/New York: Peter Lang.

Luskin Robert C. & Fishkin James S. (2002): "Deliberation and Better Citizens". Available at http://cdd.stanford.edu/research/papers/2002/

Luskin, Robert C., Fishkin, James S. & Jowell, Roger (2002): 'Considered Opinions: Deliberative Polling in Britain'. *British Journal of Political Science* (32), 480-487.

Macedo, Stephen (ed.) (1999): *Deliberative Politics: Essays on Democracy and Disagreement*. New York: Oxford University Press.

Mansbridge J. (2010): "Deliberative Polling as the Gold Standard". *The Good Society* 19 (1), 55-62.

McNamara, Kathleen R. (2002): "Rational Fictions: Central Bank Independence and the Social Logic of Delegation". *West European Politics*25 (1),47-76.

Mutz, D. (2002): "The Consequences of Cross-Cutting Networks for Political Participation". *American Journal of Political Science* 46 (4): 838-55.

Mutz, Diana C. (2008): "Is Deliberative Democracy a Falsifiable Theory?" *Annual Review of Political Science* 11, 521–538.

Neblo, Michael (2007): "Family Disputes: Diversity in Defining and Measuring Deliberation". *Swiss Political Science Review* 13 (4), 527–557.

Norris P. (ed.) (1999): *Critical Citizens*. Oxford: Oxford University Press.

Parkinson, John (2006): *Deliberating in the Real World: Problems of Legitimacy in Deliberative Democracy*. Oxford: Oxford University Press.

Rossi, J. (1997): "Participation Run Amok: The Costs of Mass Participation for Deliberative Agency Decision-Making". *Northwestern University Law* Review 92, 173-249.

Ryfe, David M. (2005): "Does Deliberative Democracy Work?" *Annual Review of Political Science* 8, 49–71.

Scharpf, Fritz W. (1999): *Governing in Europe: Effective and Democratic?* Oxford University Press.

Shapiro, I. (1999): "Enough of deliberation: Politics is about interests and power". S. Macedo (Ed.), *Deliberative Politics: Essays on Democracy and Disagreement* New York: Oxford University Press, 28-38).

Sintomer Y, & Maillard J., (2007): "The limits to local participation and deliberation in the French '*politique de la ville*'". *European Journal of Political Research* 46 (4), 503–529.

Siu, Alice (2008): *Look Who's Talking: Examining Social Influence, Opinion Change and Argument Quality in Deliberation*. Dissertation. Stanford University, Department of Communication and Committee of Graduate Studies.

Steenbergen, Marco R.; Bächtiger, André; Spörndli, Markus & Steiner, Jürg (2003): "Measuring Political Deliberation: A Discourse Quality Index". *Comparative European Politics* 1(1), 21–48.

Steiner, Jürg; Bächtiger, André; Spörndli, Markus & Steenbergen, Marco R. (2004): *Deliberative Politics in Action*. Cambridge: Cambridge University Press.

Sunstein, Cass R. (2002): "The Law of Polarization". *The Journal of Political Philosophy* 10 (2), 175–196.

Thompson, Dennis F. (2008): "Deliberative Democratic Theory and Empirical Political Science". *Annual Review of Political Science* 11:497-520.

Wagner, A. F., Dufor, M. & Schneider, F. (2003): Satisfaction not Guaranteed – Institutions and Satisfaction with Democracy in Western Europe. CESifo Working Paper n.910.

Young, Iris M. (2000): *Inclusion and Democracy*. Oxford: Oxford University Press.

Williams, B. A. & Metheny, A. R. (1995): Democracy, dialogue, and environmental disputes: The contested languages of social regulation. New Haven, CT: Yale University Press.

Witte, John F. (1980): *Democracy, Authority, and Alienation in Work: Workers' Participation in an American Corporation*. Chicago: University of Chicago Press.

Wright, Ronald F. (1992). Why Not Administrative Grand Juries? *Administrative Law Review* 44, 465-521.

Innovating Democracy Online?
Evaluating the Finnish Virtual Polity Experiment in Citizen Deliberation

Kim Strandberg/Kimmo Grönlund

Introduction

Partisan forms of political participation have been in decline in mature representative democracies over the recent decades. Likewise, the traditional forms of political engagement are no longer deeply rooted in the values and preferences, nor manifested in the behavior, of younger generations of citizens (Kippen & Jenkins 2004: 254; Inglehart & Welzel 2005; Dalton, 2007; Kies 2010). Contemporary democracies have even been assessed as being "thin" (Barber 1984), or having become "audience" democracies (Manin 1997). Both epithets pertain to the fact that representative democracy and its traditional actors and institutions are less and less capable of involving citizens in the political process.

 It is hardly surprising, against this context, that several scholars have stressed the need for an 'evolution' of democracy towards being better suited to engage citizens in decision-making (Barber 1984; Dahl 1989; Wright & Street 2007: 850). Democratic innovations may be regarded as one strand of tangible expressions of these theoretical desires. Democratic innovations are, in simple terms, examples of real-life solutions trying to improve, or at least supplement, representative democracy by creating channels for direct citizen participation. As stated in the introduction to this book, democratic innovations mainly fall into two types: aggregation or deliberation. This chapter concerns an example of the latter: a Finnish experiment in on-line citizen deliberation. Within recent decades, there has been a surge for the deliberative notion, which particularly stresses the importance of public discussion between free and equal citizens. Dryzek (2000: 1) summarizes what he calls the "deliberative turn" as the point of view that "the essence of democracy itself is now widely taken to be deliberation, as opposed to voting and interest aggregation".

Turning to the actual implementation of deliberative theory, though, several obstacles have been highlighted by scholars. In particular, concerns regarding how citizen deliberation could be made manageable in large scale societies have been raised (Fishkin 1995; Coleman & Goetze 2001; Wright & Street 2007). Lately, though, several types of deliberative mini-publics, e.g. citizen juries, consensus conferences and deliberative polls[1] (Dryzek & Goodin 2006), have attempted to address both practical and theoretical challenges.

Nonetheless, even though these innovations are a step forward in organizing and facilitating true deliberative discussions in practice, they are unfortunately both cost and labor intensive (Luskin et al. 2006).

Over the last decade and a half, the rapid growth of information and communication technology (henceforth abbreviated to ICTs) has seen scholars raising their hopes over ICTs being a new convenient means for engaging citizens in politics (e.g. Barber 1984: 151; Dahl 1989: 519-522; Budge 1996: 28-31). Correspondingly, scholars have also looked upon ICTs as one potential solution for some of the scale-problems (Dahl 1989; Fishkin 1995) associated with carrying out deliberative discussions (e.g. Price & Capella 2002; Luskin et al. 2006). For instance, bringing together a large number of citizens for deliberating is rather easily carried out on-line, since citizens can take part more or less regardless of physical location (Coleman & Goetze 2001; Wright & Street 2007: 852; Strandberg 2008: 72). Also, on a theoretical note, Wright and Street (2007: 851) observe that "… [T]he technical characteristics of the Internet […] have led to the creation of a 'virtual world' that establishes the conditions for deliberative democracy".

Nonetheless, despite the fact that ICTs have several features which may foster deliberation, scholars have been concerned with the ways in which the use of ICTs for citizen discussion may turn out. Interestingly, we note that many of the concerns bear resemblance to some of the criteria for evaluating democratic innovations which was mentioned in the framework of this volume. Specifically, pertaining to the criteria of inclusive participation, scholars have noted 'polarization' tendencies (Sunstein 2001; Wilhelm 1999: 172-183) in on-line citizen discussions, as well as 'digital divides' upon examining the social or demographic composition of participants in on-line discussion (e.g. Norris 2001; Strandberg 2008). In addition, regarding the frameworks' criteria of deliberation, there is also evidence of on-line citizens' discussion not readily living up to qualitative standards of true deliberative conversations (Papacharissi 2002: 16; Jankowski & Van Os 2004: 190; Strandberg 2005; 2008). Still, many scholars maintain that the Internet might be appropriate for citizen deliberations, if the discussion venues themselves were designed to be suitable for achieving such discussions (cf. Luskin et al. 2006; Wright & Street 2007).

In this chapter, we study the feasibility of conducting on-line deliberation through evaluating a controlled experiment. This experiment was something of a pilot study and it was organized in Finland in spring 2008. The experiment was one of the first full-scale on-line experiments in citizen deliberation using live video and audio conducted in Europe[2]. This so-called Virtual Polity[3] venue was designed to establish conditions suitable for citizen deliberation. In the following section we present the chapter's theoretical backdrop.

Theoretical Background

Citizen Deliberation

The theory of deliberative democracy essentially stresses the significance of free and equal citizens engaging in fact-based argumentation and discussion (Elster 1998). Such a process is believed to result in policies that fulfill the idea of a common good better than a plain aggregation of individual preferences (e.g. Gutmann & Thompson 2004). In particular, when decisions are reached in discussions where individual views need to be justified and opposing arguments need to be considered seriously, the process is perceived to push individuals' values and preferences towards a collective understanding (Barber 1984; Gutmann & Thompson 1996).

According to Grönlund et al. (2010), changes in values and opinions are not the only effects of deliberation. Reporting from a face-to-face experiment, they find positive side-effects or "civic virtues" – such as increased knowledge and interpersonal trust as well as an increased readiness for voluntary collective action. This notion is supported by several studies. For instance, studies on deliberative polls (Fishkin et al. 2000; Luskin et al. 2002) have found that participants increased their knowledge of the issue of deliberation after taking part in a discussion event. Other studies suggest that participation in deliberations may positively affect civic skills (Fung 2003) and also the participants' feelings of internal political efficacy (Gastil 2000: 358; Smith & Wales 2000, Hansen 2004, 287). This increase of skills and efficacy may, in turn, augment the propensity of participating in political or societal actions. It can also be assumed that trust in political institutions and external political efficacy may be positively affected by participation in deliberations. Grönlund et al. (2010) argue that: "As the deliberators learn and understand the complexities related to political issues, they may become more understanding and trusting of the procedures and actors of representative democracy". Finally, as to interpersonal trust, the need for taking other people into consideration when deliberating might also have positive bearing (Barber 1984). Likewise, the deliberative setting where, ideally, people with various social backgrounds are 'forced' to take each other's view into account and dishonest behavior can lead to less credibility and trustworthiness in the eyes of other deliberators, is perceived to be beneficial for interpersonal trust (Dryzek & List 2003).

Deliberation is perceived to affect citizens in several ways, as evident from the discussion hitherto. It is also noteworthy that several of the effects perceived here bear direct resemblance to many of the criteria – e.g. effectiveness and legitimacy, deliberative quality and enlightened citizens – for evaluating democratic innovations listed in the book's framework. In the next section, we will discuss what bearing ICTs may have on these, and other, aspects of deliberative democratic innovations.

The Prospect of Deliberating On-Line

In the introduction to this chapter, we mentioned that an array of social science scholars have looked upon ICTs as a suitable venue for carrying out citizen deliberations (e.g. Coleman & Goetze 2001; Price & Capella 2002; Luskin et al. 2006). There are several reasons for this optimism. Firstly, using the Internet for conveying and organizing deliberative discussions is practically and logistically convenient compared to the vast amount of resources required for off-line deliberation events (Luskin et al. 2006). In an excellent summary of this line of thought, Hauben and Hauben (1997: 319) state that: "...the democratic ideas of some great political thinkers are becoming practical". Moreover, partly because of these practical benefits in bringing together large numbers of citizens, several leading scholars in democratic theory have even thought about the prospects of ICTs bringing about broader changes to democracy by increasing citizens' involvement in politics and decision-making (e.g. Barber 1984; Dahl 1989: 519-522; Budge 1996).

However, with time, there have been some doubts concerning the arguably rather techno-deterministic view that ICTs *per se* serve to improve democracy. After all, ICTs are not inherently democratic and will serve to innovate and improve democracy only if they are employed in ways beneficial to democracy. One strand of skepticism concerns the inclusive aspects of ICTs: firstly, as regards this, a scholarly debate about whether political activity on-line will reach beyond certain social strata (i.e. those with resources for the equipment needed to take part) or the already active citizens (i.e. those with enough motivation) has been noticeable (e.g. Hill & Hughes 1998; Davis 1999; Norris 2001). Concerning on-line citizen deliberation, for instance, citizens arguably need to have a strong interest in discussing politics in order to take part. Secondly, also pertaining to the inclusiveness aspect of ICTs in politics, other scholars, too, argue that the skills required for using ICTs may exclude certain groups of citizens, for instance the elderly (e.g. Kies 2010: 67). The risk, in summary, could be that on-line discussions become too isolated and exclusive to have any real connection either to the general public or to public policies (Wright & Street 2007: 852).

A second focus of the skepticism about the benefits of ICTs for deliberative democracy concerns discussion quality. According to deliberative democratic theory, the essence of deliberation lies in the quality of the deliberative process, i.e. the nature of the actual discussion between citizens. Rather alarmingly, several scholars have shown that on-line discussions often do not meet the ideals of truly deliberative discussions (e.g. Wilhelm 1999; Jankowski

& Van Selm 2000; Strandberg 2008). Specifically, the large extent of hasty opinions and notable abundance of severely conflict-laden discussions found on-line have been cause for concern (e.g. Papacharissi 2002: 16; Strandberg 2005; 2008).

Regardless of the skepticism, though, we argue that it would be premature to dismiss the prospects of deliberating via ICTs only based on evidence from existing on-line discussion forums which are often of an ad-hoc nature (cf. Wright and Street 2007: 850). In other words, if on-line citizens' discussions are left to their own devices, there is a high risk of failing to meet deliberative ideals. But if these discussions are carefully designed, they can be deliberative. In essence thus, the need for carefully constructing on-line deliberative democratic innovations is apparent. Hitherto, an increasing number of research and policy activities have been carried out within the field of innovations in electronic deliberation (e.g. Price & Capella 2002; Muhlberger 2005; Luskin et al. 2006; Shane 2008). Many of these innovations and experiments have combined face-to-face discussion with on-line elements and have addressed deliberative democracy directly. As a common denominator, the experiments in these studies have designed the discussion venue stringently á priori in order to better achieve conditions suitable for citizen deliberation. We will now briefly report on some of the findings from these studies.

Price and Capella (2002: 313-320), reporting on a year-long on-line citizens' discussion project, found several interesting effects which were rather similar to findings from other studies of citizen deliberation off-line (cf. Fishkin et al. 2000; Gastil 2000; Smith & Wales 2000; Luskin et al. 2002; Fung 2003). Firstly, they found that the participants' opinions changed after deliberation. Secondly, the participants increased their political knowledge and their appreciation of the arguments of others improved. Finally, Price and Capella note that taking part in the on-line deliberations enhanced the participants' propensity to vote and participate in societal activities. In another study reporting on two deliberative polls, one off-line and one on-line event, Luskin et al. (2006) generally found more effects for off-line deliberation than on-line. Still, some of their findings for the on-line Deliberative Poll™ merit attention here. As far as learning and knowledge were concerned, the participants of the on-line deliberative poll became significantly more knowledgeable compared to a control group after taking part in the event. Furthermore, the authors note that the participants' attitudes and opinions concerning the topic of the deliberative poll changed significantly. Muhlberger (2005), reporting on findings from the so-called Virtual Agora on-line deliberation project, provides somewhat different results. Regarding changes of opinion in particular, he states that these took place due to information handed out at the deliberation events and *not* due to the actual deliberation (Muhlberger 2005: 8). This was tested using an information only group in the experiment. Still, Muhlberger shows that deliberation did make the groups' opinions more coherent. He also mentions (2005: 11) that the "community-mindedness" of the participants rose.

The brief summary of studies reporting on democratic innovations in electronic deliberation shows that there could be a potential for on-line deliberation, that is, under suitable conditions. Obviously, research in on-line deliberation is still relatively new and continuously growing; hence the evaluation of the Finnish citizen deliberation experiment to be carried out in this chapter will hopefully provide more useful insights into the prospects and feasibility of employing ICTs in citizen deliberation. The next section presents the evaluation areas relevant for the Virtual Polity experiment after which the design and methods are presented and discussed.

Evaluation Areas

On a general level, the main area of interest in this chapter is to examine the prospects of on-line deliberation by evaluating a deliberation experiment in light of the democratic criteria stated in the volume's framework. However, as such, not all of the five democratic criteria, or their specific indicators, are *ex post facto* applicable to the present experiment (which was originally designed for other purposes and other research questions). Thus, we have opted for focusing on the following of the volume's criteria in this chapter (letters are the same as used in the volume's introduction):

(a) Inclusive participation and technical obstacles
(b) Legitimacy
(c) Enlightened citizens and democratic education

Most of these criteria are examined using quantitative data. However, the aspect of technical obstacles (i.e. which we added to the framework's criteria of inclusive participation) will be addressed by the use of observations and annotations. It should also be noted that the indicators used in this chapter do not readily correspond to all of those listed in Table 1.2 in the book's framework. We have nonetheless made significant efforts to analyze our data in ways as similar to the book's criteria as possible. Before looking at the findings of this analysis, though, we present the design and methods of the Virtual Polity experiment in the following section.

Design and Methods

The Virtual Polity experiment in citizen deliberation was carried out in spring 2008. Thematically, it focused on nuclear energy and energy policy; the discussion topic was whether a sixth nuclear plant should be built in Finland. The experiment was a pilot experiment originally aiming at testing how on-line deliberation works in practice and also to the effects of deliberating on the participating citizens. By employing experimental designs and replicating an earlier face-to-face experiment (e.g. Grönlund et al. 2009) , even by using live webcam streaming and audio, the Virtual Polity pilot was one of the first large-scale on-line deliberative experiments conducted in Europe. Speaking in terms of general designs, the experiment applied a pre-test post-test control group experimental design. Several surveys were used at different stages of the experiment; a pre-test survey was initially answered electronically by both the participants and the control group. Thereafter, surveys were employed for the participants at different stages of the experiment in order to assess both the effects of deliberation and to measure knowledge gains. After deliberation, a post-test survey was answered by the participants. The post-test survey was also repeated two months after the experiment in order to see the long-term effects of deliberating. At this point, the control group also answered the post-test survey. Various surveys used in the experiment are summarized in Table 7.1.

The focus of the surveys was mainly the participants' opinions concerning energy issues, their feelings of internal and external efficacy, their political knowledge, levels of interpersonal and general trust as well as their propensity for political activity. In the analyses conducted in this chapter, we will use these measures in a manner suitable for the volume's criteria for evaluating democratic innovations. In practice, this means that some of the original measures can be used as such while some are slightly adjusted.

The Virtual Polity experiment used random group allocation into treatment groups and a control group. A random sample of 6,000 Finnish adult citizens was invited to participate. The participants were promised free technical equipment and a voucher as compensation for their participation (see Iyengar et al. 2003 for a comparable procedure). Eventually, merely 147 citizens volunteered for the experiment. This was discouraging, since we strived for a large number of volunteers in order to achieve an effective number of 144 participants, i.e. 12 groups with 12 persons in each. Based on earlier mini-publics, we could anticipate a drop-off rate of at least 25 per cent. Unfortunately, only 79 participants completed the deliberative sessions. There were several reasons for this: some citizens did not turn up and some dropped off during the course of the experiment.

Table 7.1 *The Phases of the Virtual Polity Experiment*

March 2008	Baseline survey for treatment groups and control group (T1)
April 2008	Survey measuring knowledge (T2)
	Reading information material about nuclear power
	Watching recordings of expert panel discussions
	A short poll of 7 questions (T3)
	Discussions in small groups 2-4 hours
	Decision making in the small groups 1 hour
	Final survey including measurement of knowledge (T4)
June 2008	Follow up survey for treatment groups and control group (T5)

The deliberation sessions were held at weekends in April and May 2008 via the Virtual Polity website. Each small-n discussion group had one session in total. Contrary to many on-line deliberations thus far (e.g. Price & Capella 2002; Luskin et al. 2006), the sessions were carried out with the use of *both* live audio and webcam streaming. The flow of discussion was set so that only one participant could talk at any given time. A text-based chat option was also available for use in case the participants experienced problems with audio or video streaming. This text-chat was also used by the moderator for posting technical information not directly related to the actual discussion. The discussion room also contained a whiteboard window in which the moderator listed the topics suggested by the participants in order to create an agenda for discussion. The on-line discussions lasted for a couple of hours, varying mainly according to group size. The moderator initially held a short introduction and helped the participants in getting the video and audio streaming to work. Otherwise, the moderator had mainly an observational role in the discussions. The participants filled out a post-deliberation survey (T4) immediately after the sessions had ended.

Findings

The findings are presented in three sections, one for each of the evaluation criteria relevant to the Virtual Polity experiment.

Inclusive Participation and Technical Obstacles

Inclusive Participation

The first criterion for which we will present findings is the criterion of inclusive participation. In the volume's framework, it is stated that "Participatory innovations would attract a multitude of citizens who do not get involved in traditional participation". We will examine this question in a twofold way: Firstly, we compare, in Table 7.2, the basic demographic traits of our participants with those of the Finnish population in general. Secondly, in Tables 7.3 and 7.4, we compare the political interest, engagement and level of propensity for untraditional forms of political activity for the participants and the general population. Our data do not, however, allow for any analysis of the "effective participation"-indicator which is thus omitted from the inclusiveness criterion.

Judging from Table 7.2, the participants of the Virtual Polity experiment (and the control group as well) were for most part representative of the Finnish population in general in terms of demographic traits. An overrepresentation of males and citizens aged 25 to 34 years were perhaps the most notable exceptions to this demographic pattern[4]. We continue the analysis by looking further at factors related to political and societal engagement.

Generally, the participants appeared to be more interested in politics than the Finnish population at large; roughly 87 per cent were either very or somewhat interested, compared to 61 per cent of the population as a whole. However, the volunteers, neither the participants nor the control group, were members of political parties to any larger extent than the population at large. In terms of traditional forms of participation, the Virtual Polity experiment was rather representative of the Finnish population. Table 7.4, finally, analyses the political engagement aspect by examining the participants' propensity for taking part in various somewhat *unconventional* forms of political activities in comparison to the general public.

The findings presented in Table 7.4 further strengthen the notion that the participants volunteering for the on-line deliberation experiment were relatively engaged and interested citizens. Additionally, it might not be so surprising that the volunteers score highly on a scale measuring alternative forms of participation, seeing as an experiment in deliberation is one such *alternative* participatory activity as well. So, to that extent we can tentatively conclude our analysis of inclusiveness by stating that the Virtual Polity experiment seemingly did attract "...citizens who do not get involved in traditional participation".

Table 7.2 Demographic Characteristics of Virtual Polity Participants, Control Group Members and Finnish Population

	Participants		Control group		Finnish population	
	%	N	%	N	%	N
Gender						
male	62.0	49	57.1	56	49.4	702
female	38.0	30	42.9	42	50.6	720
Age						
18-24	14.1	11	10.4	10	9.8	139
25-34	23.1	18	14.6	14	15.3	217
35-44	16.7	13	15.6	15	13.6	193
45-54	17.9	14	13.5	13	15.9	226
55-64	19.2	15	29.2	28	20.0	285
64-	9.0	7	16.7	16	25.5	362
Education						
primary	10.2	8	10.4	10	17.1	243
vocational	32.9	26	42.2	41	42.8	608
upper secondary	17.7	14	14.4	14	18.0	256
polytechnic	24.1	19	15.5	15	6.8	96
university	15.2	12	17.5	17	14.7	209
Household income						
under 10,000 €	12.0	9	2.1	2	10.6	129
10,000-20.000 €	10.7	8	9.5	9	20.4	249
20,001-30,000 €	8.0	6	16.8	16	18.5	226
30.001-40,000 €	21.3	16	18.9	18	15.4	188
40,001-50,000 €	13.3	10	14.7	14	11.5	140
50,001-60,000 €	14.7	11	14.7	14	10.1	123
60,001-90,000 €	10.7	8	14.7	14	9.8	119
over 90,000 €	9.3	7	8.4	8	3.7	45
Living area						
in city centre	16.5	13	32.7	2	24.3	345
in suburb to larger city	32.9	26	29.6	29	44.0	625
municipal centre	24.1	19	17.3	17	20.3	289
in rural environment	26.6	21	20.4	20	11.5	163

Table 7.3 Political Engagement

	Participants		Control group		Finnish population	
	%	N	%	N	%	N
Political interest						
very interested	29.1	23	17.7	17	16.7	238
somewhat interested	58.2	46	60.4	58	44.7	636
rather uninterested	11.4	9	18.8	18	31.3	445
very uninterested	1.3	1	3.1	3	7.2	103
Party membership						
active member	8.9	7	3.1	3	5.5	55
passive member	8.9	7	6.1	6	8.6	86
not member	82.3	65	90.8	89	85.8	857
Union membership						
active member	8.9	7	10.2	10	8.2	83
passive member	53.2	42	51.0	50	41.4	417
not member	38.0	30	38.8	38	50.4	508

Table 7.4 Propensity for Political Activity (standardized index 0-1)

Propensity for political activity	N	Mean	Std.dev.
Participants	79	.58	.19
Control group	98	.48	.20
Finnish population	1,331	.43	.22

Note: *The scale is constructed based on 8 items asking the respondents whether they have taken part or would consider taking part in the following activities: write to a newspaper's public section; contact a politician regarding an important matter; sign a petition; take part in a boycott or similar consumer's strike; take part in a peaceful demonstration; demonstrate civil disobedience by taking part in non-violent illegal activity; take part in a demonstration where violence has occurred previously; use force to achieve one's goals.*

Technical Obstacles

In considering the inclusiveness of the Virtual Polity experiment, it is also relevant to note that the on-line Virtual Polity experiment helped shed light on several obstacles – mostly due to the technology itself – for on-line deliberative innovations to overcome (see Grönlund et al. 2009 for more detailed discussion). The first obstacle is server capacity, which ideally should just be a prerequisite for a functioning on-line deliberation event. However, albeit many measures had been taken to avoid it, several groups experienced IT-problems related to server capacity in our experiment. Naturally, a face-to-face deliberation is safe from such problems, making innovations in on-line deliberation more hazardous to carry out. Another troublesome aspect of on-line deliberations deals with what Kies (2010: 67) calls digital divides in computer skills. In the Virtual Polity experiment traces of this were manifested by many participants experiencing problems in setting up their webcams and headsets, being forced to use text-based interaction instead. In that sense, participation did not take place on equal terms for all participants and, thus, was not up to deliberative standards (Grönlund et al. 2009: 197). Still, with time, people will probably become more accustomed to using such technical equipments and this issue should not be as apparent in future on-line deliberations. Finally, we also observed that our on-line deliberation was somewhat hindered by limited broadband capacity on the part of some participants. Again, though, this ought to be less of a problem when broadband speeds develop over time.

Our brief evaluation of the technical obstacles regarding inclusiveness in the Virtual Polity experiment undoubtedly leads us to a somewhat skeptical summary. At the present moment, emulating ideal deliberation settings — i.e. comparable to those stated in the literature (see Strandberg 2008) — is rather challenging. However, observations made by the moderators of the group discussions still give cause for optimism[5]; they regarded the quality and flow of the discussion as good. Consequently, if the quality of discussion was indeed rather satisfying already, it is perceivable that democratic innovations in on-line deliberation may become even closer to fulfilling qualitative ideals since the technical obstacles ought to diminish.

Legitimacy

The second evaluation criterion is legitimacy. This is, of course, a very multifaceted notion (see Easton 1965). Bearing this in mind, the following analysis is by no means to be regarded as a strict measure of legitimacy. Rather, we chose to follow the line of thought of this volume's framework (pp. 24) stating that "...proponents of democratic innovations argue that citizens would accept the political system, decisions, or even politicians with more enthusiasm if they were involved in the political process". In testing this assumption for the Virtual Polity experiment we look at two types of indicators: the participants' feeling of external political efficacy and their trust in political institutions.

Table 7.5 shows that taking part in the on-line deliberation did not affect the participants' feelings of efficacy. Apparently, even though the deliberative setting forces people to learn about and discuss complex issues (Gastil 2000: 358; Smith & Wales 2000; Grönlund et al. 2010; Setälä et al. 2010), only one experiment is not enough for boosting efficacy. Looking at how the participation in the VP experiment affected the participants' trust for institutions there were likewise no significant effects to be found due to participation in the experiment. This leads us to summarize that from the point of view of legitimacy in the eyes of the citizens, the Virtual Polity deliberation innovation did not have any effect, either negative or positive.

Table 7.5 Development of Feelings of Political Efficacy and Trust for Institutions in the Experiment- and Control Group

	Participants			Control group		
	Pre-test	Post-test	Change	Pre-test	Post-test	Change
External efficacy						
People can exert influence through voting	3.42	3.46	0.04	3.42	3.39	-0.03
An ordinary citizen cannot influence politics	1.95	2.11	0.16	2.29	2.17	-0.12
On the whole, democracy works well in Finland	2.99	3.13	0.14	3.18	3.07	-0.11
Trust for institutions						
The parliament	2.77	2.79	0.02	2.61	2.55	-0.06
The judicial system	3.08	3.13	0.05	2.97	3.00	0.03
The police	3.27	3.22	-0.05	3.27	3.22	-0.05
Politicians	2.15	2.16	0.01	2.06	2.02	-0.04

Note: Items marked with a * show a significant development within the group. Figures are group averages on a scale 1-5 where 1 stands for disagreeing totally with the statement and 5 for agreeing totally.

Enlightened Citizens And Democratic Education

Increased knowledge concerning the topic of discussion is a common effect of deliberation (e.g. Fishkin et al. 2000; Luskin et al. 2002; Grönlund et al. 2010). In our evaluation of the criteria of enlightened citizens, knowledge and learning regarding the issue of discussion are in focus, as well. Arguably, it is logical to expect increased knowledge due to deliberation; participants learn about, discuss and debate the issue of the deliberation. Still, it has been argued that the information material used as a part of the deliberative design might affect knowledge more than the actual group discussions (e.g. Muhlberger 2005). In our analysis of knowledge gains, we account for this possibility by separating the items whose answers could be found in the pre-discussion information package from other knowledge-related items (Table 7.6)[6].

Table 7.6 Knowledge Gains

	Participants (N=79)		
	Pre-test	Post-test	Change
Items found in the information material (0-6)	2.96	3.35	*0.39
Other energy policy items (0-4)	2.22	2.26	0.04
General political knowledge items (0-5)	3.59	3.48	-0.11

Note: *Items marked with a * show a significant development within the treatment group (paired samples t-test). Bolded items differ significantly between the vote and statement groups (independent samples t-test).*

The findings presented in Table 7.6 show that the participants indeed increased their knowledge – but only for the items found in the pre-discussion information material. There were no significant knowledge changes in the other items on energy policy.

Turning to the notion of democratic education, the framework to the volume operationalizes this as improved civic skills. In evaluating the impact of the present on-line experiment *vis-à-vis* civic skills we opt for focusing on how participation affected the citizens' feelings of internal political efficacy (Table 7.7). Concerning this, it is proposed that deliberators may increase their civic skills and feeling of internal political efficacy after deliberating, since deliberating forces them to "practice" and learn the ways of political reasoning and decision-making (Gastil 2000: 358; Smith & Wales 2000).

However, based on the finding in Table 7.7 we are not able to find any effects on internal efficacy due to taking part in the on-line deliberation. This could, of course, be due to the fact that taking part in only one session is not adequate for achieving such effects. Another possible explanation is that the participants became more aware of the epistemic complexity of the nuclear power issue and more uncertain about their own political competence. Nonetheless, the summary of the evaluation of the Virtual Polity experiment in light of enlightened citizenship and democratic education is that, in general, the experiment did not have profound effects (Grönlund et al. 2010).

Table 7.7 Development of Internal Efficacy in the Experiment- and Control Group

	Participants			Control group		
	Pre-test	Post-test	Change	Pre-test	Post-test	Change
Internal efficacy						
Sometimes politics seems so complicated that an ordinary citizen cannot really understand what is going on	2.99	3.06	0.07	2.04	1.97	-0.07
I know more about politics and government than most of my fellow citizens	2.56	2.65	0.09	2.67	2.42	-0.25

Note: *Items marked with a * show a significant development within the treatment group (paired samples t-test). Bolded items differ significantly between the vote and statement groups (independent samples t-test).*

Conclusions

Recap

In this chapter we have evaluated an experiment in on-line deliberation in light of three evaluation criteria. To conclude our chapter, then, we will now bring the findings together in order to provide an overarching assessment — to the extent a single pilot experiment ought to be evaluated in light of criteria depicting democratic ideals — of whether the Virtual Polity democratic innovation shows any promise of being able to "refine" representative democracy.

Looking at the results as regards the evaluation criteria, the general impression is ambiguous. On the one hand, the VP experiment was inclusive in the sense that the composition of participants was mostly representative of the Finnish population in general. The annotations concerning deliberative quality made by the moderators were also quite optimistic. On the other hand, technical obstacles nonetheless had an adverse impact on the inclusiveness of the participation. Moreover, participation in the on-line deliberation had no effect on the citizens' perceptions of legitimacy of the political system. Neither could a high degree of citizen enlightenment or democratic education be detected. In summary, thus, the evaluation of the present experiment demonstrates that one innovation in on-line deliberation is unlikely to be beneficial to democracy in all respects. Naturally, additional experimental research is needed in order to address this matter more thoroughly.

Taking a broader approach on our findings, beyond the evaluation of democratic innovations, what bearing do they have for the prospects of using ICTs in citizen deliberation? First and foremost, as mentioned in the presentation of our data and methods, the lack of interest shown (147 volunteers of 6,000 invitations) by the Finnish citizens for taking part in our experiment should be stressed. We are, of course, unable to judge whether this is due to digital divides (e.g. Norris 2001; Kies 2010), technophobia or lack of interest in the topic of discussion. Either way, this is a challenge for future on-line experiments in deliberation to deal with. While on-line venues *a priori* solve many of the scale problems with deliberating in large societies (Fishkin 1995), the actual implementation of the deliberation may turn out to be far from the ideal. We also find it hard to support Hauben and Hauben's (1997: 319) notion that "...the ideas of some great political thinkers are becoming practical..." when taking all the technical problems encountered in the Virtual Polity experiment into account. If on-line deliberations ought to try to emulate face-to-face off-line settings — including live video and audio — technical obstacles will most likely always be a challenge.

In conclusion, the Virtual Polity experiment in on-line citizen deliberation served its purpose in testing democratic innovations in practice. Our intention was to test the feasibility of carrying out on-line deliberations and to compare how on-line discussions come out in comparison with face-to-face settings. Regardless of several observed challenges, most notably the difficulties in recruiting volunteers and problems related to technology, we remain optimistic about the feasibility of being able to design and carry out deliberative discussions on-line.

References

Barber, B. R. (1984). Strong democracy: participatory politics for a new age. Los Angeles: University of California Press.

Budge, I. (1996). The new challenge of direct democracy. Oxford: Blackwell.

Coleman, S. & Goetze. J. (2001). Bowling Together: Online Public Engagement in; Policy Deliberation. London: Hansard Society. Retrieved May, 20, 2009 from http://www.bowlingtogether.net /about.html

Dahl, R. A. (1989). Demokratin och dess Antagonister [Democracy and its Critics]. New Haven: Yale University Press.

Dalton, R.J. (2000). The decline of party identifications. In R. J. Dalton & M. P. Wattenberg (Eds.), Parties Without Partisans: Political Change in Advanced Industrial Democracies (pp. 19-36). New York: Oxford University Press.

Dalton, R. J. (2007). The good citizen: how a younger generation is reshaping American politics. Washington: CQ Press.

Davis, R. (1999). The Web of politics: the Internet's impact on the American political system. New York: Oxford University Press.

Dryzek, J. S. (2000). Deliberative democracy and beyond: Liberals, critics, contestations. New York: Oxford University Press.

Dryzek, J. S. & Goodin, R. E. (2006). Reconciling pluralism and consensus as political ideals. Politics and Society, 34, 219-244.

Dryzek, J. & C. List. (2003). Social choice theory and deliberative democracy: a reconciliation. British Journal of Political Science, 33, 1-28.

Easton, D. (1965). A systems analysis of Political life. Chicago: The University of Chicago Press.

Elster, J. (1998). The market and the forum: three varieties of political theory, in J. Elster & A. Hylland (Eds.), Foundations of Social Choice Theory (pp. 103-132). Cambridge: Cambridge University Press.

Fishkin, J. S. (1995). The voice of the people: public opinion and democracy. New Haven: Yale University Press.

Fishkin, J. S., Luskin, R. C. & Jowell, R. (2000). Deliberative polling and public consultation. Parliamentary Affairs, 53, 657-666.

Fung, A. (2003). Recipes for public spheres: eight institutional design choices and their consequences. Journal of Political Philosophy, 11, 338-367.

Gastil, J. (2000). Is face-to-face deliberation a luxury or a necessity. Political Communication, 17, 357-361.

Grönlund, K., Setälä, :, & Herne, K. (2010). Deliberation and civic virtue - lessons from a citizen deliberation experiment. European Political Science Review, 2(1), 95-117.

Grönlund, K, Strandberg, K. & Himmelroos, S. (2009). The challenge of deliberative democracy online - a comparison of face-to-face and virtual experiments in citizen deliberation. Information Polity, 14, 187-203.

Gutmann, A. & Thompson, D. (1996). Democracy and disagreement. Why moral conflict cannot be avoided in politics, and what to do about it. Cambridge: The Belknap Press of Harvard University Press.

Habermas, J. (1981). The theory of communicative action: reason and the rationalization of society. Cambridge, MIT Press.

Habermas, J. (1996). Between facts and norms: contributions to a discourse theory of law and democracy. Cambridge: Polity Press.

Hansen, K. M. (2004). Deliberative Democracy and Opinion Formation. Odense: University Press of Southern Denmark.

Hauben, M. & Hauben, R. (1997). Netizens. London: Wiley/IEEE Computer Society Press.

Hill, K. A. & Hughes, J. E. (1998). Cyberpolitics: citizen activism in the age of the Internet. New York: Rowman & Littlefield.

Inglehart, R. & Welzel, C. (2005). Modernization, cultural change and democracy. The human development sequence. New York: Cambridge University Press.

Iyengar, S., Luskin, R. C. & Fishkin, J. S. (2003, August-September). Facilitating informed public opinion: evidence on face-to-face and online deliberative polls'. Paper presented at the Annual Meeting of the American Political Science Association, Philadelphia.

Jankowski, N. & Van Selm, M. (2000). The promise and practice of public debate in cyberspace. In K. L. Hacker & J. Van Dijk (Eds.), Digital Democracy: Issues of Theory and Practice (pp. 149-166). London: Sage.

Jankowski, N. & Van Os, R. (2004). Internet-based political discourse: a case study of electronic democracy in Hoogeveen. In P. M. Shane (Ed.), Democracy Online: The Prospects for Political Renewal Through the Internet (pp. 181-195). New York: Routledge.

Kies, R. (2010). Promises and Limits of Web-deliberation. New York: Palgrave Macmillan.

Kippens, G. & Jenkins, G. (2004). The challenge of e-democracy for political parties. In P. M. Shane (Ed.), Democracy Online: The Prospects for Political Renewal Through the Internet (pp. 253-267). New York: Routledge.

Luskin, R. C., Fishkin, J. E. & Jowell, R. (2002). Considered opinions: deliberative polling in Britain. British Journal of Political Science, 32, 455-487.

Luskin, R. C., Fishkin, J. E. & Iyengar, S. (2006). Considered opinions on U.S. foreign policy: evidence from online and face-to-face deliberative polling. California: The Center for Deliberative Democracy.

Mair, P. & Van Biezen, I. (2002). Party membership in twenty European democracies, 1989-2000'. Party Politics, 7, 5-21.

Manin, B. (1997). The Principles of Representative Government. Cambridge University Press.

Muhlberger, P. (2005). The Virtual Agora project: a research design for studying democratic deliberation. Journal of Public Deliberation, 1(1).

Norris, P. (2001). Digital Divide: Civic Engagement, Information Poverty, and the Internet Worldwide. Cambridge University Press.

Papacharissi, Z. (2002). The virtual sphere: the Internet as a public sphere. New Media & Society, 4, 9-27.

Price, V. & Capella, J. N. (2002). Online deliberation and its influence: the Electronic Dialogue project in campaign 2000. IT & Society, 1, 303-329.

Scarrow, S. E. (2000). Parties without members? Party organization in a changing electoral environment. In R. J. Dalton & M. P. Wattenberg (Eds.), Parties Without Partisans: Political Change in Advanced Industrial Democracies (pp. 79-101). New York: Oxford University Press.

Setälä, M., Grönlund, K. & Herne, K. 2010 Citizen Deliberation on Nuclear Power: A Comparison of Two Decision-Making Methods. Political Studies DETAILS TO BE INSERTED.

Smith, G. & Wales, C. (2000). Citizens' juries and deliberative democracy. Political Studies, 48, 51-65.

Shane, P. (2008). Building democracy through online citizen deliberation. A framework for action. Ohio State University.

Strandberg, K. (2005). 'Town Hall' Meetings for the Masses or 'Social Clubs' for the Motivated? – A Study of Citizens' Discussions on the Internet. World Political Science Review, 1, 1-19.

Strandberg, K. (2008). Public Deliberation goes On-Line? – An Analysis of citizens' political discussions on the Internet prior to the Finnish parliamentary elections in 2007. Javnost-The Public, 15, 71-90.

Sunstein, C. (2001). Republic.com. Princeton: Princeton University Press.

Wilhelm, A. (1999). Virtual sounding boards: how deliberative is online political discussion?. In B. N. Haugue & B. Loader (Eds.), Digital democracy: discourse and decision making in the information age (pp. 153-178). London: Routledge.

Wright, S. & Street, J. (2007). Democracy, deliberation and design: the case of online discussion forums. New Media & Society, 9, 849-869.

Democratic Innovations and Deliberative Quality –Two Ways of Capturing the Challenging Deliberation Criteria

Staffan Himmelroos

Introduction

In recent years the debate on democratic theory has come to be dominated by the concept of deliberative democracy, and in its trail a plethora of democratic innovations with a strong emphasis on democratic deliberation have emerged (Gutmann & Thompson 2004, Smith 2009). The purpose outlined in the introduction of the book is to use a criteria-based approach in order to compare such democratic innovations. And if we hope to gain a better understanding of the potential of different democratic innovations, a comparative approach is certainly desirable. A comparative approach might, however, prove problematic if the knowledge of certain criteria is insufficient to start with, and I will argue that this is a potential challenge when evaluating the quality of the deliberation in democratic innovations.

Democratic innovations are often perceived as a cure to different democratic malaises, because they promise to make the political decision-making process more inclusive and promote the enlightenment of citizens by engaging them in democratic deliberation. Empirical research on the processes of democratic deliberation is, however, quite thin, leaving us with little evidence of how real-world deliberations actually play out (Ryfe 2005). To the extent rigorous empirical research has been carried out, the focus has predominantly been on the outcome or effects, whereas the process that is expected to generate these outcomes often seems to have been taken for granted. For all we know, the outcome may as well be the result of various social mechanisms and underlying power structures, rather than inclusive and enlightened discussion between citizens (Andersen & Hansen 2007: 539; Ryfe 2005: 54).

And if our understanding of the quality of deliberation is inadequate, how can we expect to be able to do proper comparisons? The focus in this chapter will, therefore, lie on a specific criterion, deliberation, or ways of capturing the quality of deliberation to be more exact, rather than taking a wider perspective for comparative purposes. To evaluate the procedural quality of deliberation in democratic innovations we need to have a good understanding of what citizen deliberation entails and what the standards of a qualitative deliberative procedure are. I will discuss the theoretical challenges related to capturing deliberation, and show how two measures with different origins, but a similar purpose, can provide us with the necessary tools to capture the deliberative quality of democratic innovations.

The Deliberative Process in Theory and Practice

The Ideal Process

According to a generally acknowledged understanding within deliberative theory, democratic deliberation must take place between equal participants interacting with carefully weighed reasons and morally justified arguments in a context of mutual respect (Habermas 1981; Cohen 1989; Dryzek 1990; Chambers 1996; Bohman 1996; Gutmann & Thompson 1996). What does this imply? First of all, all participants should be recognised as having equal standing through the process, where they can propose issues for the agenda, propose solutions to the issues on the agenda, and offer reasons in support or criticism of proposed solutions. However, ideal deliberation requires not only the logical justification of assertions and validity claims; the arguments should also have intrinsic characteristics that make them compelling to others. That is, there should be a sense of empathy or solidarity that allows the participants to consider the well-being of others and of the community at large (Cohen 1989).

An interactive process relies on the participants paying attention to and understanding the claims and arguments put forward by others. To achieve that there must be a fundamental respect for other participants and their arguments. Without respect deliberation can never bridge different views or stands that must act alongside each other in every pluralist society. According to the political philosopher T.M. Scanlon (see Chambers 1996), a reasonable person is not simply the person who has good reasons for her actions; it is also a person who is willing to listen to objections, who is open to suggestions, and who will re-evaluate a position in the light of new evidence.

How would a process that fulfils these requirements unfold? Habermas's theory of communicative action (1981) constitutes perhaps the most complete normative account of deliberative communication. According to this ideal, the participants make their case for the better argument only by reasoned argumentation. Arguments that do not meet the requirements of the listener are rejected. This subsequently leads to a successive sorting of arguments. The ones that are not accepted are sorted out, while the ones that win acceptation live on. This can be seen as an indication of the force of the better argument. The process is driven on by the evaluation and correction of the arguments. The force of the better argument rejects all propositions that cannot be accepted by everyone and eventually produces an outcome that all can agree on (Habermas 1996; Eriksen & Weigård 2003).

Too Rational – Too Rigid?

As we have seen, democratic deliberation takes on quite rigorous standards concerning the reflective capacities of the participants. Individuals are assumed to be able to consider and arrange their specific preferences and values relative to their sense of higher order good, or at least be able to incorporate the good of others with their own view. They are also assumed to be able to take the perspective of others and thus fairly consider the claims of another person in that person's terms. Moreover, they should consider not only the personal value of specific actions or outcomes, but also the common value of general principles of interaction. (Rosenberg 2004)

Many are, thus, sceptical of whether real-world deliberation can be compared to the ideal at all, and whether only capacity for rational discourse should be decisive for our understanding of deliberation. The Habermasian ideal speech situation has been strongly criticised for relying on an assumption that under ideal conditions language would be fully transparent, i.e. its meaning is accessible to all. This is a characterisation of speech highly contested in post-structuralism, where following Foucault, language is seen as thoroughly and intractably implicated in power (Kohn 2000: 410). These critics believe that since linguistic capability is hierarchically distributed, discourses will always be hegemonic in nature and subjugate them to power (cf. Sanders 1997, Mouffe 1999).

The problem with discourses is that they may constrain, as well as enable thoughts, speech, and action. Every discourse embodies some conception of common sense and acceptable knowledge, and thus, it may act as an expression of power by recognising some interests as valid while repressing others (Dryzek & Niemeyer 2008: 2). It has been suggested that Habermasian rational discourse represents a form of communication that is characteristic of some groups, while it tends to exclude others.

Political theorist Iris Marion Young (2000) claims that in order for everyone to be able to participate on an equal basis, we need to take a less restrictive view on deliberation. Young emphasises that an inclusive democracy should not only respect the pluralism of views and interests in society, but also the pluralism of expression. Communication based on rhetoric, greetings and narratives could be used as tools for deliberation by giving a voice to people who depend on more emotional forms of expression. It is important to recognise that democratic discourse includes many kinds of communication; otherwise an important part of the deliberative process may be disregarded or overlooked. Since the way we express ourselves is part of our language, it is difficult to limit deliberation by linguistic norms for what constitutes "correct" argumentation or rational communication, at least if one hopes to respect the pluralism of modern society.

Most proponents of deliberative democracy readily admit that there will always be some constraints limiting the ideal of a communicative rationality. James Fishkin (1997: 41) thinks that in order to embrace a more realistic understanding of deliberation, "a great deal of incompleteness must be tolerated" and Habermas (1996: 323) himself concedes that "rational discourses have an improbable character and are like islands in an ocean of everyday praxis". It is, thus, quite clear that rational discourse can hardly act as the sole evaluative standard of deliberation; we need other evaluative standards to complete the framework. Otherwise it would be likely that only fragments of the process are actually captured and that any such measurements of real-world deliberations would give a much-distorted picture of the deliberative process as a whole[96].

Even though I agree with the notion that empirical studies must encompass something beyond the Habermasian communicative rationality, and give us an understanding of other phenomena that may influence the process, the solution may not be as simple as expanding the concept of deliberation to encompass additional forms of communication like narratives, rhetoric, greetings etc. When you stretch a concept it will inevitably become more elusive. If you include other forms of communication in the concept of deliberation, much like Young (2000) suggests, it will be harder to define where deliberation begins and where it ends (Elstub 2006; Steiner 2009). There is also considerable uncertainty regarding the alternative forms of communication that could or should be added to the concept of deliberation. Since they cannot be deduced from the theory as such, their relationship to deliberation remains somewhat unclear.

Dialogue as a Prerequisite for Effective Deliberation

Regardless of approach, we need to outline a definition of the deliberative process that enables us to capture something beyond the communicative rationality, and give us an understanding of other phenomena that may influence the process, without disconnecting it from the fundamental principles at the heart of the deliberative theory. Since expanding the concept of deliberation is not an entirely unproblematic solution, we should look into other ways of capturing real-world deliberation. My suggestion is an approach that emphasises the underlying notion of dialogue inherent to all forms of inter-subjective deliberation, rather than exclusively focusing on the specific forms of communication or types of discourse that the concept of deliberation should include.

Why then should we look to theories of dialogue when trying to capture the deliberative process? First of all, the dialogic approach is receiving in-

---

96 For a more elaborate discussion on this see e.g. Bächtiger et al (2010).

creasing attention within the fields of linguistics and communication studies, and some scholars have also begun to link the notions of deliberation and dialogue (cf. Burkhalter et al. 2002; Barge 2002; Walsh 2007; Kim & Kim 2008; Escobar 2009). Secondly, deliberation and dialogue share many important features. Interaction as it is portrayed in the deliberative ideals resembles to that of dialogic communication, where speaking is seen as intertwined with listening and understanding. In dialogue, each speaker incorporates and reinterprets the other's contributions in his or her own way (Bohman 1996: 55-63). The speaker is continuously listener-oriented, attending to the communicative activity he shares with his interlocutor. The listener, in turn, is speaker-oriented, aiming at understanding what the speaker intends to make known (Linell 1998: 109). We cannot engage in dialogue by ourselves, and much like in the search for the better argument, our particular contributions form a part of a whole that we cannot determine or fully control ourselves.

James Bohman (1996) explains the relationship between dialogue and deliberation, by portraying dialogue as a particular joint action with the special characteristics necessary for deliberation. Rational discourse is to be understood as a second order communication, while dialogue is a wider and less normatively regulated concept than discourse, which takes place in actual dialogue. Deliberation as a democratic discourse can be described as dialogue with a particular goal; it presupposes agreement on basic rules and standards of rationality, and is thus more demanding than dialogue. Dialogue is the mere give and take of reasons. It does not necessarily aim to produce well-justified claims; rather, it aims to produce claims that are wide enough in scope and sufficiently justified to be accountable to an indefinite public of fellow citizens (Bohman 1996: 57). Dialogue could perhaps best be understood as a necessary prerequisite for effective communication and, thus, also for deliberation.

How can dialogue help us understand and evaluate deliberation? Sociolinguist Per Linell (1998: 14) emphasises that "dialogue and communication involve, by definition, some kind of coordination (or cooperation), coherence, reciprocity and mutuality, but empirically these properties are never present in their entirety." A normative account of dialogue, such as the Habermasian ideal speech situation, characterised by certain values like clarity, egalitarianism, mutuality, consensus etc., will automatically exclude self-interest, power, emotions, misunderstandings, partial knowledge and vagueness, which are all amply represented in real social life.

Linell (1998, 2009) explains that by adopting a descriptive notion of dialogue, rather than an idealistic Habermasian one, we are free to explore empirical differences among discursive activities in terms of (a)symmetries, reciprocities, mutualities etc. Through a dialogical perspective all forms of connections can be examined, no matter what the discursive attire. This way normatively valuable contributions of rational discourse as well as other forms of discourse can be compared based on the underlying structure of dialogue. It must, how-

165

ever, be noted that while this approach certainly allows for an examination of the underlying structure in a deliberative process, it will not illuminate specific features or effects of different forms of discourse, like rhetorical appeals to emotions or the power of narratives. It will, however, capture their function in the dialogic structure.

Capturing Deliberative Quality

Where and how to Examine the Process of Deliberation?

Democratic innovations are not only a way of renewing democracy; as a vehicle for deliberative processes they are also potent tools for empirical research. Since democratic discourse is an elusive concept that can be quite hard to measure, institutionalised forms of deliberative democracy, such as mini-publics and other democratic innovations, provide a suitable setting for empirical analysis of the deliberative process. To counter different inequalities that may distort the deliberative process, different counter-measures are generally applied (cf. Smith 2009; Brown 2006). Random sampling is often used in analysis to bring about an inclusive process in which all relevant views are represented; neutral and balanced information material is distributed in order to contribute to the deliberative capacity of the participants by equipping them with a basic command of the issue at hand; also, basic rules of conduct and moderators are a common way of ensuring a civilised debate. Furthermore, since a constructive environment is expected to elicit favourable conditions for deliberation, it would also allow for the rigorous testing of different theoretical assumptions.

But even though the design of the deliberative process is pivotal to the workings of the deliberative process, my concern here is not with institutional design but with ways of evaluating the quality of deliberation. To be able to gather empirical data we need to operationalise our theoretical dimensions, in this case the deliberative ideal of rational discourse and the dialogic structure. Furthermore, we are interested in the distribution of discursive activity among the participants in order to establish whether the deliberative process can be considered fair and inclusive. We subsequently need a measure or combination of measures that capture, (a) the activity of the participants, (b) the level of rational discourse, and (c) the structure of dialogue. Since we need to examine the actual interaction between the participants in democratic forums, some type of content analysis would seem the most appropriate.

The fundamental idea of content analysis is to deduce speech or text to a number of categories, giving the opportunity to look at both frequencies of different categorisations, and how they are connected to particular actors (Krippendorf 2003; Brydér 1985).

While there have been other attempts at developing content analytical measures for the analysis of the deliberative process (see Dutwin 2002; Holzinger 2004; Stromer-Galley 2007 etc.[97]), the most interesting and perhaps most advanced instrument developed for this purpose is the Discourse Quality Index (DQI for short) by Steiner et al. (2004).

The DQI was originally developed as a discourse measure for deliberative quality in parliamentary debates, and while it mainly draws on Habermasian discourse ethics, other theories of deliberative democracy have also been incorporated in the measure. The strong and apparent connections to the core of deliberative theory combined with its functional outlook sets it apart from most, if not all, other attempts at analysing the deliberative process. It has also been met with considerable support from deliberative theorists (Habermas 2005; Thompson 2008), which can be considered a strong indication of its validity. Considering how well it fits with the purpose of measuring rational discourse, it seems like an adequate point of departure for an analysis of the deliberative process.

Regardless of how valid the DQI is as a measure of deliberative quality, it has certain weaknesses when it comes to examining citizen deliberation. First, there is a theoretical challenge; the DQI was constructed to measure the very heart of deliberative theory, i.e. communicative rationality. This brings us back to the issue discussed in the theoretical chapter concerning the limits of a standard of evaluation based solely on a rational discourse. Second, the DQI is quite distinctly shaped by what it was set out to analyse, namely parliamentary debates; democratic forums relying on citizen deliberation can be quite different from parliamentary debates (see Wales et al. 2009; Himmelroos 2010). The communication between citizens tends for instance to be more dialogical than parliamentary debates, where the interaction easily becomes quite structured and monological. While the exchange of arguments certainly can be more erratic in citizen deliberation, it is usually also more dynamic and organic in its development. Citizen deliberation will very likely include a higher degree of both misunderstandings and cooperation before common definitions are reached or goals can be set up.

In order to capture the underlying dialogue and the more fragmented deliberative process of citizen deliberation the analysis is completed by a measurement instrument called (Initiative/Response) IR-analysis. The IR-analysis is a method for looking at how the sender and receiver are connected within a conversation, and was originally developed by Per Linell and Lennart Gustavsson (1987) for linguistic research. What makes the instrument interesting for em-

---

97 Not including all the measures developed for text-based internet communication (cf. Janssen & Kies 2004)

pirical scholars interested in deliberative democracy is, not only its capacity to examine interaction, but also the fact that it was used already in 2003 by Theodorsson for the analysis of small group deliberation (Theodorsson 2003). If nothing else, this indicates that IR-analysis can give us a better understanding deliberative processes.

Primarily IR-analysis captures elements of both working communication and different disturbances or deviations in dialogue (Theodorsson 2003). However, although it presents a picture of the dynamics of communication, it will not tell us anything about specific types of discourse. It will, however, give us a wider perspective of how communication is structured within the deliberative process, as it is strictly functional to its nature and not bound by a certain understanding of what makes up good reasons. IR-analysis makes it possible to obtain all kinds of communication, whether it lies close to or very far from what can be considered rational discourse. And, consequently, it can tell us something about the structure of all communication, irrespective of whether it falls on the inside or outside of the frame of ideal deliberation.

Applying the two Measures of Deliberative Quality

The original DQI was composed of seven indicators[98] deduced from deliberative theory. Based on a pilot study using DQI in the context of citizen deliberation (Himmelroos 2010), some indicators have been modified, while others that can be measured more accurately in other ways have been left out altogether. The modified measure of discourse quality includes four indicators: *(I) Level of Justification, (II) Content of Justification, (III) Respect* and *(IV) Reciprocity*. The modifications were mainly due to the fact that some indicators are predisposed by the purpose of the original measure, i.e. capturing discourse quality in a parliamentary setting. In many cases, lay citizens are not as easily divided into factions or group interests as are elected representatives. When distinct groups or factions cannot visibly be discerned, it can e.g. be extremely hard to tell whether participants are respectful or considerate toward a view different from their own, or whether they just concur because they share the same view.

Whatever the form of the *(I) justification*, the crucial point is that the participants present their arguments in a logically coherent way, so that other participants can understand the argument. The tighter the connection between premises and conclusions, the more coherent the justification is and the more

---

98 Participation, Level of Justification, Content of Justification, Respect toward groups to be helped (empathy), Respect toward the demands of others, Respect toward counterarguments, and Constructive Politics.

useful it will be for deliberation (Steiner et al. 2004: 21). According to the deliberative ideal, arguments should, however, not only be logical and coherent, but also expressed in terms of the common good. Appeals to the common good can take different forms. *(II) Content of justification* aims to capture the reason behind one's argumentation. Are you only looking out for your own interests or are you taking others' interests into consideration, as well? On the one hand, the common good may be stated in utilitarian terms, i.e. as the best solution for the greatest number of people (Mill 1859). The common good may also be expressed through the difference principle in the sense that the common good is best served if the least advantaged are helped (Rawls 1971).

In order to create an environment where arguments can be appreciated at least a modicum of respect is needed. As noted before, citizen deliberation may not be as factional as parliamentary debates, and the level of respect is therefore captured by looking for instances of disrespect. Two types of respect are included in this measure. *(IIIa) Internal respect* measures how respectful participants are towards each other or, in this case, if they have been disrespectful. The use of say, inflammatory rhetoric is an indicator that interlocutors are not very interested in finding agreement, persuading their opponents or easing conflict (Chambers 1996: 209). *(IIIb) External respect* on the other hand, measures empathy towards a person or group under discussion. It shows the ability to take the perspective of someone else, the type of enlarged 'mentality' that deliberative democracy is expected to induce.

Deliberation also relies on the fact that everyone reflects on what is being said and evaluates each argument and the way it relates to his own opinions (Bohman 1996). The last indicator *(IV) reciprocity*, can therefore perhaps best be understood by looking at how participants treat arguments that contradict their own, or whether they touch upon them at all (Steiner et al. 2004). Another way to identify whether the participants act in a reciprocal manner would be to see if different (conflicting) demands are weighed or compared to each other by a participant.

The IR-analysis was developed to capture the dynamics of interactive communication as it appears locally in the dialogue, i.e. it tries to capture the immediate value of speech or utterance. This is an essential requirement if the analysis is to mirror the dynamics of the dialogue (Linell and Gustavsson 1987: 6). The idea is to illustrate the mutual interdependence between how the participants act and react, and that communication cannot be understood as independent actions or speech acts produced by separate individuals (Linell & Gustavsson 1987).

The fundamental components of IR-analysis are initiatives and responses. An initiative is a starting point or new development in the dialogue. It could be a question, a request, or simply a different view that is presented (Theodorsson 2003). Making an initiative implies that a part in a social situation sends a message directed to a receiver or audience. Generally the one who makes the initiative wants to know something about or change something in the receiver's cognitive, emotive and/or connotative status. Usually one also seeks a response. By taking an initiative in a discussion one tries to influence the immediately following development of the interaction (Linell & Gustavsson 1987).

Like in the case of the DQI, the IR-analysis has been slightly modified to fit the purpose of the study. In this case however, the content of the measure has been kept intact, but the appearance has been altered to better match that of the discourse quality measure. In the original measure, each type of utterance was represented by a specific symbol ($<$, $=$, $<$ $>$ etc.) depending on what features it included. Now these same features have been organised into four indicators with individual categories: *(a) strength of initiative, (b) turn-taking, (c) adequacy of response*, and finally two *(d) exceptions*.

Initiatives are recognised by their catalytic character and defined by how strongly they affect the immediately following conversation and how strongly they influence the response of the interlocutor(s). First, a distinction is made between *(a) strong and weak initiatives*. Strong initiatives explicitly want to guide the ongoing discussion, while weak initiatives try to voice an opinion, or more implicitly get a response. A command or explicit question would be typical strong initiatives, while more generally presenting one's own view would be a weak one (Linell & Gustavsson 1987).

The response part represents, on the other hand, how speeches connect backwards and in what way preceding speeches influence them. It is characterised by the way it connects to the preceding initiative, to what part of the preceding speech it is connected, and by how it complies to demands presented in the initiative (Linell and Gustavsson 1987; Johansson-Hidén 1998). The second indicator of the IR-analysis describes the shift from one speech act to another, i.e. *(b) turn-taking*. In open interaction anyone can respond to an initiative, while in other cases initiatives may be directed at an individual or a specific group. If someone answers an initiative directed to someone else, it should be considered "stolen". Interruptions can also be considered a similar form of "theft", at least if the previous speaker is not allowed to immediately return to the interrupted initiative. There is also the possibility that if no one picks up an initiative that the same person will repeat it or respond to it himself, and thus make a so called self-linked connection. (Linell & Gustavsson 1987; Johansson-Hidén 1998)

Table 8.1 Indicators of Discourse Quality

I. Level of Justification

0: no justification, presents only his/her point of view

1: inferior justification; conclusion(s) embedded in (an) incomplete inference(s), no linkage is made as to why Y will contribute to X

2: qualified justification; one conclusion embedded in a complete inference, other incomplete inferences may be present, a linkage is made as to why Y will contribute to X

3: sophisticated justification; more than one conclusion, each embedded in a complete inference

II. Content of Justification

0: explicit statement concerning group/ self- interest

1: neutral statement; no reference to group or self- interest, but no reference to common good either

2: explicit reference to common good in utilitarian or collective terms

3: explicit statement in terms of the common good with reference to the difference principle

IIIa. Internal respect

0: disrespect; explicitly negative statement concerning other participants and their views

1: implicit respect; no explicitly negative statement concerning other participants and their views

IIIb. External respect

0: disrespect; explicitly negative statement concerning the group under discussion

1: implicit respect; no explicitly negative statement concerning the group under discussion

IV. Reciprocity

0: No reference to demand of others or self-linked reference

1: Reference to a demand presented by another participant

2: Considers counter-argument to own demand own argumentation or compares/weighs different arguments

---

The third indicator is *(c) adequacy,* by which is meant how well the response meets the initiative. In this case, it can be helpful to see what the connection looks like. A fully adequate response is supposed to be both focally and locally connected to the initiative, i.e. the connection should be direct both time- and topic-wise (Linell & Gustavsson 1987: 49). A response lacking either focality or locality fails to meet the requirements of the initiative in some way. Usually this is because the recipient lacks the will, capacity or knowledge to give a direct or adequate response (Linell & Gustavsson 1987: 53). There are two *(d) exceptions* to these categories, which are either utterances that are completely inadequate, i.e. they are incomprehensible and include no recognisable initiative or response, or utterances that carry a little of both, but in which the roles are quite ambiguous, e.g. a clarification, which is plainly a response to a preceding initiative, but in the form of a question.

The measure for discourse quality is directly connected to central features in the theory of deliberative democracy, thereby making interpretations fairly straightforward. First, a distinction is made between relevant and irrelevant parts in each speech, and only speeches with relevant parts are coded. A relevant part is one that contains a demand, i.e. a proposal for what should be done (or not). The emphasis on demands by Steiner et al. (2004) stems from the idea that demands stipulate what ought to be done, and this normative character puts them at the centre of discourse ethics (Steiner et al. 2004: 55). Secondly, the discourse quality measure relies on an idea that deliberative actions can be placed on a continuum from no deliberation, with insufficient justification and disrespect, to ideal deliberation, with sophisticated justifications and respectful communication. Each speech, containing a demand, can be placed anywhere on this scale and thus give us an understanding of how close the discussion is to ideal deliberation. The higher a score a speech act receives on the indicators, the closer the speaker is to the ideal of communicative rationality.

The measurement of dialogue is, however, a little harder to interpret. The interaction between initiatives and responses reveals the elementary dynamics of dialogue. In the IR-analysis, initiatives and responses are seen as abstract units, moves in a communicative game, not as factual claims. Each speech can both have initiative- and response like features and thereby reflect different parts or aspects of a claim or input (Linell & Gustavsson 1987: 15).

A working dialogue is depicted by a balance where participants' speeches relieve each other and every speech by one part connects to the preceding speech of another part, while also producing something that elicits a response. In this weave of mutual recognition, each speech brings about, or produces new content and the participants indicate how they have understood the preceding speech of the other parts, or how they intended their previous speech.

Moments of balanced dialogue are, however, a feature of dialogue that occurs only fleetingly, separated by various disturbances. There are a variety of reasons as to why dialogues do not evolve into endless homogeneous threads of balanced dialogue. Communication can fail in many different ways; initiatives may be ignored, which may be both the cause and effect of self-linked connections; it may have to do with misunderstandings, the disregard of certain types of communication or with one part interrupting the other; speeches may also be used to control the development of the discussion, by introducing new topics without responding to any previous initiative or by connecting to a topic previously discussed rather than the ones at hand. Much like some speeches try to control the development, some simply act as a response to previous initiatives, rather than trying to engage in a continuous weave of dialogue.

Evaluating Standards of Deliberation

What will two different measures tell us about the overall standard of deliberation? Since the dialogue measure is a much broader measure than the one for discourse quality, they will measure partly different things, just as they should. But this does not mean that it is without interest to examine how they co-vary. While there are distinct differences between the discourse quality and dialogue measures, they also have several features in common, and most importantly both are content analytical in character and use speeches or utterances as the unit of analysis. This makes it relatively easy to present and compare findings from the two instruments. The measures can obviously interact in different ways, but are there any specific standards that we should expect to be upheld for the process to be considered democratic?

In the best of worlds, everyone would take part in a reciprocal exchange of high quality arguments; but this is a rare case in the real world. If there is a considerable amount of discussion that fall outside the parameters of ideal rational discourse, and especially if some groups are less likely to engage in it than others, an expanded concept of deliberation might be in order, so as to realise a more inclusive evaluation of deliberation. A dialogic approach recognizes that discussions have their shortcomings and never can be perfectly balanced, but the amount of balanced dialogue, and the possible deviations from it, will tell us how each individual has managed to take part in the dialogic process.

Table 8.2 Indicators of Dialogic Communication

---

a. *Strength of the initiative*

0: No initiative: the speech includes only a response to a preceding initiative
1: Weak initiative: implicit question or developing line of argument (new aspect)
2: Strong initiative: explicit question or request

b. *Turn-taking*

0: No response: the speech includes only an initiative, no response to a preceding initiative
1: Open connection: Participant responds to an initiative without an anticipatory character
2: Tied connection: Participant responds to an initiative directed to him
3: Stolen: Responds to an initiative directed to someone else or interrupts another participant
4: Self-linked connection: Responds to or repeats their own initiative

c. *Adequacy of response*

0: No response: the speech includes only an initiative, no response to a preceding initiative
1: Adequate response: the response has a clear connection to the initiative, both time and association-wise
2: Non-local response: A non-local response is connected to an earlier topic, but at a time when the discussion clearly has moved on
3: Non-focal response: A non-focal response is attached to the current topic, but connects to some other aspect than was intended by the initiative, by a more or less far-fetched association

d. *Exceptions*

(*) Reparation or clarification: short clarifying question or correction
(*) Non-adequate speech: completely irrelevant speech, i.e. cannot be categorised with an initiative or response

---

As long as the balanced connections are fairly equally distributed among participants, while there are differences in the level of rational discourse, it is only a question of how rational we expect the discussions to be. However, if some individuals have a greater tendency towards being involved in misunderstandings or, if they tend to produce independent initiatives rather than take part in the ongoing debate, we would have to question how inclusive the dialogue actually is. If only some participants take part in the dialogue, stretching the concept of deliberation beyond rational argumentation might have little effect, since there are people who are systematically disadvantaged and whose points of view will never catch the attention of others, regardless of how deliberation is defined. If some were systematically disadvantaged regardless of measure, the deliberative process could hardly be considered fair and equal, which would inevitably put the democratic qualities of deliberation in doubt.

We should also be aware of the fact that deliberative processes may have different goals. A working dialogue may be enough for some purposes, e.g. to help us look for common ground or, if we hope to throw some light on a specific issue by gathering all available perspectives. If, on the other hand, we expect people to change their minds and actually come to some kind of decision, we would probably have to stress the rationality of the process, as well as a fairly high standard of reciprocity. Decision-making based on interaction alone requires a normative logic that all parts can follow, and a reciprocal acknowledgement through which a shared view can be established. As this short discussion already shows, it is difficult to set any specific standards for the quality of deliberation. Democratic innovations relying on deliberative processes may make use of deliberation in very different ways and this obviously affects the expectations on the standards to be met. Subsequently, it must be made clear what is to be expected from the deliberative procedure in order to evaluate its success.

Conclusion

At the outset I argued that there is a potential risk in comparing democratic innovations, if the different criteria are not fully understood. I further argued that this is the case for the quality of deliberation criterion, since the deliberative processes that are presumed to bring about reasoned and democratic outcomes have not been sufficiently examined. Subsequently, I set out to look for ways of examining deliberation procedures in democratic innovations. I have discussed the difficulty of satisfying both the assumptions of the deliberative ideal and the challenges of a real-world deliberation in these measurements. I have further argued for the benefits of using mini-publics in this type of research since, (a) democratic innovations such as mini-publics offer a constructive environment for deliberation and (b) they give us an opportunity to capture the process of citizen deliberation.

To capture the deliberative quality we will need instruments that can help us answer whether the process can be considered fair and equal, and how well it matches the assumptions made in deliberative theory. To do that we must operationalise the concept of democratic deliberation; we need to identify valid and reliable indicators that can help to describe the process and content of citizen deliberation. I have argued that two instruments, the DQI and IR-analysis (with a few minor alterations), are particularly appropriate for the purpose of examining mechanisms and functions of the deliberative process, since they have apparent connections to the normative literature on democratic deliberation and are well grounded in empirical analysis. Using these indicators of rational discourse and interactive dynamics in the analysis of deliberative processes taking place within democratic innovations will provide us with a better understanding of both the deliberative process and deliberative capacity of ordinary citizens, thereby helping us understand the extent to which democratic innovations can be considered useful, useless or potentially even harmful, when it comes to addressing deficits of democracy.

References

Andersen, Vibeke Normann & Hansen, Kasper M. (2007). How deliberation makes better citizens: The Danish Deliberative Poll on the euro. *European Journal of Political Research*, Vol. 46: 531–556

Barge, J. Kevin. (2002). 'Enlarging the meaning of group deliberation', in Frey, Lawrence R. (Ed.) New directions in group communication. Thousand Oaks/London: Sage Publications.

Bohman, James. (1996). *Public Deliberation. Pluralism, Complexity and Democracy*. Cambridge: The MIT Press.

Brown, Mark B. (2006). Survey Article: Citizen Panels and the Concept of Representation. *The Journal of Political Philosophy*. Volume 14, No. 2; 203-225.

Brydér, Tom. (1985). *Innehållsanalys som idé och metod*. Åbo: Åbo Akademi.

Burkhalter, Stephanie; John Gastil; & Todd Kelshaw. (2002). 'A conceptual definition and theoretical model of public deliberation in small face-to-face groups'. Communication Theory. 12; pp.398-422.

Bächtiger, André; Niemeyer, Simon; Neblo, Michael; Steenbergen, Marco & Steiner, Jürg. (2010). Disentangling Diversity in Deliberative Democracy: Competing Theories, Their Blind Spots and Complementarities. *Journal of Political Philosophy* Vol. 18, No. 1; 32–63

Chambers, Simone. 1996. *Reasonable Democracy*. Ithaca: Cornell University Press.

Cohen, Joshua. 1989 (1997). Deliberation and Democratic Legitimacy. In James Bohman & William Rehg (eds.), *Deliberative Democracy: Essays on Reason and Politics*. Cambridge: The MIT Press.

Dryzek, John. (1990). *Discursive Democracy: Politics, Policy, and Political Science*. Cambridge: Cambridge University Press.

Dryzek, John & Niemeyer, Simon. (2008). Discursive Representation. *American Political Science Review*. Vol. 102, No. 4: 481-493.

Dutwin, David. (2002). *Can People Talk Politics? A Study of Deliberative Democracy*. Unpublished dissertation.

Elstub, Stephen. (2006). A double-edged sword: the increasing diversity of deliberative democracy. *Contemporary Politics*. Vol. 12, No. 3-4; 301-309.

Eriksen, Erik & Weigård, Jarle. (2003). *Understanding Habermas. Communicative action and deliberative democracy*. London: Continuum Press.

Escobar, Oliver. (2009). The Dialogic Turn: Dialogue for Deliberation. *In-Spire Journal of Law, Politics and Societies*. Vol. 4, No. 2: 42-70.

Fishkin, James S. (1997). *Voice of the People*. New Haven: Yale University Press.

Gutmann, Amy & Thompson, Dennis. (1996). *Democracy and Disagreement. Why moral conflict cannot be avoided in politics, and what to do about it*. Cambridge: The Belknap Press of Harvard University Press.

Gutmann, Amy & Thompson, Dennis (2004). *Why Deliberative Democracy*. Princeton: Princeton University Press.

Habermas, Jürgen. 1981 (1991). *Theory of Communicative Action. Vol 1. Reason and the Rationalization of Society*. Cambridge, Polity Press.

Habermas, Jürgen. (1996). *Between Facts and Norms. Contributions to a Discourse Theory of Law and Democracy*. Cambridge, MIT Press.

Habermas, Jürgen. (2005). Concluding Comments on Empirical Approaches to Deliberative Politics. *Acta Politica* Vol. 40; 384-392.

Himmelroos, Staffan. (2010). *Medborgare i demokratiska samtal – verktyg för analys av deliberativa processer*. Åbo Akademi, Licentiate thesis.

Holzinger, Katharina (2004). Bargaining through Arguing: An Empirical Analysis Based on Speech Act Theory. *Political Communication* Vol. 21 No 2: 195-222.

Janssen, Davy & Kies, Raphaël. (2004). *Online Forums and Deliberative Democracy: Hypotheses, Variables and Methodologies*. E-Working papers 2004/01. http://www.edemocracycentre.ch/edcadmin/images/onlineforums.pdf 20.8.2009.

Johansson-Hidén, Birgitta. (1998). *Analyzing talk in the workplace group: Dynamics, dominance and coherence*. Karlstad, Högskoletryckeriet.

Kim, Joohan & Eun Joo Kim. (2008). Theorizing dialogic deliberation: everyday political talk as communicative action and dialogue. Communication Theory.Vol 18; pp.51-70.

Kohn, Margaret. (2000). Language, Power and Persuasion: Toward a Critique of Deliberative Democracy. *Constellations*. Volume 7, No. 3; 408-429.

Krippendorf, Klaus. (2003.) *An introduction to its methodology*. Beverly Hills, CA : Sage.

Linell, Per & Gustavsson, Lennart. (1987). *Initiativ och respons: om dialogens dynamik, dominans och koherens*. Linköping: Universitetet i Linköping.

Linell, Per. (1998). *Approaching Dialogue: Talk, interaction and contexts in dialogical perspectives*. Philadelphia: John Benjamins Publishing.

Linell, Per. (2009). *Rethinking Language, Mind and World Dialogically*. Charlotte, NC: Information Age Publishing.

Mill, John Stuart. 1859 (1988). *On Liberty*. Harmondsworth: Penguin.

Mouffe, Chantal. (1999). Deliberative Democracy or Agonistic Pluralism. *Social Research* Vol. 66 (3).

Rawls, John. (1971). *A Theory of Justice*. Oxford: Clarendon Press.

Rosenberg, Shawn. (2004). *Reconstructing the Concept of Democratic Deliberation*. http://repositories.cdlib.org/csd/04-02/ 20.8.2009.

Ryfe, David M. (2005). Does Deliberative Democracy Work? *Annual Review of Political Science*. Vol 8; 41.

Sanders, Lynn M. (1997). Against Deliberation. *Political Theory* Vol. 25, No. 3.

Smith, Graham. (2009). Democratic Innovations: Designing Institutions for Citizen Participation. Cambridge, Cambridge University Press.

Steiner, Jürg; Bächtiger, André; Spröndli, Markus; Steenberger, Marco R. (2004). *Deliberative Politics in Action. Analysing Parliamentay Discourse*. Cambridge: Cambridge University Press.

Steiner, Jürg. (2009). Concept stretching: the case of deliberation. *European Political Science* Vol.7: 186-190.

Stromer-Galley, Jennifer. (2007). Assessing Deliberative Quality: A Coding Scheme. *Journal of Public Deliberation* Vol. 3, No. 1.

Theodorsson, Annika. (2003). *Samtala både länge och väl. Deliberativ demokrati i tre föräldrakooperativ och dess effekter på deltagarna.* Göteborg: Göteborgs universitet.

Thompson, Dennis F. (2008). Deliberative Democratic Theory and Empirical Science. *The Annual Review of Political Science.* Vol. 11: 497-520.

Young, Iris Marion. (2000). *Inclusion and Democracy.* New York: Oxford University Press.

Wales, Corinne; Cotterill, Sarah & Smith, Graham. (2009). *Do citizens *deliberate* in on-line discussion forums? Preliminary findings from an Internet experiment.* Paper presented at the ECPR general conference in Potsdam 10-12.9.2009.

Walsh, Kathrine Cramer. (2007). The Democratic Potential of Civic Dialogue. In Shawn Rosenberg (ed.) *Deliberation, Participation and Democracy: Can the People Govern?* New York: Palgrave Macmillan.

Deliberation and Aggregation in Different Forms of Direct Democracy

Maija Setälä

Introduction

Institutions of direct democracy allow citizens to participate directly in raising issues on the political agenda and making decisions on these issues by voting. The most important institutions of direct democracy are popular initiatives and referendums.[99] In most systems of representative democracy, direct democratic institutions have played only a marginal role, whereas in a few cases they have actually shaped the overall functioning of the political system. What are the benefits and pitfalls of direct democratic procedures? In terms of the evaluative framework outlined in this book, particular attention is paid to the extent to which direct democratic practices enhance deliberative and inclusive decision-making and enlightened citizenship.

Deliberative democrats have often expressed concerns about practices of direct democracy. The most important criticism is that these forms of participation are based on the aggregation of people's preferences rather than on deliberation. Votes expressing preferences are counted in referendums, and popular initiatives and petitions involve the collection of a certain number of signatures. Furthermore, direct democratic practices do not necessarily support public deliberation either in parliaments or in the wider public sphere, and some direct democratic procedures in fact replace or undermine parliamentary deliberations.

This chapter analyses the forums and sequences of deliberation and aggregation in different procedures of direct democracy, that is, in so-called government-initiated referendums and different forms of referendums that can be used to veto parliamentary decisions. Furthermore, also different practices of popular initiatives are analyzed, both initiatives dealt with in parliaments (agenda initiatives) and those leading to a referendum (full-scale initiatives). The aim of the chapter is to explore from a deliberative perspective the positive

---

99 Sometimes also the institution of the recall is considered a form of direct democracy (see e.g. Cronin 1989, 125-156). However, as the institution of the recall deals with the position of elected representatives, it falls beyond the scope of this chapter.

aspects and the problems of different direct democratic procedures, paying particular attention to the sequencing of public deliberation and preference aggregation at different forums (see e.g. Goodin 2005). Examples of direct democratic practices in Europe are used to illustrate the analysis. The chapter concludes with some recommendations concerning how direct democratic institutions should be designed, and how the quality of deliberation could be improved in direct democratic campaigns.

Theoretical Points of Departure

Theories of deliberative democracy have dominated democratic theoretical debate during the past two decades (Dryzek 2000), although the central ideas of deliberative democracy are by no means new. According to the theory of deliberative democracy, collective decisions should be based on a process of reciprocal reason-giving among equal and autonomous citizens or their representatives. Arguments put forward in democratic deliberation should be considered equally by their merits, in other words, by the epistemic and moral qualities of the arguments. Democratic deliberation can thus be distinguished from strategic communication (e.g. bargaining) where arguments are not judged by their merits, but rather on the basis of power resources, such as institutional, economic and physical power, which can be mobilized in support of political claims.

The idea of deliberative democracy is often associated with micro-level deliberation in different institutional settings, such as parliaments (especially parliamentary committees) and in various deliberative citizen forums, especially so-called deliberative mini-publics. However, many theorists emphasize that deliberative democracy should be understood as a macro-political system, in which the process of collective decision-making is responsive to various claims and demands arising from civil society and capable of accommodating them in a process of democratic deliberation. The interaction between autonomous civil society and formal democratic institutions, most notably parliaments, seems to be a central element in deliberative democracy understood as a macro political system (see e.g Habermas 1996).

Democratic deliberation should be an inclusive process of reciprocal reason-giving where arguments are judged by their merits only, in other words, by the consistency and the epistemic qualities of arguments as well as reasonableness of the claims put forward. Some theorists have criticized this 'standard' account of democratic deliberation for the reason that the emphasis on rational and sophisticated argumentation may, in fact, lead to an exclusion of certain viewpoints. In her book *Inclusion and Democracy* (2000), Iris Marion Young distinguishes different ways in which people can be excluded from the process of democratic deliberation. Young makes a distinction between external and internal exclusion. External exclusion means that certain relevant perspectives are not allowed to be presented in public deliberation or decision-making. As examples of external exclusion Young (2000, 54-55) mentions the disenfranchisement of certain groups of people, and *de facto* exclusion of citizens (or their elected representatives) from actual decision-making processes. Internal exclusion rather concerns the dynamics of the deliberative process. Young (2000, 55-56) gives various examples of internal exclusion where certain viewpoints and interests are favoured in the deliberative process, whereas others are dismissed or ignored.

The ideal processes of inclusive reciprocal justification are probably best achieved in certain institutional contexts. Like other democratic theorists, also deliberative democrats seem to have great faith in representative institutions, most notably parliaments, in which different political claims are articulated and debated. Famously, John Stuart Mill (1861/1851, 282) argued that the parliament is a 'Congress of Opinions' where representatives test each other's arguments. As a consequence of the exchange of arguments between representatives of different opinions, even people on the losing side can accept the decision, because they are convinced by the arguments put forward in support of the decision.

The institutional design of parliaments should enhance inclusiveness, accountability and the quality of deliberation. Under the conditions of universal suffrage and fair electoral rules, parliamentary deliberations can be assumed to be relatively inclusive, as elected representatives are expected to articulate the concerns of their constituents. The elected representatives should also be accountable to the wider public. The publicity of parliamentary plenary sessions furthers this goal because it allows constituents both to monitor and to give feedback on the parliamentary work. At the same time, different viewpoints must be reconciled in parliamentary proceedings, especially in parliamentary committees. Deliberations in committees are often conducted in secrecy, which enhances trust and openness to the arguments of others among parliamentarians. In fact, some deliberative democrats have suggested that parliamentary work should combine both forums in which deliberations take place in secrecy and forums for public deliberation (Elster 1998).

Arguably, the process of democratic deliberation has a capacity to generate consensus, although recently it has been argued that we should expect 'meta-consensus' rather than unanimity as the outcome of deliberation (Dryzek and Niemeyer 2006). Moreover, it has been emphasized that the quest for a consensus may not always be compatible with the idea of deliberation. There are fears that the requirement of a consensus brings about group pressures and other social mechanisms which hinder deliberation. For this reason, it seems necessary that even deliberative bodies may end by voting. The main theorists of deliberative democracy admit the necessity of voting in real world political decision-making. For example, Habermas (1996, 306) argues as follows: "Political deliberation, however, must be concluded by majority decision in view of pressures to decide". Parliamentary procedures rely heavily on voting, although for example committee work often aims at consensual outcomes.

Of course, the above-mentioned is a highly idealized picture of parliamentary decision-making, and in reality factors like government-opposition division and party discipline shape the parliamentary discussions and bring about patterns of external and internal exclusion in parliamentary debates. Moreover, although there are certain elements in parliamentary procedures which can be expected to enhance the reciprocal exchange of arguments, it seems obvious that processes of policy-making in parliaments are based on a mix of deliberation and various forms of strategic communication, such as bargaining (for empirical evidence, see Holzinger 2004).

Many deliberative democrats have been relatively skeptical about the prospects of some forms of mass participation, such as referendums and elections, to enhance deliberation in the public sphere (Chambers 2001). Unlike parliamentary votes that are cast under the public eye, secret ballot is used in referendums and, consequently, unlike parliamentarians, voters do not need to publicly justify their choices. Moreover, voting in mass electorates does not provide incentives for making informed and considered choices. This insight was powerfully captured already in Downs' notion of 'rational ignorance' introduced in his *Economic Theory of Democracy* (1957). In nation-wide referendums, like large-scale elections, individual voters' likelihood to be decisive with respect to the outcome is close to zero, and for this reason citizens may not be very motivated to invest time and effort in reflecting on political issues. This view has received support in many empirical studies on direct democratic votes (for summary, see e.g. Kriesi 2005). On the basis of empirical research, it appears that people participating in referendums rely on information shortcuts and cues instead of considering different arguments presented in favour of different alternatives.

Simone Chambers (2001) has argued that majority rule, in particular, is hard to reconcile with deliberation. The use of the majority rule easily leads to an adversary style of argumentation between those who support and those who oppose the policy proposals, which in turn easily leads to group polarization. In his account of 'strong democracy', Benjamin Barber (1984) suggests multi-option ballots because they potentially support processes in which the alternatives are actually judged by their merits. Chambers (2001) argues that the Borda rule, which allows people order the alternatives according to their preference orderings should be more reconcilable with deliberation. The Borda rule favours the alternatives which are not at least widely objected, and so it seems to encourage people to moderate their views. In reality, most referendum votes have included only two alternatives, yes or no, to a policy proposal. Multi-option referendums have been relatively rare events, and they have usually relied on the plurality rule as a voting rule.

In the evaluation of institutions of direct democracy, the focus on deliberation and aggregation may be considered too narrow in many respects. Most notably, the focus on these two modes of reaching a decision is not particularly helpful for understanding how the political agenda is set. Several democratic theorists (e.g. Dahl 1989, 112-4) have argued that democratic procedures do not just involve decision-making but also processes of agenda-setting which, in fact, precede the decision-making stage. From the perspective of deliberative democracy, this seems to mean that every citizen should have equal access to the public sphere where political problems are defined and different claims are articulated. Moreover, different arguments and claims should be judged reasonably in the course of democratic deliberation.

Popular initiatives seem to open the political agenda for novel viewpoints emerging from civil society. Opening the political agenda could in many cases be considered valuable from the perspective of deliberative democracy. Iris Marion Young (2000, 172-180), for example, argues that from the perspective of inclusiveness, it is particularly important that members of marginalized or suppressed groups form 'counter-publics', which challenge prevailing political discourses. Initiatives may be important in challenging the established political discourses, and helping to mobilize different 'counter-publics'. Based on a study of Swiss popular initiatives, Kriesi and Wisler (1996) conclude that grass-root organizations and new social movements are active users of popular initiatives. Also, new and marginalized political parties have used initiatives to gain publicity for their policy goals. In this respect, organizing an initiative campaign may be the first step which helps new political groupings to enter the domain of electoral competition. These findings support the view that popular initiatives actually enhance inclusiveness in the policy-making process.

However, although the number of signatures required for initiatives tend to represent a small proportion of the whole electorate, the process of making an initiative always includes the challenge of organizing collective action. Making an initiative calls for sufficient resources in order to be able to campaign successfully for the initiative and to collect the required number of signatures. At the outset, it looks as if the distribution of the resources needed for an initiative seems to reflect the distribution of material and political resources. In this respect, the organization of a popular initiative may be beyond the reach of truly marginalized groups in the society. This may be the reason why for example Bowler and Donovan (2002) have found that in the context of US states, the availability of an initiative institution may have a negative impact on the political efficacy among ethnic minorities. Bowler and Donovan's finding casts some doubts on the view that popular initiatives enhance inclusiveness. The capacity of various groups to actually use initiative instruments varies between societies and it also seems to depend on the more detailed regulations of the initiative procedure. [100]

Deliberation and Aggregation in Different Forms of Direct Democracy: a Sequential Analysis

Robert Goodin (2005; 2009) has argued that the principle 'first talk then vote' should be followed in democratic decision-making. In other words, decision-making procedures should encourage the exchange of arguments between citizens or representatives before voting. As pointed out above, the term 'direct democracy' refers to a variety of procedures which allow citizens to get involved in political agenda-setting and decision-making. These procedures vary significantly in terms of how they interact with parliamentary procedures. From the point of view of this chapter, it is important to analyze the sequencing of different stages in the policy-making process, including agenda-setting, 'talk' in the parliament and in referendum campaigns and 'vote' in the parliament and in referendums. Different procedures of direct democracy prove to be very different in this respect.

In the following, I will present a schematic analysis of the sequences of agenda-setting, deliberation and voting in various direct democratic procedures used in European democracies. The aim is to identify the stages of talk and vote in each direct democratic procedure (the moments of talk are italicized). It must be pointed out that the stages of talk provide *chances* for deliberation but this does not necessarily mean that good quality deliberation actually takes place. As will be pointed out in the following, different direct democratic procedures provide different *incentives* for political actors to deliberate. The description of the sequences of talk and vote is followed by a brief discussion, from the point of view of deliberate democracy theory, about the potential benefits and drawbacks of each direct democratic procedure.

---

100 One explanation for the differences in the experiences in Switzerland and in the US states could be the fact that in Switzerland, signatures required for an initiative are collected by volunteers, not by professional PR companies which is the case in many US states.

Type 1. Government-Initiated Referendums (Plebiscites)

Government-Initiated Binding Referendums

Government's proposal $\longrightarrow$ government's/president's request for a referendum $\rightarrow$ *referendum campaign* $\rightarrow$ referendum (decision)

In these variants of plebiscites, it is usually the president who has the right to trigger a binding referendum on a governmental proposal. These kinds of institutions exist mostly in countries with presidential or semi-presidential political systems. In the European context, the most notable example is France, where the president has the right to trigger a referendum under certain circumstances. French presidents have actually used these rights on several occasions (see Morel 2001). In France, referendums have often come up when the government and the parliament have disagreed on a particular policy proposal.

It is notable that government-initiated binding referendums are actually used *in place* of parliamentary procedures. Referendums can thus be used to bypass parliamentary procedures, which seems particularly problematic from the perspective of deliberative democracy. Indeed, these kinds of referendums are sometimes motivated by the willingness to emphasize the position of the president in relation to the parliament. In addition to undermining the position of the parliament, these types of referendums are sometimes explicitly framed as votes of confidence for the head of the state. As a consequence of such a framing, deliberations related to the actual issue may have played a relatively minor role during referendum campaigns.

Government-Initiated Advisory Referendums

Government's proposal $\rightarrow$ government's (parliamentary majority's) request for referendum $\rightarrow$ *referendum campaign* $\rightarrow$ referendum $\rightarrow$ *parliamentary debate* $\rightarrow$parliamentary vote (decision)

Government-initiated advisory referendums are often also called plebiscites as they represent a purely top-down procedure. These types of referendums have been used in most European democracies; they are particularly wide-spread in countries which have not experienced other types of referendums (see e.g. Morel 2001). In some countries (e.g. Finland, Sweden) the right of a parliamentary majority to initiate an advisory referendum is constitutionally regulated, whereas in others (e.g. Norway, the UK) the right of the parliamentary majority to call for a referendum is simply based on the principle of parliamentary sovereignty. In government-initiated advisory referendums, the government (and the parliamentary majority supporting it) is both the agenda-setter and the initiator of the referendum. The demand for government-initiated advisory referendums is likely to come up in situations where the governmental party or coalition is divided on an issue and hence, becomes willing to delegate the resolution of the issue to the electorate. These types of referendums have also been used to legitimize some important decisions, such as participation in the European integration.

Government-initiated advisory referendums precede the procedures of parliamentary deliberation and decision-making. In principle, the parliamentarians are not constrained by the result of the referendum, and the parliamentary majority could make a decision which is against the outcome of the referendum. However, in practice, it may be very difficult for the parliamentarians not to follow the result of the referendum when they make decisions in the parliamentary arena. In fact, formally advisory referendums have turned out to be *de facto* binding at least if we look at the government-initiated referendums at the national level in Europe.[101] This can be regarded as problematic because it implies that government-initiated referendums may undermine parliamentary deliberations. Parliamentarians do not need to take a considered position concerning the issue as such; they may simply adopt the position supported by the majority of the people in the referendum. From the point of view of governmental parties, this may be particularly tempting when government-initiated referendums are used on divisive issues which threaten the unity of the government.

Type 2. Mandatory Referendum (Binding)

Government's proposal → *parliamentary debate* and decision → *referendum campaign* → referendum (decision)

As the term already indicates, mandatory referendums are constitutionally required on certain types of issues, typically constitutional amendments. The rationale behind constitutional referendums is that the basic rules of the society need to enjoy a high degree of public support, and a constitutional referendum is regarded as a necessity for achieving such support. This type of rationale is endorsed by various democratic theorists, both those who represent liberal constitutionalism (e.g. Mueller 1997) and those who represent a more republican or deliberative view of democracy (e.g. Ackerman 1998). For example, the Swiss, Danish and Irish Constitutions require that all constitutional amendments are submitted to a referendum. More recently, the idea of constitutional

---

101 However, the picture looks somewhat different if we look at government-initiated referendums at the local level.

referendums has also been discussed in the context of supra-national governance. Habermas (2008, 103-104), for example, has called for an EU-wide constitutional referendum for legitimizing the deepening of the European integration process.

The government introducing a proposal for a constitutional amendment anticipates the requirement for a referendum and thus, needs to ensure that the proposal can gain popular support in a mandatory referendum. Parliamentary parties should be well motivated to campaign for or against the constitutional amendments, and therefore mandatory referendums can be regarded as instruments used to enhance 're-iterated' deliberation where parliamentary deliberations are followed by a process of public deliberation in which representatives justify their choices in the public sphere (cf. Gutmann & Thompson 1996, 137-144).

However, some deliberative theorists (e.g. Chambers 2001) have been concerned about the impact of constitutional referendums on parliamentary deliberations. Chambers argues that the anticipation of a constitutional referendum may 'derail' parliamentary deliberations, that is, hinder actual exchange of arguments. This is particularly likely to happen when there is a clear-cut division of opinions based, for example, on (ethnic, linguistic or other) identities among the electorate. Instead of truly exchanging arguments, supporters and opponents of the constitutional change use parliamentary debates to appeal to their own voters and to mobilize them in a referendum. According to Chambers, this undermines parliamentary deliberations and has potentially polarizing effects.

Type 3. Rejective Referendums

Government's proposal → *parliamentary debate* → parliamentary vote (decision) → minority (parliamentary or popular) request for referendum → *referendum campaign* → referendum (decision)

The rejective referendum provides an opportunity for minority groups to veto a piece of legislation passed by the parliament. Typically, the rejective referendum needs to be triggered within a certain period of time after the parliament has passed a law but before it has been enacted. The referendum can be initiated by a parliamentary minority (e.g. 1/3 of parliamentarians in Denmark), or a number of citizens (50,000 voters in Switzerland) or some other political actors.[102] Like mandatory referendums, rejective referendums also serve as a check on parliamentary legislation. In other words, rejective referendums take place after parliamentary deliberations and decision-making. In this respect, parliamentary parties should be well prepared and motivated to justify publicly their positions in favour of or against the law passed by the parliament. Like mandatory referendums, rejective referendums could thus enhance the kind of re-iterated deliberation called for by the theorists of deliberative democracy.

Rejective referendums protect the interests of minorities, and so the threat of a referendum encourages the majorities to consider the opinions of minorities already when laws are drafted. In this respect, the anticipation of rejective referendums can be expected to reinforce consensual forms of policy-making. Indeed, the provision for a citizen-initiated rejective referendum can be regarded as the primary reason why in the Swiss government all major parties have been included since 1959. (Trechsel & Kriesi 1996, 202-204.) At least from a theoretical perspective, citizen-initiated rejective referendums could be expected to enhance inclusiveness of deliberations on the parliamentary arena, as they cannot simply be avoided by log-rolling among parliamentary parties (Setälä 2006).

The so-called abrogative referendum follows the same sequences as rejective referendums, the only difference being that in abrogative referendums the decision made by the parliament is actually enacted before the referendum is requested. When it comes to the sequential analysis, this detail should not have much of an impact. However, the most well-known example of abrogative referendums, the Italian 'referendum abrogativo', is in many respects different from rejective referendums. In the Italian abrogative referendum, there are no limits in terms of the time between the enactment of a law and the request of the abrogation of the law. This makes it possible to use the abrogative referendum to repeal any law, regardless of how long it has been in force. In this respect, the Italian abrogative referendum has many similarities with popular initiatives as it can be used to achieve legislative changes. (Uleri 2002).

---

102 Also the Slovenian Constitution provides for a rejective referendum which can be triggered by 40,000 voters. (Schiller & Setälä 2012a, 13)

Type 4. Full-Scale Initiatives

4.1. Full-Scale Initiative

Citizens' proposal including request for referendum → *referendum campaign* → referendum (decision)

In popular initiatives, a group of citizens have both an opportunity to raise an issue on the political agenda and to demand a popular vote on the issue in question. The practices of popular initiatives vary to a large extent, especially in terms of the extent to which the parliament is involved in the process. In countries such as Hungary, Latvia and Lithuania, for example, the topic of a popular initiative is not deliberated by the parliament before the popular vote. In these variants of the popular initiative, the popular vote follows from the initiative more or less automatically. In this respect, the institution of the popular initiative actually provides an alternative channel of legislation *vis-a-vis* parliamentary procedures. Such popular initiatives and votes are used *in place* of parliamentary procedures, which may bring about conflicts between representative institutions and direct legislation as well as inconsistencies in policy-making. This has been considered a major problem in the Californian practice of popular initiatives, in particular (cf. Ferejohn 2008, 193-195).

Furthermore, these types of initiatives can be considered problematic from a deliberative perspective, because there may be huge variation in the deliberative quality of initiative and ballot campaigns. In those European countries where initiatives are constitutionally provided (Latvia, Lithuania, Hungary), there are also very high procedural hurdles, such as high signature thresholds and restrictions on the issues allowed, which actually make the use of initiatives difficult and uncommon. This means that the use of initiatives is completely out of the reach of marginalized groups and raises questions about the capacity of initiatives to enhance inclusiveness in policy-making (Schiller & Setälä 2012b).

Full-Scale Initiative with Parliamentary Negotiations

Citizens' proposal including a request for a referendum → *parliamentary negotiations* (→ counterproposal)→ *referendum campaign* → referendum (decision)
Or,
Citizens' proposal including a request for referendum →*parliamentary negotiations* → withdrawal of the initiative→ parliamentary ballot (decision)

Unlike in the above-mentioned countries, there are institutionalized parliamentary procedures concerning popular initiatives in Switzerland. After an initiative is signed by 100,000 voters and successfully submitted to a parliament, it will undergo a process of negotiations in which the parliamentary parties (representing the grand coalition government) and the initiators are involved. In many cases, the government agrees to make some legislative changes according to the demands of the initiators. If the initiators are satisfied with the proposal, they may withdraw their initiative. Otherwise, the initiative is submitted to a popular vote.

In Swiss popular votes, voters often need to take a position on both the popular initiative and the governmental counterproposal. In case both of these are supported by a (double) majority of voters, the decision is made based on an additional question which asks for the voters' preference on the two proposals (Trechsel & Kriesi 1996; Lutz 2012). The parliamentary negotiation phase in the Swiss practice of popular initiatives seems to help prevent such conflicts between representative and direct legislation as appear to have become a problem in the other variant of citizens' initiatives.

Type 5. Agenda Initiatives

Citizens' law proposal → *parliamentary debate* → parliamentary vote (decision)

The agenda initiative allows a certain number of citizens to put forward a legislative proposal which will be discussed and voted on by the parliament. Agenda initiatives are relatively widely adopted in European democracies, such as Austria, Spain, Poland and, more recently, the Netherlands and Finland. A variant of agenda initiatives, the European Citizens' Initiative, was adopted at the EU level as a part of the Lisbon Treaty. As a contrast to other agenda initiatives which are dealt with in parliament, the European Citizens' Initiative is submitted to the European Commission (Kaufmann 2012). In the context of representative democracies, agenda initiatives may represent a feasible compromise between those who support the idea of parliamentary democracy and those who support the expansion of people's direct involvement in policy-making. Because the number of signatures required for an agenda initiative is usually relatively low compared to full-scale initiatives, the use of these kinds of institutions seems to be more easily within the reach of marginalized groups.

Overall, agenda initiatives appear to be comparatively weak institutions, because they do not change the distribution of institutional power in political systems. In this respect, it may be asked whether they can be regarded as a form of direct democracy. However, when it comes to the actual political impacts of agenda initiatives, there are considerable differences between the practices in different countries. Most agenda initiatives do not usually gain such public visibility as full-scale initiatives. Still, agenda initiatives have gained relatively much public attention in Austria where they have been used by opposition parties (Giese 2012). In some countries, most notably in Poland, parliamentary procedures concerning agenda initiatives have been carefully outlined. This has increased the political weight of initiatives and ensures that parliamentarians cannot so easily dismiss popular initiatives (e.g. Rytel-Warzocha 2012).

How to Improve the Deliberative Qualities of Direct Democratic Campaigns?

Apparently, the impact of direct democratic instruments on the quality of deliberation varies considerably in the parliamentary arena, and the sequencing of various procedures seems to be the key here. Naturally, the sequential analysis can give rise to theoretical expectations, and the empirical reality often seems much more complicated. However, there is no question that certain forms of government-initiated referendums and popular initiatives actually eliminate chances of parliamentary deliberations, and that they create different incentives for representatives to deliberate on the issue.

Another question is whether the sequencing of parliamentary and direct democratic procedures influences the quality of referendum campaigns. It is possible that there are some systematic differences across different institutional designs. There are theoretical arguments and also some empirical evidence that the discursive engagement of political elites is the key to the quality of referendum campaigns. Kriesi (2005), for example, finds that in Swiss direct democratic votes, voters are more likely to make their decisions based on arguments when the campaigns are intensive and the issues familiar.

Institutions of direct democracy provide different kinds of incentive structures for political actors, especially for political elites, to engage in referendum campaigns. The motivations of political elites to participate in referendum campaigns may depend on the sequencing of parliamentary and direct democratic procedures. In general, the fact that the parliament has made a decision on the issue before the popular vote could be expected to encourage political elites to engage in referendum campaigns. Especially mandatory and rejective referendums encourage governmental parties to defend their policy choices publicly before the ballot, and this kind of a re-iterated deliberation could potentially have some positive effects on the quality of referendum campaigns.

The question still remains: How do we encourage people participating in referendums to consider arguments related to the issue? It has been pointed out on several occasions that referendums easily become votes on the government's popularity rather than on the actual issue at hand. There is also some empirical evidence of these so-called 'second order' effects of referendums (see e.g. Franklin 2002; Svensson 2002). The question of institutional design may appear also in relation to second order effects. It has been argued that second order effects are more likely to take place in government-initiated referendums, where the government both triggers the referendum and sets its agenda. Indeed, sometimes governments actually frame the referendum as a vote of confidence of their own position in order to mobilize their supporters. The possible variation in issue voting in different direct democratic procedures is a question which calls for further empirical research.

Assuming that a referendum campaign actually focuses on the right issue, there is still a risk that the adversary style of referendum campaigns polarizes public opinion rather than helps to achieve constructive dialogue between various sides on the issue. The problems of reconciling mass participation and deliberation seem to be acute. As pointed out above, multi-option referendums could help to avoid the polarizing dynamics related to majoritarian decisions. Moreover, as far as advisory referendums are concerned, multi-option referendums could also help highlighting the responsibility of the parliamentarians to make the final decision. Having said this, it must be pointed out that, from a deliberative perspective, the use of so-called deliberative mini-publics could be regarded as a much more recommendable way of consulting people's opinions on policy issues than advisory referendums. The term deliberative mini-public refers to forums of citizen deliberation where participants are expected to represent the population at large (Dryzek and Goodin 2006). The most well-known formats of deliberative mini-publics are citizens' juries, deliberative polls and consensus conferences.[103]

Deliberative democrats have also suggested the use of deliberative mini-publics as a potential cure for the bad deliberative quality of referendum campaigns. As deliberative mini-publics include only a fraction of the whole elec-

---

103 The representativeness of participants is achieved either by recruiting participants through random sampling or selecting a group of participants which represent different socio-economic groups (for the idea of representativeness in deliberative mini-publics, see Brown 2006). Citizen deliberation in mini-publics should be informed, equal and balanced. Normally, participants of mini-publics interact with experts and stakeholders, and they participate in facilitated deliberations in small groups. Some deliberative mini-publics finish with the formulation of a written statement on the issue discussed, whereas in others only individual participants' opinions are aggregated. Most notably, deliberative polls do not enforce consensus but rather rely on the measurement of individual preferences before and after deliberation. Deliberative mini-publics have been used to consult policy-makers, to enhance public debate on a salient issue, and in some cases, purely for research purposes. Only in a few cases, deliberative mini-publics have actually been vested with power to make collective decisions.

torate, their impact on the overall political debate is deemed minor unless the impacts of deliberations are somehow 'amplified'. The boldest suggestion has probably been made by Ackerman and Fishkin (2002) who suggest that a specific national holiday, a Deliberation Day, should precede any major national election or referendum. Their idea is that all voters are expected to participate in deliberative discussions organized in their neighborhood. In other words, instead of a deliberative mini-public, Ackerman and Fishkin are recommending a deliberative 'macro-public' including the whole electorate.

The extensive media coverage of deliberative mini-publics has often been regarded as another, perhaps more feasible solution to the problem of how to amplify the effects of deliberation. Examples of these types of procedures are the Australian referendum on the republican constitution in 1999 and the Danish referendum on the euro in 2003. In both cases, widely broadcasted deliberative polls were organised in conjunction with referendum campaigns, and the media coverage on these deliberative polls arguably contributed to the public discussion and opinion (Fishkin 2003; Andersen and Hansen 2007). However, there may have been too much optimism as regards the capacity of the media coverage of deliberative mini-publics to transform the character of referendum campaigns. There are concerns that the media coverage of deliberative events follows the adversary style which often characterises referendum campaigns more generally. Instead of focusing on the arguments put forward in the course of deliberation, the coverage focuses on the question which side 'wins' deliberation.

In fact, some authors have suggested that instead of media coverage, there should be other ways of boosting the effects of deliberation in mini-publics. The example of the Citizens' Assembly on electoral reform in British Columbia in 2005 offers some ideas on how this could be accomplished (Warren & Pearse 2008). In this case, the Citizens' Assembly was assigned the task of defining a new, alternative electoral system for the first-by-the-post system used in the province. The assembly consisted of 160 citizen representatives who, after several months of deliberations, almost unanimously suggested Single Transferable Vote as a new electoral system. The proposal by the assembly was submitted to a referendum where 57.7 per cent of the voters supported the new electoral system. However, this was not sufficient to pass the 60 per cent supermajority requirement set for the ballot vote.

There are studies based on surveys showing that a large proportion - about 60 per cent - of the electorate was aware of the Citizens' Assembly. Also, a large share of the electorate regarded it as a trusted source of information when they were making their voting decision on the issue. The basis of trust varied across the electorate; some trusted the Assembly because it consisted of ordinary people, whereas others trusted it because its members became experts on the issue during the process (Cutler et. al. 2008). It is also notable that the public visibility of the Assembly was enhanced by the fact that the participants of the Citizens' Assembly did not only deliberate among themselves, but they also participated in public hearings in various parts of the province.

Another possible way to increase the deliberative quality of referendum campaigns is to use deliberative mini-publics as sources of voting recommendations. The consensus government in Switzerland issues a voting recommendation routinely before each popular vote. A voting recommendation includes the main arguments for and against the proposal at stake, and a brief justification for the position taken by the government. A system of voting recommendations such as this may not be applicable to 'normal' parliamentary systems where recommendations given by the government would most likely be trusted by the supporters of governmental parties only.

However, one could imagine that instead of the government, a deliberative mini-public could deliberate on and draft a voting recommendation distributed among voters. Obviously, this kind of a voting recommendation should include the main arguments for and against the proposition, as well as a justification for the position taken on the issue. This kind of procedure has recently been experimented with in Oregon, where two citizens' initiatives were reviewed by a deliberative citizen panel. The statements of the panel were distributed among voters as part of a Voters' Pamphlet (Gastil & Knobloch 2012.)

Concluding Remarks

Direct democratic institutions, especially referendums, appear to provide inclusive and effective participation. Referendums also seem to have strong legitimizing impacts. Popular initiatives allow citizens to raise political issues on the agenda and, if the thresholds are not too high, this should improve the inclusiveness of the policy-making process. However, as is the case concerning any other democratic innovations, the democratic credentials of institutions of direct democracy are, to some extent, debatable. Especially in terms of criteria such as deliberation and enlightened citizen participation, direct democratic institutions may first appear defective.

In this paper, it has been argued that a more careful analysis of the role of direct democratic institutions may provide a more refined picture. The democratic credentials of direct democratic institutions depend on the role they play in the entire policy-making process. This paper has suggested that these institutions should not be evaluated only on their own, but more attention should be paid to the ways in which they are sequenced with the primary mode of decision-making, that is, institutions and practices of representative democracy.

The sequential analysis of direct democratic procedures used in Europe shows that government-initiated referendums replace and, in case of advisory referendums, undermine parliamentary deliberations. In some cases, popular initiatives may create conflicts between representative and direct democratic procedures, whereas the Swiss system of parliamentary negotiations helps avoiding some of these deficiencies. At the same time, citizen-initiated rejective referendums may have a potential to enhance inclusive deliberation in the parliamentary arena as well as communication between elected representatives and voters.

Summing up, different direct democratic institutions have different impacts. In many cases, they provide inclusive and effective participation and they can enhance legitimacy. Furthermore, under certain circumstances they might enhance deliberation among citizens and influence citizens' enlightenment in a positive way.

References

Ackerman, Bruce (1998): *We the People: Transformation*. Cambridge, Ma: Harvard University Press.

Ackerman, Bruce & Fishkin, James S. (2002): Deliberation Day. *The Journal of Political Philosophy*, 10: 129-152.

Andersen, Vibeke Normann & Hansen, Kasper M. (2007): How deliberation makes better citizens: The Danish Deliberative Poll on the euro. *European Journal of Political Research* 46: 531-556.

Barber, Benjamin (1984): *Strong Democracy. Participatory Politics for a New Age*. Berkeley: University of California Press.

Bowler, Shaun & Donovan, Todd (2002): Democracy, Institutions and Attitudes about Citizen Influence on Government. *British Journal of Political Science*, 32:2, 371-390.

Brown, Mark (2006): Survey Article: Citizen Panels and the Concept of Representation. *The Journal of Political Philosophy* 14 (2): 203-225.

Chambers, Simone (2001): Constitutional Referendums and Democratic Deliberation. In Matthew Mendelson & Andrew Parkin (eds): *Referendum democracy: citizens, elites, and deliberation referendum campaigns*. Basingstoke: Palgrave, pp. 231-255.

Cronin, Thomas E. (1989): Direct Democracy. The Politics of Initiative, Referendum, and Recall. Cambridge, Ma: Harvard University Press.

Cutler, Fred; Johnston, Richard; Carty, Kenneth R., Blais, André & Fournier, Patrick (2008): Deliberation, information, and trust: the British Columbia Citizens' Assembly as an agenda setter. In Mark E. Warren & Hilary Pearse (eds): *Designing Deliberative Democracy. The British Columbia Citizens' Assembly*. Cambridge: Cambridge University Press, pp. 166-191.

Dryzek, John (2000): Deliberative Democracy and Beyond. Liberals, Critics, Contestations. Oxford: Oxford University Press.

Dryzek, John S. & Niemeyer, Simon (2006): Reconciling Pluralism and Consensus as Political Ideals. *American Journal of Political Science*, 50, 634-649.

Dahl, Robert A (1989): *Democracy and its Critics*. New Haven and London: Yale University Press.

Downs, Anthony (1957): *An Economic Theory of Democracy.* HarperCollins, New York.

Dryzek, John S. & Goodin, Robert E. (2006): Deliberative Impacts: The Macro-Political Uptake of Mini-Publics. *Politics and Society,* 34: 219-244.

Elster, Jon (1998): Deliberation and Constitution Making. In Jon Elster (ed.), *Deliberative Democracy.* Cambridge: Cambridge University Press, pp. 97-122.

Ferejohn, John (2008): Conclusion: the Citizens' Assembly Model. In Warren, Mark E. & Pearse, Hilary (2008): *Designing Deliberative Democracy. The British Columbia Citizens' Assembly.* Cambridge: Cambridge University Press, pp. 192-213.

Fishkin, James S. (2003): Consulting the public through deliberative polling. *Journal of Policy Analysis and Management:* 22: 128-133.

Franklin, Mark (2002): Learning from the Danish Case: A Comment on Palle Svensson's Critique of the Franklin Thesis. *European Journal of Political Research* 40: 31-56.

Gastil, John & Knobloch, Katie (2012): Evaluation Report to the Oregon State Legislature on the 2010 Oregon Citizens' Initiative Review. Department of Communication, University of Washington.

Giese, Karim (2012): The Austrian Agenda Initiative: An Instrument Dominated by Opposition Parties. In Maija Setälä & Theo Schiller (eds): *Citizens' Initiatives in Europe.* Basingstoke: Palgrave, pp. 175-192.

Goodin, Robert E. (2005): Sequencing Deliberative Moments. *Acta Politica,* 40: 182–196.

Goodin, Robert E. (2009): Innovating Democracy. Democratic Theory and Practice after the Deliberative Turn. Oxford: Oxford University Press.

Gutmann, Amy & Thompson, Dennis (1996): *Democracy and Disagreement.* Harvard: Belknap Press.

Habermas, Jürgen (1996): *Between Facts and Norms.* Cambridge, Ma: The MIT Press.

Habermas, Jürgen (2008): *Europe. The Faltering Project.* Malden Ma: Polity Press.

Holzinger, Katharina (2004): Bargaining by Arguing. An Empirical Analysis Based on Speech Act Theory. *Political Communication* 21: 195-222.

Kaufmann, Bruno (2012): Transnational 'Babystep': The European Citizens' Initiative. In Maija Setälä & Theo Schiller (eds.): *Citizens' Initiatives in Europe.* Basingstoke: Palgrave, pp. 228-242.

Kriesi, Hanspeter & D. Wisler (1996): Social movements and direct democracy in Switzerland. *European Journal of Political Research* 30: 19-40.

Kriesi, Hanspeter (2005): Argument-Based Strategies in Direct-Democratic Votes: The Swiss Experience. *Acta Politica,* 40: 299-316.

Lutz, Georg (2012): Switzerland: Citizens' Initiative as a Measure to Control the Political Agenda. In Maija Setälä & Theo Schiller (eds) *Citizens' Initiatives in Europe.* Basingstoke: Palgrave, pp.17-36.

Mill, John Stuart (1861/1958): *Considerations on Representative Government.* Indianapolis & New York: The Bobbs-Merrill Company.

Morel, Laurence (2001): The Rise of Government-Initiated Referendums in Consolidated Democracies. In Matthew Mendelson & Andrew Parkin (eds): *Referendum democracy: citizens, elites, and deliberation referendum campaigns.* Basingstoke: Palgrave, pp. 47-64.

Mueller, Dennis (1997): Federalism and the European Union: a constitutional perspective. *Public Choice* 90: 255-280.

Rytel-Warzocha, Anna (2012): Popular Initiatives in Poland: Citizens' Empowerment or Keeping up Appearances? In Maija Setälä & Theo Schiller (eds): *Citizens' Initiatives in Europe*. Basingstoke: Palgrave, pp. 212-227.

Schiller, Theo & Setälä, Maija (2012a): Introduction. In Maija Setälä & Theo Schiller (eds): *Citizens' Initiatives in Europe*. Basingstoke: Palgrave, pp. 1-14.

Schiller, Theo & Setälä, Maija (2012b): Conclusions. In Maija Setälä & Theo Schiller (eds): *Citizens' Initiatives in Europe*. Basingstoke: Palgrave, pp. 243-259.

Setälä, Maija (2006): On the Problems of Responsibility and Accountability in Referendums. *European Journal of Political Research*, 45 (5): 701-723.

Svensson, Palle (2002): Five Danish Referendums on the European Community and Union: A Critical Assessment of the Franklin Thesis. *European Journal of Political Research*, 41: 733-750.

Trechsel, Alexander H. & Kriesi, Hanspeter (1996): Switzerland: the referendum and initiative as a centerpiece of the political system. In Michael Gallagher & Piervincenzo Uleri (eds.): *The Referendum Experience in Europe*. Basingstoke: Macmillan Press, pp. 185-208.

Uleri, PierVincenzo (2002): On referendum voting in Italy: YES, NO or non-vote? How Italian parties learned to control referendums. *European Journal of Political Research*, 41: 863-883.

Warren, Mark E. & Pearse, Hilary (2008): *Designing Deliberative Democracy. The British Columbia Citizens' Assembly*. Cambridge: Cambridge University Press.

Young, Iris Marion (2000): *Inclusion and Democracy*. Oxford: Oxford University Press.

The Local Recall Revisited: An Old Tool for Inclusive and Effective Participation in New Democracies[104]

Michael L. Smith

Introduction

At first glance, the recall process – the process in which citizens can remove an elected official or body from office by popular vote – hardly seems innovative. First mentioned by Aristotle,[105] the recall has a history both intertwined with and as long as the citizen's initiative and legislative referendum, though used more sporadically. While the initiative and referendum give citizens the voice to decide major policy issues, the recall focuses not on the policies but the policy-maker, since it allows voters to directly assess the performance of elected politicians – or entire electoral bodies, in proportional systems – by subjecting them to the possibility of losing their mandate before their electoral term is over. The recall is institutionally diverse: it can be either full or mixed, depending on who initiates the referendum process, and take either the separate-elections or the recall-and-replacement formats.[106] Recalls also vary by

104 This chapter was made possible by the support of the Czech Science Foundation through grant no. 403/07/1608, "The Politics of Local Referendums in Central Europe" as well as by grant no. VG20102013029 of the Czech Ministry of Interior, "Reducing Security Threats from Corruption and Organized Crime in the Czech Republic."

105 In the Constitution of Athens, Part 43 Aristotle explains that one of the duties of the Council of Five Hundred was to evaluate the performance of the "sovereign assembly." In that assembly "the people have to ratify the continuance of the magistrates in office, if they are performing their duties properly, and…. impeachments are introduced by those who wish to do so…" This ratification/impeachment process could be an ancient version of the modern recall.

106 A full recall takes place when citizens are involved in both petitioning for and then voting in the recall referendum. In a mixed recall, citizens are involved in only one of the two processes, such as when they may vote in the recall but on the basis of a decision by Parliament (IDEA 2008). In the separate-elections format, a referendum on the recall of a politician or political body is held; if the recall is successful, a replacement election is then scheduled. In the recall-and-replacement format, the referendum and the replacement election take place at the same time, in which the results of the replacement election are valid only if the incumbent is

whether turnout quorums are imposed for the results to be valid. Overall, in the countries where the recall process is institutionalized, the device is generally seen as a mechanism for democratic accountability between elections, particularly in cases where an elected politician refuses to resign (or cannot be impeached), but is accused of incompetence, bribery, or other gross violations of moral conduct.

Relatively 'old' democratic devices as the recall can become innovative when they are applied to new and unexpected contexts, thus serving as fresh solutions to problems like civic apathy or corruption that are deep-rooted and difficult to prevent (G. Smith 2009). While it is believed that the recall at the level of local politics is practiced most extensively in the U.S. states (Cronin 1989), over the last two decades the device has become increasingly used in two new democracies of post-communist Europe – Poland and Slovakia – which have seen dozens of disgruntled communities oust mayors and local councils from power, often due to perceptions of corruption and mismanagement. In those countries, the *local recall is arguably one of the most important innovations in citizen empowerment that have been implemented in recent years*. In both countries, the recall was enshrined in national legislation at the same time as local government reforms introduced the direct election of mayors. Previously, mayors in both countries were accountable to their respective local councils, which appointed and recalled them; under the new rules, mayors are accountable to the people (who can vote and recall them) and face a checks-and-balances system with local councils. In such new democracies where citizens are overwhelmingly distrustful of politicians and where civil society is weak, it was thought that the introduction of the recall could both foster citizen empowerment in local politics while also tackling the seemingly endless problem of irresponsible (and irresponsive) government. A primary goal of this chapter is to assess the recall process as a tool for innovative democracy and whether it offers a form of decision-making suitable for dealing with major controversies at the local level.

The recall process has remained one of the least researched areas of democratic politics. One reason is that the device is so sporadically used, particularly at the national level, which has made it difficult to evaluate its impact. Altman (2005) points out that the 2004 referendum to recall Venezuelan President Chavez from office nearly led the country to civil war (in part due to alleged political interference in both the signature collection process and in the recall

---

successfully recalled. One of the main differences between the formats is that in the recall-and-replacement format political attention does not focus only on the politician being recalled, but also gravitates towards campaigns of other candidates seeking political office. In both formats, a recalled politician could plausibly run as a candidate in the replacement election.

vote), and cautions that the recall's impact can vary considerably by institutional context. Arguably the recall event most researched by political scientists is the successful recall of California Governor Gray Davis.[107] On the basis of that case, Shaw, McKenzie and Underwood (2005) argued that the recall-and-replacement format disadvantages incumbent parties, who have to both defend the incumbent while also campaigning for a party replacement. Others found that ethnic cleavages (Segura and Fraga 2008), strategic voting (Alvarez, Kiewiet and Sinclair 2006), and corporate lobbying (Cressman 2007) played a mayor role in the recall vote. Since those are also features of ordinary electoral politics, it is not surprising that Bowler and Cain (2006: 8) perceived the California recall as "just another election" in which the "constitutional, orderly, and peaceful replacement of one leader by another" took place.

In terms of local politics, most research has focused on the U.S., where 36 states have legislation enabling recalls at the municipal level. Within an average five-year period, one in ten local governments experience an attempt to recall an elected official in those states (Bowler and Cain 2006). Cain, Anderson, and Eaton (2006) found that campaigns to recall mayors organized by groups of citizens were more successful than campaigns organized by institutional interests. They also found that mayors are more likely to be recalled in the recall-and-replacement format than in the separate-elections format. Lastly, those authors also claimed that the number of signatures required for a petition does not have an impact on the success of a recall proposal to get on the ballot. Other institutional determinants do not seem to have an effect on the ability of citizens to recall state officials in different U.S. states (Mixon 2000).

Since the empirical data on the recall process at the local level is piecemeal and the literature is relatively small, there has been little systematic attempt to evaluate the local recall as a mechanism of democratic governance. This chapter takes a step in that direction by evaluating the recall process in the only two post-communist countries where national legislation enables local residents to use that device: Poland (since 1992) and Slovakia (since 2002). Building on the work of Lástič (2005, 2007, 2011) and Piasecki (2005, 2011), the chapter will first give an overview of the basic elements of Polish and Slovak legislation on

---

107 According to the official petition, the accusation made against Davis was that he had engaged in "gross mismanagement of California finances by overspending taxpayers' money, threatening public safety by cutting funds to local governments, failing to account for the exorbitant cost of the energy fiasco, and failing in general to deal with the state's major problems until they get to the crisis stage." 55% of Californian voters voted to recall Davis (turnout was 61%, or nearly 5 million voters); in the replacement election, 49% voted in favor of Schwarzenegger, securing a margin of over 1.5 million votes over his nearest competitor, Hispanic lieutenant governor Cruz Bustamante.

direct democracy at the local level. We then evaluate the recall process in Poland and Slovakia in terms of four main criteria: 1) whether citizen participation in the process is *effective*; 2) whether it is *inclusive*; 3) whether the recall helps restore *legitimacy* to public office when politicians are perceived to abuse their power; and 4) the *effectiveness* of the recall process, i.e. whether the recall helps identify and achieve collective goals of the communities under consideration.

The analysis in the chapter is based on two main data sources. First, comprehensive databases of recall events were created for both countries on the basis of data from statistical offices, media reports, and election results.[108] Those databases were used to identify overall trends in recall use in those countries. Second, 24 interviews with local politicians and activists involved in recall campaigns were conducted in six different communities (three in each country) in order to gain insight into participants' experience and evaluation of the recall process. The cases were selected on the basis of variation in recall outcome (whether successful or not), as well to achieve variation in the set of collective problems raised in those communities.

Legislation on Local Direct Democracy in Poland and Slovakia

Immediately after the collapse of communism, many countries in Central and Eastern Europe passed legislation on the local initiative and referendum, and to a lesser degree, the recall. Unified Germany is the best-known example of this. During the Cold War period Baden-Württemberg was the only German state to have local referendums (where there were roughly 300 cases since 1956), whereas all other German states passed similar legislation after German unification, most recently in Berlin. In Bavaria, there have been an eye-popping 1,457 initiatives just in the years 1995-2005 (Walter-Rogg and Gabriel 2007). According to government data, in the Czech Republic, over 150 local referendums took place between 2000 and 2008, while in Hungary 187 referendums took place between 1998-2008 (M. Smith 2007, 2009). Poland has witnessed

---

108 Polish data is from the National Electoral Commission of Poland. Since neither the Slovak government nor other authorities collect data on local recalls, the only way to collect data on Slovak recalls is through searching media databases for articles mentioning attempts at recalling mayors. Media analysis was conducted on newspapers SME, Pravda, Slovak Spectator, Nový čas, and the Slovak Press Agency for the period 2002-2008.

hundreds of local referendums and recalls since 1990, as its legislation has generally been the most favourable to practitioners of direct democracy among post-communist countries. While in most Western European countries (besides Germany and Switzerland) local referendums are merely consultative in nature, i.e. not binding on local government, in much of Central and Eastern Europe local referendum results are binding if a legislatively established turnout quorum is met (Council of Europe 2000).

Poland and Slovakia are the only two countries in Europe where local recalls are legally permitted nationwide. Both countries use the separate-elections format and impose turnout quorums for the recall (but not in the replacement election) to be valid. The countries vary considerably in the use of the recall device (it is much less common in Slovakia), in part due to differences in their legislative histories.

Polish regulations on local direct democracy have undergone several phases of legislative development. In the first phase of democratic reform, the Act on Local Self-government of March 1990 established that local referendums are one of two ways municipal self-administration is to be carried out (the other way is decision-making by local council), and differentiated between obligatory local referendums, such as in the introduction of local taxes, and facultative local referendums, in the case of other matters important for the community. The Law on Local Referendums of October 1991 established the specific rules for carrying out local referendums in Poland. Initially, recall referendums were to be called if local residents collected signatures of 20% of registered voters and would be valid if 50% of the electorate voted. Since there are three types of municipality (*gmina*) in Poland – rural, urban, and urban-rural – recalls can take place in all three types. Two months after the law went into force, it was amended so that signatures of only 10% of registered voters were necessary, and outcomes were valid with a reduced 30% turnout quorum (Olejniczak-Szałowska 2002; Piasecki 2005). In September 1995, the Law on Local Referendums was amended so that recalls can neither take place in the last six months of the electoral term nor in the first 12 months of an electoral term. It also clearly stated that only citizens can initiate a campaign to recall the local council. Also in 1995, the Highest Administrative Court ruled that recall referendums couldn't take place at the same time as local referendums on other municipal issues.

In the second phase of democratic reform in Poland, which focused on political reform at the meso-level of government (Swianiewicz and Herbst 2002; Wollmann and Lankina 2003), a new Law on Local Referendums was passed in September 2000 that enabled referendums at the county and regional level. Legislation on the direct election of mayors was also part of the territorial reform package. The amended referendum law thus enabled the recall of mayors as of 2003, which can be initiated by either citizens or the local council. However, if a local council calls for a recall referendum of the mayor, and if the recall is not successful, then the local council has to be dissolved, which has led to practically no recalls of that type (Piasecki 2005).

In the most recent phase of reform, in July 2005 another amendment of the referendum law was passed (taking effect at the time of the 2006 local elections) that abolished the 30% turnout quorum and stated that recall elections are valid, when turnout reaches 3/5 of the level of the turnout achieved in the prior election of the political entity being recalled. This means that if 5,000 voters voted in a mayoral election, the mayor can be recalled if in the recall referendum at least 3,000 voters turn out, the majority of whom vote in favour of recalling him. By tying the turnout quorum to a municipality's prior turnout record, the amendment has the potential to decouple referendum validity from demographic conditions, such as population size, that strongly shape aggregate turnout (M. Smith 2009, 2011). In other words, the amendment has the effect of generally reducing the turnout quorum for larger towns and cities (as well as possibly increasing it in smaller communities), so that the chances of achieving a successful recall election are more evenly distributed among municipalities of different size, all else being equal.

In summary, Polish legislation on the local recall has become increasingly expansive (from recalls of local councils, to recalls of councils, mayors, and elected officials of county and regional governments) as well as more favourable to those initiating a recall campaign (reductions in signature collection requirements as well as in turnout quorums). As we will discuss in the following section, these legislative changes have had a positive impact on the effectiveness of citizen-initiated recall campaigns.

Slovakia, by contrast, has had a very weak legislative framework for all forms of local direct democracy. As discussed by Lástič (2005, 2007, 2011), the clauses relating to local referendums and recalls in the main Law 369/1990 on Local Government were amended a spectacular 27 times between 1990 and 2005. As was the case with the frequent changes to the Slovak constitution in the 1990s, the amendments to the Local Government Act seem to have little or no justification in referendum practice (as the state administration does not collect data on local referendums and recalls, it can hardly evaluate them), but was rather the result of the calculus of political parties to steer legislative rules to their advantage. The reasons behind some legislative changes are more clear-cut than others; for example, in 1998, in reaction to the Štúrovo referendum where the local government organized a referendum against Slovak NATO membership, the Slovak parliament passed legislation stating that local referendums can only be held on issues in the competency of local government, rather than on issues a local government finds important. In 2001, parliament also passed legislation instituting not only the direct election of mayors (Law No. 6/2001 on Local Government), but also their possible recall by local citizens. The law also established a separation of powers between the mayor and the local council, and provided the mayor with extensive executive powers over local administration and in chairing meetings of the local council.

The same law also detailed regulations for the recall process. Paragraph 13a of the amendment states that the local council shall call a referendum on the recall of the mayor if 1) at least 30% of registered voters in the municipality demand it via a petition; or 2) the mayor engages in gross and repeated acts of negligence, if he breaks constitutional law, or if he is either absent or not duly performing the office of mayor for a period of 6 months. As in Poland, once the signatures are collected, the local council has to approve by majority vote that the legal conditions for a recall have been met.[109] Lastly, as with the case of local referendums, the results of a recall of a mayor are valid *if at least 50% of registered voters vote in the recall*. The frequent changes in legislation, coupled with relatively restrictive rules and the 50% turnout quorum, have meant that there have been less than 50 recall campaigns in the country since 2002.

Citizen Participation in the Local Recall: is it Effective?

If participatory innovations are to help bring about political change, citizen involvement in them has to be effective. Effective participation means that citizens' contributions in a participatory process are not simply dismissed or ignored, but are actually taken into account in deliberations and decision-making (Fung and Wright 2001; Warren 2006; Smith 2009). In most of Central and Eastern Europe, as well as in Germany and Switzerland, the institutions of direct democracy are not simply consultative, but are *legally binding* on government. This means that if direct democracy campaigns are relatively accessible, i.e. easy to carry out, those campaigns would also represent an effective means for ordinary citizens to shape or change local government policy.

In fact, the effectiveness of binding direct democracy devices – e.g. the relative ease with which citizens can organize initiatives when governments are

---

109 In the local referendums and recalls in the U.S., the local clerk, who is typically non-partisan, has the responsibility for verifying the eligibility of a petition for a recall. The fact that in Central Europe this decision-making is done directly by local councils has led to many cases of politicizing the petition process – particularly if local residents propose initiatives directly against the policies of the local council – in which local councils would find rather spurious or quite formalistic reasons to justify not calling referendums. Many of such cases have went to administrative or civil court, illustrating the importance of the judicial system in interpreting and upholding referendum law (Smith 2007).

irresponsive, or the ease with which legislatures can defer decision-making to citizens on fundamentally important topics and treaties – contributes to their immense popularity around the world. Asked whether referendum use was a good or bad thing, respondents in the Anglo-Saxon countries of Australia, New Zealand, Canada and the U.S. states of California and Washington have given resounding popular approval of the device by margins of around 65% (good thing) to around 5% (bad thing) (Bowler, Donovan, Carp 2007). In a 1997 Eurobarometer survey, respondents across the 15-EU states agreed, by a 71.5% to 28.5% margin, that the Swiss system of direct democracy works well and should be considered in their home countries. In the USA, no state that has adopted institutions of direct democracy at the state level has ever gotten rid of them, and in fact more and more states are adopting those institutions for the first time.

Turning to the recall process, effective participation depends on trade-offs in two key institutional features: 1) the rules according to which citizens can petition to remove a politician or political body from office, and 2) the turnout quorum in the recall vote. In terms of the petition, if the number of signatures needed for the petition were "too high," then there would be less frequent recall campaigns, though the campaigns that can meet high signature requirements likely have wide popular support among the electorate. If the signature requirement is "too low," then there would be more frequent recall campaigns, though it would be conceivable that very small groups of residents would be able to use the device to challenge and discredit popularly elected officials. Similarly, high turnout quorums would mean that few recall votes would be successful, but it also implies that the recalls that do succeed have overwhelming support of the local population. By contrast, low turnout quorums (or non-existent quorums, as in the USA) imply that many recalls could be successful, but with the prospect that elected officials could be ousted from office by only a small fraction of the total electorate. Taking these trade-offs into account, one could hypothesize that the recall process is most effective when legislation strikes a balance between the benefits and costs of high and low signature requirements and quorums. Such a balance helps ensure that direct democracy institutions are not manipulated by very small groups, but at the same time ensures that civic groups that initiate campaigns with wide popular support have a good chance to succeed.

Another important consideration is that demographic conditions do influence the degree of effective participation. If a signature requirement is set at 10% of the electorate for all municipalities, then it would be much easier for campaigners to collect those signatures in small villages compared to large cities. Similarly, if the turnout quorum were to be for example 50%, recalls would be possible in the villages, but nearly impossible to organize in cities, since urban voters are often less likely to vote than rural ones, particularly in a one-off recall event that is not tied to any other election. In fact, in Poland prior to 2005 (when the recall quorum was set to 3/5 of the turnout level achieved in the prior election of the political entity being recalled), there were practically no recalls in larger cities due to the 30% turnout quorum. In 1992 in Krakow, local residents seeking to recall the city council found it impossible to collect the more than 54,000 signatures that would have been necessary to call the referendum (Piasecki 2005). In 2000, at the time when Andrzej Lepper's Self-Defence Party organized a national campaign to block major roads to protest against the economic situation of Polish farmers, Self-Defence collaborated with merchants from a local market in Jelenia Gora to organize a referendum on the recall of the city council. Despite the wide publicity of the campaign, only 14% of registered voters voted in the referendum, which once again underscores the difficulty of organizing referendum campaigns in urban contexts.

Beyond individual cases, we can use comprehensive data on the local recall in Poland and Slovakia to better understand citizens' chances of successfully recalling local councils and mayors. In Poland, between 1992-2000, when it was possible to recall only local councils (so-called rural, urban, and rural-urban *gmina*), there were 275 such recalls (Figure 10.1), but only a small percentage resulted in the successful recall of the local council (Figure 10.2). While institutional learning, combined with improved legislative conditions, likely contributed to the increasing effectiveness of the recall between electoral periods, successful recalls of local councils have never exceeded 16% of the total for any given electoral period.

However, once it was possible for Polish citizens to directly elect and recall their mayors, the number of council recalls declined significantly, with citizens turning their attention instead to the mayors. In recent electoral periods, attempts at recalling mayors have been more frequent than council recalls as well as roughly twice as likely to lead to successful outcomes. While there have been fewer recalls in the 2007-2010 electoral term (during which time the 3/5 turnout rule is in effect), 17.6% of those cases have resulted in valid recalls. The new turnout threshold does increase the chances of reaching valid results: recall referendums in Piwniczna-Zdrój (turnout of 29.4%), Dorohusk (28.5%), Zgierz (26.0%), Zduńska Wola (29.1%), all of which took place in 2008, had binding outcomes under the current legislation, but would have been invalid under the prior 30% quorum. The new quorum rules also made it possible for the mayor of the city of Lodz, the third-largest city in Poland, to be recalled in early 2010 even with a recall turnout of only 22%.

In summary, Figures 10.1 and 10.2 lead to the inference that more is not necessarily better: over successive electoral periods, the number of local recalls in Poland has declined, but the degree of effective participation – in the sense of successful recall campaigns – has increased. While we have pointed to the role of legislative conditions in facilitating this development, a number of other factors could play a role as well: the ability of campaigners to learn from the successes and failures of campaigns in other towns, the expansion of web blogs and other forums for residents to discuss local issues more effectively, or the professionalization of Polish civil society (Rose-Ackerman 2007; Domański 2009). More research is needed, particularly by local scholars, to better understand the above trends.

In Slovakia, by contrast, neither the Slovak government nor other public institutions monitor or collect data on recall campaigns. Thus, the only way to count the number of cases is by conducting content analyses of Slovakia media sources over the given period, searching for any article using the word "recall" (*odvolanie* in Slovak). The present author did this using the national dailies *SME*, *Pravda*, *Nový čas*, *Slovak Spectator*, and the *Slovak Press Agency* for the period 2002-2008. During that time, it was possible to identify at least 36 campaigns aimed at recalling Slovak mayors, 25 of which led to actual recall votes. Of those 25, at least 13 led to the successful recall of mayors.[110] This suggests that even though the overall frequency of recall campaigns in Slovakia is much lower than in Poland, the effectiveness of the device is in fact higher.

---

110 All recalls above the turnout quorum were in favor of recalling the mayor. It should be noted that I have not been able to determine the results of 5 of the 25 recalls above; if some of those were also successful, the number of successful cases would be even higher.

*Figure 10.1: The Recall of Local Councils and Mayors in Poland, 1992-2010
(Municipalities are differentiated between rural and urban ones. Combined mayor-
council recalls include simultaneous recalls of both institutions regardless of their ur-
ban/rural character.)*

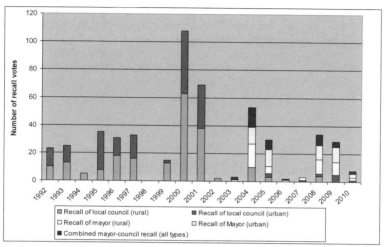

Source: Central Statistical Office of Poland

*Figure 10.2 The Effectiveness of the Local Recall in Poland.
Figure depicts the share of recalls in the given electoral period leading to successful
outcomes (i.e. the actual removal of the local council or mayor from office).*

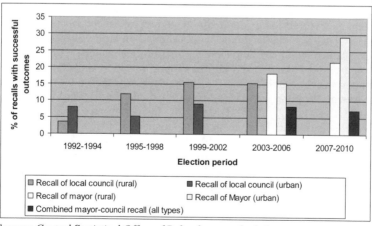

Source: Central Statistical Office of Poland, own calculations.

209

The lower number of Slovak recall campaigns could be due to a number of factors. As discussed above, the recall device is newer (since 2003) and comes with a 50% turnout threshold, which likely deters many would-be activists. Further, while Slovakia has a seventh of the population of Poland, it has a larger number of local governments (there are 2,929 municipalities in Slovakia, compared to 2,479 in Poland). In other words, Slovak municipalities are smaller in both population and territorial size than Polish ones, leading their budgets to be considerably smaller as well, which could imply fewer big-money controversies or fewer cases of major financial mismanagement. As suggested above, the high entry costs (turnout thresholds) for Slovak recalls leads to fewer cases but also a higher rate of success when campaigns are credible.

Citizen Participation in the Local Recall: is it Inclusive?

As an aggregative voting procedure, the recall process is inherently inclusive in the sense that any citizen with the right to vote can participate in the recall process, including the organization of recall petitions. However, critics of direct democracy, including the recall, claim that direct democracy devices are exclusionary, particularly to minority groups, and thus harmful to democratic politics as such. Since a referendum vote is based on majority rule, it is believed that social groups in the numerical majority, such as whites in Western societies, will be able to dominate referendum outcomes in ways that harm the rights and interests of minorities. In the context of local recalls in Poland and Slovakia, does the empirical evidence suggest that the recall process is exclusionary, or on the contrary, is a source of citizen empowerment for minorities, the poor, and others who challenge the 'establishment' in local government?

The claim that direct democracy is harmful to minority rights is often based on examples like the well-known Proposition 13 in California, which reduced tax revenues of the state and disproportionately shifted the costs of public services on the poor, minorities, women and others who were forced to pay higher user fees (Schrag 1998). Historically, initiatives have also been used to prohibit same-sex marriages, to prevent Japanese from owning land, and to deny affirmative action to women and ethnic minorities (Cronin 1989).

However, more systematic studies of the topic of minority rights have challenged whether, as a whole, whites or other majority groups dominate referendum outcomes. Focusing on California, Hajnal and Louch (2001) identified 45 initiatives from 1978-2000 that were of crucial importance to Latino and other minority communities. Proposition 13 on limiting property taxes (passed), Proposition 10 on limiting rent control (failed), and Proposition 165 on limiting welfare benefits (failed) are all examples of initiatives for which minority groups have affected interests. The authors found that the probability that a member of a racial group would be on the "winning side" of an initiative concerning issues that "minorities deem important" was 59% for whites, 59% for African-Americans, 52% for Latinos and 59% for Asian-Americans. That is, whites and minorities as a whole have a similar opportunity to support or challenge initiatives that concern them, and to do so with comparable success.

The scholarly literature has thus found mixed results concerning the effects of direct democracy on minority rights. Another point of consideration is that direct democracy has its own 'checks-and-balances' in the form of judicial review by the courts. We should take note that Parliaments and other representative institutions have also banned same-sex marriage, passed discriminatory legislation, and imposed large tax burdens on the poor. Both representative and direct democracy are subject to the same constitutions and constitutional courts, and both are equally subject to judicial review. Both forms of democratic decision-making can lead to unjust outcomes, and courts are responsible for protecting minority rights regardless of the form of decision-making originally used (Center for Responsive Government 1992).

Focusing on the local recalls in Central Europe, the key question to pose is what kind of impact the recall process has for national minorities, particularly the Roma, and other socially excluded communities. Since Slovakia has relatively large Roma and Hungarian minority populations, we will use Slovak cases to begin to answer the question above. Further examples, particularly of ethnically mixed communities are discussed in the following two sections of the chapter.

First, we should reiterate that between 2002-2008, at least 25 referendums on the recall of mayors took place in Slovakia (that compares to 126 recall cases taking place in Poland over the same time period). Recall attempts are most frequent in the rural areas of the Banskobystrický region, particularly in the district Rimavská Sobota, which has a large Hungarian population, and in the Košický region, which has a relatively dense network of Roma communities. Recalls are least common in larger cities and localities close to Bratislava. Many of the municipalities where recalls have taken place are located in areas of the country with higher degrees of social exclusion (Gajdoš 2005), thus suffering from high unemployment, poor public infrastructure and transport accessibility, and low levels of education, human capital, and population density (municipalities with less than 500 residents). One would expect that as mayors fail to sufficiently address (or are somewhat powerless to address) the economic situation of their community, they may face recall attempts from disappointed citizens demanding greater change.

In Slovakia, recall attempts are particularly common in ethnically divided communities i.e. those with large Roma or Hungarian populations, which also tend to be in areas with high levels of social exclusion. One of the most well-known cases concerning Roma took place in 2003 in the village of Richnava, where the population is estimated to be 60% Roma, where Roma unemployment is nearly 100% and where there is not even reliable water or electricity connections. The non-profit Roma Council of Slovakia (*Rada Romù Slovenska*) initiated a petition to recall the mayor for his lack of ability to address the plight of Roma residents. In the January 2004 recall vote, 600 of the 1,090 registered voters turned out, 510 (85%) of whom voted to successfully recall the mayor. While the mayor initially refused to accept the results of the referendum, he had little choice but to do so, after a criminal investigation on him was initiated for his refusal to leave office.[9] That case emphasizes the role that the legal system plays in enforcing referendum results when they are valid and rejecting them if they are unconstitutional or infringe upon civil rights.

By contrast, in the village of Žehra, which like Richnava has a large Roma community and a history of poverty and ethnic tensions,[111] the 2004 recall was not initiated by an NGO or local residents, but by the local council, which criticized the mayor for not disclosing enough information about the financial condition of the municipality.[112] Despite the problems the council voiced, only 262 of 756 registered voters turned out to vote in the recall.[113] Since recalls initiated by local councils do not involve civic campaigns, it is difficult for local residents to gain sufficient information about them. In similar referendums on the recall of the mayor initiated by local councils, such as in the municipalities of Pohorelá in 2004 or Marianka in 2005, not a single one has been successful in reaching the 50% turnout threshold for binding outcomes.

While these cases are only reflective of the Slovak experience with the recall, they do suggest that it would be incorrect to automatically assume that the recall process is detrimental to minorities. In the cases above, Roma communities used the recall process as a tool to empower them *vis-a-vis* local governments that were not responsive to their needs. There is no evidence that the recall has been used to further exclude already marginalized minority groups from local politics. While the recall device is not always effective in bringing about a change in municipal leadership, it can be an important mechanism for minority groups themselves to demand that local government reflects the needs of all of its constituents.

---

111 SME, "V Žehre po hromadnej bitke vládne napätie a obavy," 26. 8.2003; SME, "Zástupcu starostu obvinili z úžerníctva," 30. 8.2003.

112 Korzár, "Referendum rozhodne, či budú v Žehre nové voľby starostu," 5.6.2004.

113 SME, "Referendum v Žehre je neplatné, starostu neodvolali," 8.6.2004.

Democratic Legitimacy: Using the Recall to Restore the Sanctity of Public Office

Recall campaigns often occur in contexts where residents believe that local government has suffered a major decline in its perceived legitimacy, such as through various scandals and perceived abuses of public office. Since it is often the case that there is insufficient evidence to convict a politician for malfeasance or corrupt behavior, the recall process provides a legally recognized and legitimate way for residents to decide themselves, whether the mandates of elected officials continue to hold the public trust. To illustrate the role of the recall in restoring public legitimacy, we will use two in-depth cases that gained nationwide attention in their respective countries: Piwniczna-Zdrój in Poland, and Veľký Meder in Slovakia.

Piwniczna-Zdrój (pop. 10,500) is a Polish mountain spa town near the Slovak border, famous for its mineral water and skiing. While the town was a major ski center in the past, the lack of modern tourist infrastructure and outdated lifts has made it less competitive to more modern ski resorts in southern Poland. The development of a new, modern ski resort on Kicarz mountain close to the town center was one of the main themes of the November 2006 municipal elections. By promising to develop the Kicarz ski area and on the basis of her former status as Vice-President for Social Security (ZUS), Joanna Leśniak won the mayoral election by defeating the incumbent mayor, Edward Bogaczyk, in the second round by a 59% to 41% margin.

Half a year after the elections, however, news broke out that Leśniak was being indicted for criminal charges relating to real estate purchases approved by her in 1998 as Vice-President of Social Security. The prices for those purchases were allegedly overestimated by several million of Polish zlotys.[114] Two years later, the state attorney investigated Leśniak for lack of public supervision. While the case had been in a district court in Łódź, she did not disclose the issue to Piwniczna-Zdrój residents prior to the 2006 mayoral elections, later insisting that she was innocent of any wrongdoing. Once the news of the criminal investigation broke out, local residents initiated a campaign to recall her from office. The main initiator of the campaign proclaimed that "we have been deceived. Never in our lives would we have supported Leśniak if we had known that she is charged with a crime."[115]

In addition to the political scandal, the development of the Kicarz ski area was also in doubt. The previous mayor of the city signed a contract with a de-

---

114 Gazeta Wyborcza Kraków, "Referendum z Kicarzem w tle," 22.5.2008.
115 Gazeta Wyborcza Kraków, "Referendum z Kicarzem w tle," 22.5.2008.

veloper to provide land for the future Kicarz ski area, which also gained the relevant building permits. After the elections, however, that contract was annulled by the local council at the initiative of the new mayor, citing, for example, the need for additional expert assessments about the possibility of landslides and the risks posed to the mineral water under the mountain. According to an interview with one of the campaigners in the recall, the mayor wanted to support another ski resort instead, which would have been further away from the city, and thus less beneficial to it. The mayor was thus in a battle between two competing ski area developments, with many local residents supportive of the Kicarz area that the mayor originally promised.

The campaigners for the recall of the mayor succeeded to collect 1,734 signatures, more than twice the 790 signatures, or 10% of registered voters, that was required by law. One of the people involved in the campaign explained the situation this way:

"Kicarz is a wonderful place, at the centre of Piwniczna, a magnificent mountain and has all necessary conditions for great skiing, such as a terrain sloped to the North. The snow hasn't been melting much and we see a great chance for development for our small town. Second, such investment would boost the local economy, for the private sector as well. More people would come here and we could be better off. That's why we cared. The current mayor promised to accomplish the investment of the ski station, however, after she was elected and appointed, her actions went in the opposite direction – against finishing the ski station project. Further, there was a possibility of getting a grant or subsidy from the European Union but unfortunately she also failed to do it. Thirdly, she lied to us about hiding the criminal action in Łódź against her. She could have told us beforehand, but if she had, I presume she wouldn't have been elected. Therefore, we called for a referendum to recall her from office."

Taking place on May 18, 2008, the recall referendum was successful, with 29.4% of registered voters turning out, the great majority of whom voted in favor of the recall. Regardless of whether the mayor was found guilty or not in the court case against her (she was later acquitted), voters in the recall felt that she deceived them both in the lack of disclosure as well as in going against an electoral promise (the ski resort issue). In the Polish context, the recall device was arguably the only effective mechanism available for residents to restore order to city hall.

Similarly, the case of Veľký Meder in Slovakia can be used to illustrate some of the benefits and limits of the recall process as a tool for dealing with public officials accused of corruption. Veľký Meder lies between Dunajska Streda and Komárno, approximately eight miles from the Hungarian border in western Slovakia. Ethnic Hungarians constitute 85% of the population of 9,113, Slovaks 14%. The city is well known as a tourist destination for its large Thermalpark, which the city developed for about 77 million crowns (about 1.8

million euros) between 2001and 2003.[116] Tourism is in fact the core of the city's economy, employing nearly 1,000 people in a city with an unemployment rate close to 30%.

Given the success of the Thermalpark, the city council wanted to expand its accommodation capacity and agreed to rent a large property next to the thermal bath to a businessperson for a symbolic 1 crown for 50 years, in exchange that the businessperson would develop year-round accommodations for visitors. According to one media report, the developer did not keep the agreement, as he built only a small complex ill-suited for winter use, and never submitted his investment plans to the local council. [117] As a result, the city council declared that it intended to cancel the rental agreement with the developer.

According to numerous media accounts of the events, the developer then visited the mayor, Samuel Lojkovič, who "allegedly promised to the renter that everything can be resolved and promised him that he will try to convince the city council to not cancel the contract. In exchange, the mayor requested from the developer the transfer of some properties to his name. In the end, the mayor demanded cash."[118] The developer then reported the bribe to the Office of the Fight against Corruption, which then organized a police raid. Acting as an *agent provocateur*, which is possible under Slovak law, the developer met the mayor at a restaurant, where the mayor allegedly accepted a bribe of 300,000 crowns (about 7800 euros). The police arrested the mayor on the spot.

Since the mayor was soon indicted on charges of accepting a bribe, it was fitting that he should no longer function as mayor of the city. The city council therefore voted to call a referendum on the recall of the mayor, which was held in November 2005. Well before the recall took place, in January 2005, the Special Court dealing with corruption-related cases reached the verdict that the mayor was guilty of accepting the bribe and sentenced him to 32 months in prison. The mayor appealed the verdict, insisting that the money was not a bribe but rather the payment of a loan that the developer owed him. The recall thus took place in the context of an appealed criminal offence.

In November, 86% of voters voted in favor of recalling the mayor. However, only 13% of the 7,316 registered voters turned out, which meant that the result was non-binding. It may have been the case that residents thought the recall was pointless, since local elections were set to take place a month later. Turnout could have been low also because the recall was based on the initiative of the local council, which usually has less publicity than initiatives based on a citizens' petition. However, in the Slovak local council and mayoral elections

---

116 TASR, „Vo Veľkom Mederi vsadili na kúpeľníctvo," 10.10.2004.

117 TASR, "Primátora Veľkého Medera obvinili z korupcie," 1.4.2005.

118 Pravda, "Svedok oddialil proces s primátorom," 26.11.2005.

of December 2006, Lojkovič was surprisingly re-elected as mayor, receiving a plurality 37% of the vote. He did not serve much of that term, since in February 2007, the High Court confirmed the guilty verdict, thus sending him to 32 months in jail and annulling his mayoral mandate.

The cases of Piwniczna-Zdrój and Veľký Meder raise several important issues regarding the potential of the recall process as a tool for restoring legitimacy to public office. First, legitimacy is very much *perceived*: what matter is whether local residents perceive an abuse of power, not how it is decided in courts. Ironically, in Piwniczna-Zdrój, the recalled mayor was later found to be aquitted of any wrongdoing concerning the property sales, whereas the mayor of Veľký Meder survived the recall vote (even securing re-election) despite being convicted of bribery.

Both cases involved controversies relating to major developments that were of vital interest to the local tourist economy, and both cases involved relatively blatant violations of public trust. Both towns are of similar size, and both are located in marginalized border areas. Despite these similarities, the opposite outcomes of the two recalls could have been due to different institutional features. The recall campaign in Piwniczna-Zdrój was organized by a local entrepreneur and seemed to have received substantial publicity; the recall in Veľký Meder was decided by the local council without prior initiative of local residents. In terms of the turnout quorum, while the recall in Piwniczna-Zdrój was valid under Polish law, it would have been invalid under the 50% quorum rule required for Veľký Meder and other Slovak municipalities. The recall in Piwniczna-Zdrój took place in the middle of the electoral term, whereas in Veľký Meder it took place just before the mayoral election, which could have influenced turnout. The mayor of Veľký Meder also could have lost the subsequent mayoral election had Slovak law required an absolute majority via a second run-off election, as is the case in Polish mayoral contests.

The two contrasting cases illustrate the importance of the recall process when local government faces a crisis of legitimacy. But since legitimacy is itself perceived, residents may not always vote in ways consistent with court rulings, established facts, or other judgments from the outside. Differing institutional contexts can also shape residents' behavior in the recall process. This does not mean that the recall is not a useful tool for restoring public legitimacy, but it does suggest that recall outcomes and whether public legitimacy is indeed in crisis depend very much on local conditions and context.

Effectiveness: Using the Recall to Achieve Policies in the Public Good

Another important tool for evaluating participatory institutions is their effectiveness in achieving policies that are seen as reflecting the common good. Though the recall process involves decision-making about an elected official rather than a public policy, controversies about public policies are often in the background (and motivate) recall campaigns. The recall process can be an effective tool for decision-making by helping resolve policy debates in a sharply divided community by holding a 'referendum' on the official most responsible for the policy; it can also be used to oust officials from power who seem to pursue special interests as opposed to collective goals. To illustrate the role of the recall in helping achieve effective policies (or reversing ill-suited ones), we will focus on two case studies, one from the small Slovak village of Čakany, the other from the Polish city of Łopuszno.

Čakany is a small village with only 555 residents in the Trnava region of south-central Slovakia. As with many other Slovak recall cases, the village has a majority ethnic Hungarian population. Ethnic cleavages, however, seemed to have played a minor role in the case, since the main actors involved were all ethnic Hungarian. In the 2006 municipal elections, the incumbent mayor of Čakany, Dezider Kiss (independent), won the election over his closest rival, Lívia Bugárová (also independent), by a slim 127 to 125 margin. The village was under-developed in ways typical for its area, i.e. lacked natural gas, sewage, and a self-sustaining economic base.

The recall campaign in Čakany has its roots in a controversy surrounding the opening of a gravel quarry in the municipality. In March 2005, the local council voted in favor of a 5 hectare quarry, intended to spur local jobs. The investor stated that "water gravel mining will take place for a period of about 17 years and will lead to the creation of two new 5 hectare bodies of water."[119] However, later in 2006 the company submitted a second investment plan to enlarge the quarry's operation to 39 years and to create an additional 23 hectare body of water.[120] The two investments would thus lead to water pools 33 hectares large, whereas the local council only approved of the roughly 10 acre quarry. According to one politician interviewed, during a public hearing in late

---

119 EIA documentation of the development project "Čakany: Water gravel mining in a mineral quarry" by the GRAVEL Land Company. The documentation is available online at http://eia.enviroportal.sk/detail/cakany:-vodna-tazba-strkopieskov-na-lozisku-nevyhradeneho-nerastu (accessed 1.9.2008).

120 Ibid.

2006 in which about 100 local citizens attended, the mayor was not able to explain the change in the size of the quarry. The project was also criticized by local residents because the quarry would probably employ only 7 people and would not provide other benefits to the local government (such as the possibility of profit-sharing). Of course, the quarry would also have significant environmental impacts, such as in terms of transport by large trucks, and risks associated with water contamination. Because the controversy was still not widely known by the December 2006 local elections, the mayor was re-elected, though narrowly, to his fourth consecutive term in office.

In March 2007, only three months after the elections, local residents submitted a petition signed by 360 people (i.e. the majority of the village) and asked the mayor to resign. When he refused to do so, a second petition, with 260 signatures, was then submitted for the purpose of recalling the mayor. According to one local councilor, the mayor refused to call a meeting of the local council (which would vote on the recall) for two months. Council members upset that the mayor "without the knowledge of the local council agreed to the enlargement of the gravel quarry in the municipality"[121] voted in favor of calling the recall referendum, which was held in May 2007. Of the 461 registered voters in the municipality, 369 voted in the recall, with 242 voting in favor. In October 2007, new elections were held, in which Lívia Bugárová, who was a critic of the mayor, won with 266 votes, over twice her closest competitor. The new leadership of the village then sought to reverse the decision of the Mining Office (which had previously approved the expanded quarry), which it succeeded to do. The village submitted a complaint at the office of attorney general, which declared the enlargement of the quarry as invalid.

While the issue of concern in Čakany was sustainable local development, in Łopuszno it was the future of local schools. In rural Polish communities the cost of managing preschools, primary and lower secondary schools often reach half of the budget of a municipality, which is responsible for running them. While preschool education is financed through a municipality's own revenues, primary and lower secondary education are financed from a general-purpose grant, called an education subvention, from the central government.[122] The amount of the subvention is based on the weighted number of students in the municipality. However, Swianiewicz and Herbst (2002) found that municipalities' expenditure on education exceeded the received subvention by 20%,

---

121 Pravda, "Takmer tridsať starostov už dovládlo," 1.12.2007.

122 Local governments are responsible for managing lower secondary schools (gimnazjum), but not upper secondary schools offering a general instruction (liceum) or vocational schools (technikum, zasadnicza szko³a zawodowa), which are the responsibility of counties [powiaty].

meaning that local governments were subsidizing schools. Per-student costs in rural communities are 30% higher than in cities because of the small size of schools and classes, which increase the share of fixed costs in total expenditures (an average primary school in a rural community has only 148 students, compared to 540 in cities). When coupled with rural communities' much lower own per capita revenues, these costs create an unsustainable situation for municipal finances and can lead to lower quality of educational instruction (ibid). For many municipalities, the only way out of the problem is to close down schools with too few students and to consolidate schools so that the number of pupils per school and classroom are higher.

The problem of the efficiency of public schools was particularly ominous in Łopuszno, which has seen its enrollment in basic schools decline from 1,344 in 1998 to 717 in 2007.[123] The municipality of Łopuszno also encompasses 30 different rural settlements, some of which had their own basic schools. After the November 2006 municipal elections, the mayor and local council of Łopuszno agreed to close down four small rural schools, including a grammar school (Gimnazjum). The 126 pupils of that school were to join the 593 pupils attending another grammar school just several hundred meters away.[124] According to one local politician interviewed, school closures were necessary because of population decline and projected declines in enrolment, dropping from 1,200 pupils in 2007 in both the basic schools and gymnasia to about 860 pupils in 2012. In his view, "the closed-down schools have been defended but, in most cases, their students are now going to well-equipped and nice schools – who are brought there by school buses with drivers and assistants – and do not want to go back to those old, neglected, and under-equipped schools. For sure, children from Snochovice [a settlement in Łopuszno where a school was closed] would not like that."

However, in addition to those school closings, in February 2008 the local council also agreed to close down 5 additional basic schools in rural settlements, affecting over 200 pupils.[125] Those school closures, in addition to the four previously announced, would leave only one grammar school and two large basic schools left in the municipality. According to one interviewee, the smaller number of schools would also enable the municipality to cope in spite of the lower subvention levels that it expects to receive in future years.

---

123 According to the educational statistics of the Regional Data bank of the Central Statistical Office of Poland.

124 Data on individual schools in Łopuszno are from the municipality's website at http://www.lopuszno.pl/index.php?option=18&action=articles_show&art_id=341& menu_id (accessed 5.11.08).

125 Gazeta Wyborcza Kielce, "Wójt Łopuszna też likwiduje szkoły," 18.2.2008.

That decision led to public outrage. At the local council meeting in February 2008 where the school closures were announced, a police officer had to maintain order due to the angry comments by roughly 100 parents and teachers present at the meeting.[126] While the mayor claimed that the municipality wasted 12 million PLZ in additional funding to those schools over the years, parents complained that the mayor thinks only about economics and not the quality of education or about how early children need to get up to go to school. To one participant, "how can we be so heartless? A school is the heart of the village, the most important place. We are making a kilometre of road instead of this?" referring to the mayor's priority of investing more funds in road infrastructure rather than education. Another resident joined that assessment, asking "The well-being of children does not count? A hole in the road is more important than children?" (ibid).

To prevent the school closures, local residents organized a recall campaign, with the recall vote set for May 2008. Despite the controversy, only 19.3% of registered voters in Łopuszno showed up at the polls, making the recall referendum for both the mayor and the local council invalid. A similar recall referendum in the nearby rural gmina of Nowy Korczyn,[127] which was also provoked by school closures, also had a low turnout (26.9%), making that result invalid as well. School-related referendums in Hungary and the Czech Republic – which have also been provoked by the same types of school closures – have characteristically low turnout, possibly because only a minority of residents (i.e. parents of small children) have an affected interest in the issue (M. Smith 2007).

In Łopuszno, it could have been the case that many local residents supported consolidating the schools, even if they were not active in expressing their views. The educational statistics for the municipality do indicate that the costs of running the schools were getting out of control. Annual primary school expenditures per enrolled pupil quadrupled in the decade up to 2006, reaching over half the municipal budget. By 2006, total basic school enrollment averaged only 14 pupils per classroom. Since the school closures began, educational costs have been reduced to 42% of the municipal budget in 2008, with pupils per classroom increasing to 19.4.[128]

---

126 Gazeta Wyborcza Kielce, "Protesty na sesji. Radni zlikwidowali pięć szkół." 20.2.2008.

127 Gazeta Wyborcza Kielce, "Podwójne referenda w Łopusznie i Nowym Korczynie," 8.4.2008.

128 Data is from the Regional Statistics Database, available online at the Central Statistical Office of Poland.

The cases of Čakany and Łopuszno, while different in many respects, suggest that the recall process can be a useful tool for reversing local policies that blatantly go against public interests. In Čakany, the politician who supported the expansion of the quarry, but without apparently first consulting the local council or residents, was recalled by an overwhelming majority. The new political leadership, which was critical of the quarry plans, was thus able to act quickly to have the relevant contracts and decisions annulled. In the absence of the recall process, the local community would not have had any other way to effectively bring about policy change.

While the majority of Čakany residents believed that the quarry expansion was not in the public interest, the same can not be said of the school closures in Łopuszno. In that case, the community was likely divided, with reasonable arguments on both side of the debate. While many residents clearly opposed the school closures, it cannot be said that the mayor and local council engaged in gross negligence or mismanagement. They rather based decisions on declining enrollment trends, rising education costs, and too few students per class. The mayor and local council has a different, perhaps equally merited, vision of the public good as did the teachers and parents. Given the complexity of the issue and that the 'public good' was less clear cut, it is not surprising that the recall vote did not achieve sufficient turnout. In that sense, reasonable turnout quorums can play a major role in annulling recall votes that garner less public interest, while also enabling the recall to remain an effective tool for reversing policies going against quite blatant cases of the public good.

Conclusion

This chapter examined the recall process as a democratic innovation that has been enshrined in legislation in two new post-communist democracies, Poland and Slovakia. The chapter sought to overview and evaluate the use of the recall at the local level by examining four key criteria that democratic innovations typically try to achieve: effective participation, inclusive participation, democratic legitimacy, and effective decision-making.

Compared to other participatory devices that are consultative in nature, the recall process can be a powerful tool for effective participation precisely due to its binding outcomes. In the context of the recall, effectiveness can also refer to the likelihood with which citizens can successfully initiate and carry out a recall campaign. That likelihood is very much conditioned by the signature gathering conditions as well as the turnout quorum. While high quorums lead to less effective participation, this should not imply that it would be ideal to have no quorums at all, since quorums can also prevent recalls from being successful if backed by only a small segment of the local population. Quorum design is also an important consideration, since fixed quorum levels (as in Slovakia) can disadvantage cities, while relative quorum levels (as in Poland) seem to provide a more level playing field for all types of local government.

It is often believed that direct democracy can lead to exclusionary politics, due to perceived lack of safeguards ensuring minority rights. This chapter has argued that such perceptions are out of place, because citizens enjoy the same constitutional protections regardless of the form of political decision-making used. Further, in the countries considered, there is little evidence that the recall process has been used to infringe upon minority rights or interests. Quite on the contrary, the chapter has found that recall use is quite common in Slovak communities that are poor, marginalized and have large minority populations, who often make use of the recall themselves. In such communities, politics can be very personal and problems difficult to solve. While the recall process is hardly the solution to all of a community's ills, it can be an important tool for inclusive participation by providing an additional mechanism for different segments of society to articulate their interests.

The recall process furthers democratic legitimacy in two ways. First, because the recall is legislatively enshrined, it is itself a legitimate mechanism in bringing about political change. In any of the interviews conducted, no respondent questioned the legitimacy of the recall process as a fair and appropriate mechanism of decision-making. Second, the recall process can also help to restore legitimacy to public office in the face of gross violations of moral conduct, such as those evidenced in the Piwniczna-Zdrój and Veľký Meder cases. The outcome of those recalls reminds us that legitimacy is always perceived, and recall outcomes can be substantially conditioned by institutional conditions. Even if the recall can have a positive impact on the public legitimacy of elected officials, it cannot be considered an objective anti-corruption device in its own right.

Lastly, the recall can serve to further effective decision-making by bringing elected officials to account who pursue policies strongly against public interests, as was indicated in the Čakany case. However, in less extreme situations, as was the case in Łopuszno, visions of the public good often depend on one's social position and perceptions of local interests. While there were many other differences between the cases, and it is thus difficult to infer much about them, it seems to be the case that the recall is most effective in helping resolve extreme and highly divisive situations in a transparent, inclusive and legitimate manner.

References

Altman, David. 2005. "Democracia Directa en el Continente Americano: ¿Auto-Legitimación Gubernamental o Censura Ciudadana?" *Política y Gobierno* 12 (2): 203-232.

Alvarez, R. Michael, D. Roderick Kiewiet & Betsy Sinclair. 2006. "Rational Voters and the Recall Election." Pp. 87-97 in Shaun Bowler and Bruce E. Cain (eds.), *Clicker Politics: Essays on the California Recall*. Upper Saddle River, N.J.: Prentice Hall.

Bowler, Shaun, Todd Donovan& Jeffrey A. Carp. 2007. "Enraged or Engaged? Preferences for Direct Citizen Participation in Affluent Democracies." *Political Research Quarterly* 60 (3): 351-362.

Bowler, Shaun & Bruce E. Cain. 2006. "Introduction." Pp. 1-16 in Shaun Bowler and Bruce E. Cain (eds.), *Clicker Politics: Essays on the California Recall*. Upper Saddle River, N.J.: Prentice Hall.

Cain, Bruce E., Melissa Cully Anderson & Annette K. Eaton. 2006. "Barriers to Recalling Elected Officials: A Cross-State Analysis of the Incidence and Success of Recall Petitions." Pp. 17-33 in Shaun Bowler and Bruce E. Cain (eds.), *Clicker Politics: Essays on the California Recall*. Upper Saddle River, N.J.: Prentice Hall.

Center for Responsive Government. 1992. *Democracy by Initiative: Shaping California's Branch of Government*. Los Angeles: California Commission on Campaign Financing, Center for Responsive Government.

Council of Europe. 2000. *Participation of Citizens in Local Public Life*. Report by the Steering Committee on Local and Regional Democracy. Strasbourg: Council of Europe.

Cressman, Derek D. 2007. The Recall's Broken Promise: How Big Money Still Runs California Politics. Sacramento: The Poplar Institute.

Cronin, Thomas. 1989. Direct Democracy: The Politics of Initiative, Referendum and Recall. Cambridge: Harvard University Press.

Domański, Jarosław. 2009. "Strategic Group Analysis of Poland's Nonprofit Organizations." *Nonprofit and Voluntary Sector Quarterly*, publication date pending (available online).

Fung, Archon & Erik Olin Wright. 2001. "Deepening Democracy: Innovations in Empowered Participatory Governance." *Politics and Society* 29 (1) 5-41.

Gajdoš, Peter. 2005. "Marginal regions in Slovakia and their developmental disposabilities." *Agricultural Economics* 51 (12): 555–563.

Hajnal, Zoltan & Hugh Louch. 2001. *Are There Winners and Losers? Race, Ethnicity and California's Initiative Process*. Sacramento: Public Policy Institute of California.

IDEA. 2008. *Direct Democracy: The International IDEA Handbook*. Stockholm: International Institute for Democracy and Electoral Assistance.

Lástič, Erik. 2005. *Inštitút referenda v ústavnom systéme SR*. Bratislava: Ústav štátu a práva SAV.

Lástič, Erik. 2007. "Referendum Experience in Slovakia: A Long and Winding Road." Pp. 189-199 in Z. Pállinger, B. Kaufmann, W. Marxer and T. Schiller (eds.), *Direct Democracy in Europe: Developments and Prospects*. Wiesbaden: VS Verlag fur Sozialwissenschaften.

Lástič, Erik. 2011. "Slovakia – Restricted Direct Democracy in Local Politics." Pp. 237-244 in T. Schiller (ed.), *Local Direct Democracy in Europe*. Wiesbaden: VS Verlag für Sozialwissenschaften.

Mixon, Franklin G. 2000. "The Control of Politicians with a Constitutional Framework: The Case of State-Level Recall Provisions." *Applied Economics* 32 (1): 81-89.

Olejniczak-Szałowska, Ewa. 2002. Referendum lokalne w świetle ustawodawstwa polskiego. Warsawa: Difin.

Piasecki, Andrzej. 2005. *Referenda w III RP*. Warsawa: Wydawnictwo naukowe PWN.
Piasecki, Andrzej. 2011. "Twenty Years of Polish Direct Democracy at the Local Level." Pp. 126-137 in T. Schiller (ed.), *Local Direct Democracy in Europe*. Wiesbaden: VS Verlag für Sozialwissenschaften.
Rose-Ackerman, Susan. 2007. "From Elections to Democracy in Central Europe: Public Participation and the Role of Civil Society." *East European Politics & Societies* 21 (1): 31-47.
Segura, Gary M. & Luis R. Fraga. 2008. "Race and the Recall: Racial and Ethnic Polarization in the California Recall Election." *American Journal of Political Science* 52 (2): 421-435.
Schrag, Peter. 1998. *Paradise Lost: California's Experience, America's Future*. Berkeley: University of California Press.
Shaw, Daron; Mark J. McKenzie & Jeffrey Underwood. 2005. "Strategic Voting in the California Recall Election." *American Politics Research* 33 (2): 216-245.
Smith, Graham. 2009. Democratic Innovations: Designing Institutions for Citizen Participation. Cambridge: Cambridge University Press.
Smith, Michael L. 2007. "Making Direct Democracy Work: Czech Local Referendums in Regional Comparison." In H. Reynaert, K. Steyvers, P. Delwit, and J.-B. Pilet (eds.), *Towards DYI Politics? Participatory and Direct Democracy at the Local Level in Europe*. Brussels: Vanden Broele Publishers.
Smith, Michael L. 2009. Občané v politice: Studie k participativní a přímé demokracii ve střední Evropě. Prague: Institute for Social and Economic Analyses.
Smith, Michael L. 2011. "The Uneasy Balance Between Participation and Representation: Local Direct Democracy in the Czech Republic." Pp. 33-53 in T. Schiller (ed.), *Local Direct Democracy in Europe*. Wiesbaden: VS Verlag für Sozialwissenschaften.
Swianiewicz, Paweł & Mikołaj J. Herbst. 2002. "Economies and diseconomies of scale in Polish local governments." Pp. 223-292 in Paweł Swianiewicz (ed.), *Consolidation or Fragmentation? The Size of Local Governments in Central and Eastern Europe*. Budapest: Open Society Institute.
Walter-Rogg, Melanie & Oscar W. Gabriel. 2007. "Direct Democracy at the Local Level in Germany." In H. Reynaert, K. Steyvers, P. Delwit, and J.-B. Pilet (eds.), *Towards DYI Politics? Participatory and Direct Democracy at the Local Level in Europe*. Brussels: Vanden Broele Publishers.
Warren, Mark E. 2006. "A Second Transformation of Democracy." Pp. 223-249 in Bruce E. Cain, Russell J. Dalton, and Susan E. Scarrow (eds.), *Democracy Transformed? Expanding Political Opportunities in Advanced Industrial Democracies*. Oxford: Oxford University Press.
Wollmann, Hellmut & Tomila Lankina. 2003. "Local Government in Poland and Hungary: From Post-Communist Reform Towards EU Accession." Pp 91-122 in Harold Baldersheim, Michal Illner and Hellmut Wollmann (eds.), *Local Democracy in Post-Communist Europe*. Opladen: Leske & Budrich.

Qualities of E-Democracy: Examples from Sweden

Gustav Lidén

Introduction

One of the themes of this book, the flaws of modern liberal democracy, is a topic that has been approached from very different angles. On a theoretical level, scholars representing different disciplines show great interest in discussing these problems and how they could be minimized. Technological innovations (e.g. Barber 2003; Rheingold 1993; Noveck 2009) are often brought up as one possible solution for strengthening liberal democracy. There is a long history of launching technological remedies for imperfections in prevailing societies. The influence of innovations such as radio and television on political systems is hard to exaggerate. They have created additional ways of linking politicians to their voters, and could increase both the amount of politically relevant information available and the extent of accountability.

It is common to argue that in many ways the most recent technological change is the most paradigmatic one, especially because of its potential to be inclusive and far-reaching. As Castells (2001, p.2) puts it: 'The Internet is a communication medium that allows, for the first time, the communication of many to many, in chosen time, on a global scale.' In just a few decades, information and communication technologies (ICTs) have dramatically changed the conditions for society in general and its political aspects, too. New concepts have been created using the prefix *e*, meaning electronic, and by combining this with political keywords such as democracy, participation and government additional applications of political processes as well as new fields of research have been created.

From a political perspective, the introduction of ICTs has resulted in many new questions and concepts. What will the future effects be of a liberal democracy that is embedded in a new technological landscape? How does this technology affect political processes or the administration of the political systems? Can e-democracy be regarded as a democratic innovation? This chapter specifically focuses on what the qualities of e-democracy could consist of and how these qualities could affect the political dimension of society. To examine this issue, e-democracy will be studied from a broad theoretical perspective, although the empirical context will be Swedish throughout. It is possible to understand the character of e-democracy by studying how Swedish municipalities work with it. In addition, analyzing material from a Swedish survey about the population's internet habits makes it possible to study variation in individuals' participation in e-democratic activities. All in all, this gives us the opportunity to examine issues of bias and potentially establish what types of bias exist in the ways in which e-democracy is used. This examination can be considered from both a supply and a demand perspective, which is important for assessing the qualities of e-democracy and evaluating its potential impact. More specifically, the supply side refers to the opportunities for e-democracy, and thus is about maintaining the channels that are preconditions for citizens' use of public e-democratic functions. The demand perspective focuses on individuals' actual use of e-democratic functions, that is, their demand for e-democracy. The nature of these conditions emphasizes that e-democracy is not a homogeneous political concept, and this is a challenge that requires precise analytical distinctions. Moreover, this material is complemented with a causal description of an e-democratic development project in one Swedish municipality. This permits us to reconstruct an example of an e-democratic development process as well as study the effects of e-democracy in relation to e-democratic qualities. The quality of the empirical material that these three examples reflect will be analysed in accordance with the framework outlined by Brigitte Geissel in the introduction of this book.

This chapter begins with a discussion of e-democracy. A historical description of its development is complemented with different theoretical perspectives on it, matched with a definition. Following this, the theoretical dimensions of e-democracy and its qualities will be discussed with the help of contributions from contemporary research. The empirical examples are then presented and finally, an analytical discussion of the qualities of e-democracy sums up the chapter.

The Development and Definition of E-Democracy

The advance of e-democracy must be studied in relation to the development of ICTs. As thoroughly proven by Castells (1996), three innovations have been crucial in this respect: microelectronics, the computer and telecommunication. Deriving from these technological landmarks, Vedel (2006) has identified three phases in the history of e-democracy. The first occurred as long ago as the 1950s and emerged in relation to the field of cybernetics. Through the introduction of early computers and their capacity to process large amounts of information, conclusions were made about technology as a means of increasing rationality in decision-making (Deutsch 1966). However, this approach was strongly criticized and more or less dissolved. The second phase of e-democracy had more of a citizen's perspective. It emerged during the 1970s and 1980s through the introduction of cable TV networks and private computers. As argued by Dutton (1992), research during this phase was unfortunately mostly ignored in political science, which is partly explained by a general scepticism about the actual impact of the technologies on representative democracy. The most recent phase in history is also the one which is most strongly associated with today's use of e-democracy. Through the internet, a widespread new medium has been established that, among other fields of application, has been used to spread political information and to make political deliberation possible.

To examine the potential impact that e-democracy can have on the political processes in a democratic society, a discussion of some of the particular characteristics of political processes online is required. Hindman (2009) points out an often ignored fact, namely that there is a difference between being able to speak and being heard. His statement does not exclude arenas on the internet. Statistics relating to internet traffic show that top political bloggers in the US represent a political elite which is similar in many ways to other privileged groups in society. That blogs, then, could be a method for guaranteeing that the ordinary citizen's voice on politics is heard is perhaps true, but since attention is drawn to only a few popular bloggers the actual impact is concentrated on these. Other inquiries add another dimension to this issue by stating that readers of political blogs also represent a politically active elite (Gil de Zúñiga et al. 2010). However, more positive claims are also included in the debate. One notion is that the rapid development of the internet, referred to as a vision of Web 2.0 where there is a higher degree of interaction associated with applications such as blogs, wikis and social networking systems, could change online politics, and therefore the internet could become more important in communication on political subjects (Breindl & Francq 2008). Other positive views are reported about the use of online discussion groups (Wojcieszak & Mutz 2009). Not surprisingly, American survey data show that engaging in political discussions online is not among the top internet activities. It is quite interesting, though, that political discussions can arise in many types of discussion groups, not just in explicitly political ones. The best quality deliberations are during discussions in which political subjects come up incidentally without being the central theme of the group. Contrary to debates that specifically political discussion groups engage in, where political opinions are both homogeneous and quite fixed, these discussions are characterized by conflicting opinions and reflexivity, which can strengthen the quality of the discussion. Proponents of e-democracy state that the strengthened opportunities to participate, made possible by ICTs lowering the barriers to inclusion and increasing the convenience of participation, have the potential to revitalize democracy (Ward & Vedel 2006). Not everyone agrees with such a statement; Levine (2002, p.124), for example, argues that 'Long before we had personal computers in our homes, there was already far too much information at the local library and newsstands for us.' A brief review of contemporary research about the actual impacts of e-democracy shows that different and sometimes opposite positions are taken.

Initially, e-democracy was closely related to the existence of electronic voting. Such a definition is, of course, too restricted since it excludes several of the political processes that are influenced by ICTs. Several attempts have been made to deal with this constraint. Hacker and van Dijk (2000, p.1) stress that the concept of e-democracy is not restricted to any particular function:

"... a collection of attempts to practise democracy without the limits of time, space and other physical conditions, using ICT [information and communication technology] or CMC [computer-mediated communication] instead, as an addition, not a replacement for traditional 'analogue' political practices."

This is a democracy that is performed through a technology which is not necessarily limited in terms of time and space, so it raises important questions about the spatial and temporal dynamic of e-democracy. Similar opinions have been presented by others (e.g. Macintosh 2004). In addition, e-democracy must be embedded in liberal democratic values. With some exceptions (Macintosh et al. 2009; Norris 2001; Schuler 1998), this idea has not been explicitly presented in earlier research. Schuler's (1998) way of deriving from Dahl's (1989) criteria of democracy and applying them to e-democracy is of particular interest. His inventory is quite discouraging since, among other things, it states that participation in e-democracy is unevenly distributed and that the internet is dominated by commercial interests that have a mandate for agenda-setting. This raises the somewhat contradictory question of how e-democracy can be more democratic (e.g. Lidén 2012). As argued elsewhere (Lidén 2011), a valid definition of e-democracy should take the above statement into account and at the same time make it clear that this phenomenon is not a dichotomy that either exists or does not exist but rather is something that can vary in its extent.

Therefore, and in line with earlier research (Hacker & van Dijk 2000; Vedel 2006), the term e-democracy which is used in this chapter will mean *the use of information and communication technologies in political processes concerning information, discussion and decision-making that are permeated by the political and civil rights that are characterized as democratic.*

Theoretical Perspectives on E-Democracy and its Qualities

Although the increasing use of ICTs in politics could have the power to revitalize democracy, this optimistic view has been questioned. As stated elsewhere in this book, innovations such as e-democracy should be considered in terms of their ability to strengthen the quality of democracy. There are frequent discussions in the literature relating to e-democracy about how inclusive political processes carried out through ICTs are. These are often addressed from the perspective of a digital divide, namely the issue of inequality in both access to technology and to information (Selwyn 2004). This phenomenon is, however, rather indistinct and the foundation for different types of discussions. As pointed out by Rose (2005), there are at least two dimensions of a digital divide, namely differences between societies and differences within them. Another duality in this concept is discussed by Min (2010), who argues that there is a considerable disparity between having physical access to the internet and having the ability to or enough interest to actually use it for political purposes. Many researchers have proved that inequalities exist within these different dimensions, but of special interest for political scientists is the impact that these inequalities will have on democracy. In the words of Taewoo Nam (2011, p.131), '...the degree of the digital divide predetermines the extent to which ICTs enhance participatory democracy via the Internet.' This means that there is a risk of actually developing a democratic divide (cf. Norris 2001, pp.235–240) where the participation in e-democratic processes is at least as skewed as it is in traditional political participation. Obviously, this development of e-democracy would not be one of the desired qualities. As noted, there is a lot of research supporting Nam's statement. Among some of the recent studies, Sylvester and McGlynn (2010) find that age, the frequency of home internet use and the use of information in newspapers all positively affect using email for contacting officials. When examining political activity on social networking sites, Nam (2011) finds other patterns of inequality that are positively related to a civic and political interest and negatively related to age. It can therefore be assumed that there is a type of bias inherent in e-democracy, and that this means that it does not supply us with a form of participation that is always inclusive or equal. As stated previously, this could affect the impact of e-democracy.

It can still be argued, however, that e-democracy is a multifaceted concept that can also be approached from an aggregated level. In doing this, it is to be expected that there is a variation in societies' achievements in terms of e-democracy, but systematizations of the factors that could help us to understand such variation are rare. One significant exception is Norris's (2001) theoretically and empirically valuable contribution. Norris identifies three broader categories of theories which can contribute to the understanding of e-democracy, and which are grounded in relevant democratic as well as technological theory. Development theories have an economic focus and state that structural changes in societies' economies result in social and political changes. Bell's (1973) paradigmatic description of the emergence of a post-industrial society is intimately related to the information technology that today's knowledge economies are dependent on. The characteristics of a post-industrial society can be crucial as factors that explain e-democracy. More specifically, an advanced and knowledge-based economy, driven by a well-educated workforce, especially when it comes to computing and internet skills, is said to be a determinant of e-democracy. From the viewpoint of technical determinism (Smith & Marx

1994), an alternative explanation is presented. Clearly, e-democracy is dependent on the right technological conditions, but whether isolated societal or technological factors are the most important determinants is an empirical question. Technological theories state that the technological infrastructure is the single most important factor for e-democracy, irrespective of the existence of a knowledge economy and socioeconomic development. Finally, Norris discusses theories of democratization as an alternative way of assessing e-democracy. Claiming that virtual politics will mirror the traditional political system, she reveals how the use of democracy can be seen as a factor explaining e-democracy but also, more indirectly, how the use of the extensive alternative theories that explain democracy can be seen (e.g. Sørensen 2008; Huntington 1991).

Continuing with Norris's empirical examination (Norris 2001, chap. 6–9), the three theories presented above are tested on countries' supply of different e-democratic functions. Beginning with government websites, Norris shows that it is the technological dimension that co-varies with the extent and qualities of these, controlling throughout for the other two theories. Continuing with the national parliamentary websites, Norris finds that both technology and the level of democracy are significant variables in explaining the supply of e-democracy. In relation to the communicative qualities of the parliamentary websites, socioeconomic development joins these two factors as significant. Turning to countries' virtual party structure, the technological dimensions are again the most essential, together with socioeconomic conditions, which also prove to be significant in some of the analyses. Finally, Norris also clarifies that technological development is important for the number of online newspapers in the world's nations. Summing up, technological conditions seem to be most important in explanations of different dimensions of the supply of e-democracy, although both the level of democracy and socioeconomic development can be relevant in some specific situations. Other examinations of e-democracy support the importance of development theories (Lee et al. 2011; Medaglia 2007) and technological theory (van der Graft & Svensson 2006), while the importance of democratization shows more ambiguous results (Lidén 2011). Together these factors should be of interest for researchers of e-democracy, additionally so since they could, in a second phase, potentially influence the quality of e-democracy.

E-Democracy In Sweden: Supply and Demand

In this chapter, e-democracy will be examined in relation to two different approaches. First, societies' supply of e-democracy will be presented. Second, individuals' activity through e-democratic functions will be presented.

Throughout this inquiry, the context is the situation in Sweden. All in all, this approach will make it possible to analyse the qualities of e-democracy on the basis of the categories put forward by Geissel in the introduction.

Supply

In order to approach e-democracy from the perspectives of both supply and demand, a multifaceted presentation of data is required. As argued by Rose (2005), this means that an important distinction must be made in relation to the explanatory factors of e-democracy. From a governmental or supply perspective, e-democracy is about the extent to which the political systems enforce a possibility of providing information and dialogue between officials and citizens using ICTs. As stated by Norris (2001), if this is achieved then several factors have been potential influences. Medaglia (2007, p.276) has shown that in relation to the development and modernization of societies a positive link exists between a local supply of e-democracy and wealth. Moreover, technological theories have been verified as important by van der Graft and Svensson (2006, p.132), who argue that the presence of the right technology positively influences the development of e-democracy. Finally, and in contrast, the importance of democratization shows more ambiguous results (Lidén 2011, p.206; van der Graft & Svensson 2006, p.132; Lee et al. 2011). More concretely, e-democracy has been regarded as both a means of promoting democracy in societies with a democratic deficit but also as a method for strengthening already highly democratic societies and increasing democratic quality. In addition to Norris's proposed theories, the importance of size has also long been emphasized both in democratic theory (Dahl & Tufte 1973) and in the explanations of e-democracy (Medaglia 2007, p.275; Saglie & Vabo 2009, pp.393–394; Wohlers 2009, p.117; Lee et al. 2011).

In Figure 11.1, a map of Sweden is presented. The local level of e-democracy throughout the 290 Swedish municipalities appears in Figure 11.1. The level of e-democracy is measured by examining the occurrence of functions concerning information and discussions on municipalities' websites and calculating these as an index ranging from 0 (low e-democracy) to 14 (high e-democracy).[129] Separating the index's underlying categorization of information and discussion shows that Swedish municipalities are, in general, more successful in supplying their citizens with relevant information than in allowing

---

129 Examples of such functions: Is the budget presented on the website?; Are there protocols from council meetings on the website?; and, Is a debate forum present on the website? The data reflects information from 2007 to 2009. See Lidén (2011) for details about this index and for references to the original data sources.

processes of discussion. One such example is that only about one quarter of the municipalities in 2008 had a discussion forum on the internet. All in all, this index is a way to measure the local form of e-democracy and the level of it that ordinary citizens meet in their respective municipalities.

As the map indicates, no municipality has a lower level of e-democracy than the value of 1.0 and the maximum level is 13.5. When considering the spatial distribution of municipalities with high and low levels of e-democracy respectively, it is hard to find any pattern that, for example, is based on the distinction between municipalities in the North and in the South or in coastal or inland areas. The explanation for this variation must thus be found elsewhere.

In Table 11.1, some of the assumed explanations of e-democracy are tested against an ordinal categorization of municipalities' level of e-democracy as low, intermediate or high.[130] Some clear and significant patterns are reported. First, more populated municipalities clearly seem to be providing their citizens with higher levels of e-democracy. This tendency is difficult to ignore and shows particular relevance for the municipalities with very high levels of e-democracy in which the population size is generally above 60,000 inhabitants. The average value for all the 290 municipalities is about half of this. Second, the share of the population with a post-secondary education also positively varies with the municipalities' level of e-democracy. To translate the information given in the table into words, the higher the level of e-democracy, the more educated the citizens are, and vice versa.

In line with earlier studies, both population size and welfare variables such as education have also proved to be important in the Swedish case. This indicates a bias in citizens' opportunities for using public e-democratic functions, and such inequalities should be taken into account when evaluating the qualities of e-democracy.

---

130 The quantitative variable was divided into three categories: low level of e-democracy (0–6), intermediate level of e-democracy (6.5–8.5) and high level of e-democracy (9–14). Care was taken to get three comparable groups consisting of approximately the same number of municipalities. See Lidén (2011) for details about the data.

Figure 11.1 Variations in E-Democracy Among Municipalities in Sweden, 2007-2009

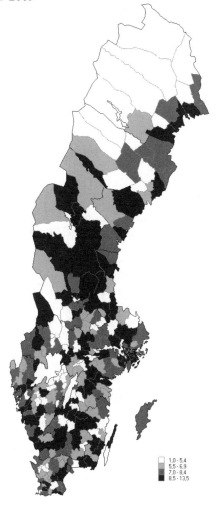

Table 11.1 Examining Assumed Explanations of E-Democracy

	Level of e-democracy		
	Low	Intermediate	High
Population size	12,516	28,365	63,286
Share of population with post-secondary education (%)	13.2	17.0	19.1

Source: See Lidén (2011) for details about the data.

Demand

The opposite dimension of e-democracy is the demand for it. If e-democracy really should strengthen representative democracy, it should not only increase the number of channels for political communication but also enhance inclusiveness and equality and create democratic processes of a higher quality. There are different opinions about how ICTs can influence civic and political engagement. Among these, two dominating positions can be discerned. The first is the argument that ICTs will be harmful to such engagement, since they constitute a multichannel medium mainly focusing on spreading entertainment that will compete with civic and political activities (Putnam 2000). The second position expects positive outcomes from the use of ICTs but can be divided into two different perspectives concerning the distribution of these effects. The first view is that technology will merely strengthen participation among those who are already interested in political and societal questions (Hindman 2009; Norris 2003). Others have argued (Barber, 2003) and empirically illustrated (Christensen & Bengtsson 2011; Taewoo 2012) that the lower barriers brought by ICTs can activate social groups of citizens that have previously been more or less excluded from politics. Scholars also seem to disagree empirically about the outcome of this question. The reported results from the meta-analysis by Boulianne (evaluating 38 earlier studies) indicate that the use of ICTs does not have a negative effect on civic and political engagement; instead, the results can be translated as positive (Boulianne 2009). However, the magnitude of these results is questionable, and mediating mechanisms such as political interests and media use count for significant shares in several of the studies.

From a micro-perspective, earlier research that tries to find explanations for individuals' engagement in e-democratic processes is quite heterogeneous. A common denominator for this research is, however, its background in political resource theory (e.g. Verba et al. 1995), and a field has emerged that examines which factors explain online activation. Bucy (2000) finds that traditional characteristics such as education influence access to the internet, while studies by Krueger (2002) and Best and Krueger (2005) stress internet skills in particular as the single most important determinant of online political participation. The latter two studies also find common results regarding the importance of an interest in politics. A more recent study by Min (2010) adds that, besides political interest and internet skills, males are more inclined than females to use the internet for political activities. Research concerning Western Europe reveals a slightly different picture than these American studies. Traditional background variables such as gender and age are significant in several studies (di Gennaro & Dutton 2006; Karlsen 2010; Norris 2003; Saglie & Vabo 2009). Regarding age, the tendency is that the likelihood for involvement in e-democracy diminishes with age, while studies show contradictory results concerning which gender is more likely to take part. These scholars can also identify the importance of the level of education and social class because their work is more closely related to resource theory. The most detailed work is Norris's (2003) study reflecting the EU-15, which creates an interesting stereotype of the typical person involved in e-democracy. The result draws a picture in which an over-representation exists among men, younger age groups, middle-class and better-educated individuals from the northern parts of Europe. Additionally, these individuals use traditional media to a greater extent and have higher levels of political knowledge and experiences of political discussions. Traditional resources therefore seem to be more important in the European context, despite one of the studies (di Gennaro & Dutton 2006) mainly verifying results from the US.

Using data from a Swedish survey that investigated people's internet habits, the assumptions above can be examined.[131] Different, potentially influencing, variables can be studied on the basis of a question about the use of the internet for accessing public information as an operationalization of individuals' e-democratic activity.[132] Beginning with the level of education, it is indicated that such activity seems to positively co-vary with the level of education, and the pattern is quite convincing. Continuing by relating e-democratic activity to

---

131 The demand side data are exclusively based on the Swedish part of the global project, World Internet Project, and have been collected by the World Internet Institute (WII) through an annual survey. This panel survey asks a representative sample of the Swedish population about their internet habits; for more information see WII 2010. To get a larger sample, data both from 2008 and 2009 are used. The used data are collected from these data sets: WII 2008; WII 2009.

132 This indicator is dichotomized and thereby divides no activity from those who express a use in taking part of public information, irrespective of how frequent. Due to some missing data the number of respondents is in the span of 2045 to 2271.

technological skills, another assumption seems to be correct. The pattern reflects that increasing knowledge of computers has a tendency to stimulate e-democratic activities. Finally, the age factor is omnipresent in discussions of internet use and the bias within it. It is only logical that the potential effect of age is also discussed in the e-democratic literature, and it is interesting to examine. From the table, it can be noted that individuals who are most active with regard to e-democracy are between 25 and 64 years old. Both young people and people over 65 indicate a lower activity. This is especially noticeable among young people, where only a third answer that they use the internet for expressing the measured e-democratic activity.

Table 11.2 Individuals' E-Democratic Activity, Level of Education, Knowledge of Computers and Age

	E-democratic activity (%)
Level of education	
Compulsory school	33.9
High school	41.5
University	58.9
Knowledge of computers	
Poor knowledge of computers	34.5
Average knowledge of computers	46.5
Great knowledge of computers	59.0
Age	
16-24 years	31.8
25-44 years	52.8
45-64 years	46.5
65 + years	41.5

Source: WII 2008; WII 2009. See WII 2010 for details about the data.

In summing up these factors a few aspects should be emphasized. First, there is a bias in terms of education, experience of computers and age that influences individuals' inclination to use e-democratic functions. Second, these results in many ways harmonize with earlier research. Authors such as di Gennaro and Dutton (2006) and Norris (2003) have, by using empirical data from different societies, underlined the positive influence of education when it comes to e-democratic activity, and the results in this examination reflect such conclusions. Also, when it comes to the importance of technological skills, this examination verifies earlier inquiries (Krueger 2002; Best & Krueger 2005). In comparison with explanations of traditional political activation, this is of course deviant. Finally, the question of age should be addressed in relation to earlier research. Contradicting the work of di Gennaro and Dutton (2006) and Norris (2003), this study shows that those in the youngest age group express a low level of activity compared to those in the older age groups. It should, however, be noted that younger people in general are also underrepresented in traditional forms of political participation, so it is hard to determine from the used data whether technology increases or decreases their use of e-democracy.

To sum up, in a Swedish context e-democracy varies both in terms of supply and demand. This means that a situation exists in which citizens are presented with different conditions for e-democratic activity related to their local government depending on where they reside. Among the factors influencing this variation are the levels of education and the population. Furthermore, another dimension also has an impact on a society's success in e-democracy. This has to do with its citizens' ability to be active in e-democracy. Individuals' education, computer experience and age tend to influence this. With regard to the framework established in the introduction concerning how to evaluate democratic innovation, in the case of e-democracy, we cannot talk about participation without bearing in mind that it is biased due to certain factors.

The Development of E-Democracy: a Swedish Case

In this section I will examine a Swedish municipality's work with e-democracy from its origin in the middle of the 1990s to 15 years after that.[133] This will allow a closer look at the impact of e-democracy on society and complement the earlier quantitative approaches.

The chosen case is the municipality of Älvkarleby. Älvkarleby is located in the middle of Sweden, about 20 kilometres south of the regional centre Gävle, in the county of Uppsala. It is a small municipality, with about 9,000 inhabitants. Since 1990, the municipality has experienced a marginal decrease in the number of inhabitants, and it also suffers from a skewed age structure, with a marked deficit of young adults. The local economy is dominated by traditional industry, mainly based on wood as raw material (Statistics Sweden 2005).

The overall level of supply of e-democracy in the municipality can be described as intermediate. In the previously presented index, Älvkarleby has a score of 6.5, slightly below the national average of 7.25.[134] Several items regarding political information are shown on the municipality's website. Among

---

133 This section draws from different types of empirical material such as interviews, records and documents.
134 It should be noted that the data for this variable reflects the time period 2007–2009.

others, protocols from the city councils and general information about the political situation can be found. Citizens can interact with decision-makers via the website by accessing the contact information of some of the leading politicians, and there is a function enabling citizens to submit complaints and opinions. In other words, the website both provides information and facilitates discussion processes (Vedel 2006).

The Development of E-Democracy in Älvkarleby

The first traits of a municipality offering its citizens e-democratic functions can be traced back to the middle of the 1990s. During this period, Älvkarleby's first official website was launched. It consisted of information of both a public and a political character. Of particular importance in this process is that the background to the initiative was a demand from local citizens and parts of the local economy. In accordance with this book's criteria of participation and legitimacy, drawing attention to how this initiative was implemented is thus a way to stress a functioning, legitimate representative democracy characterized by citizens' involvement. This idea was strengthened during the late 1990s. The work with e-democracy was then intensified, and the reason for this was, once again, citizens' initiative. This is confirmed by a civil servant employed by the municipality (Personal Interview 9 June 2010):

> – Yet, neither tools nor resources were allocated especially for this work. In that way the interest was quite limited, but all the time there was a pressure on us to develop the website and make it better.
> – Did you notice this also from the citizens?
> – Yes, yes of course. For some years it was often on the (agendas of the) meetings of the municipality board ... Viewpoints came from different quarters.

During the first years of the new millennium, a change in Älvkarleby's internal visions can be noted. First, the information society was placed on the agenda. The municipality argued that it had a significant responsibility to ensure that all citizens could access information, and that this was a condition of a vital democracy (Älvkarleby Kommun 2001). Related to this were the guidelines for employees in relation to using ICTs to a greater extent for information and communication, for example by sending out documents electronically. Second, Älvkarleby worked out a strategic vision for 2010 in which democracy and participation was one of the four core dimensions (Älvkarleby Kommun 2002). Related to this were several sub-purposes, for example to develop the forms of democracy, facilitate citizens' participation and design democratic processes characterized by transparency. Third, the municipality also made a large investment in technological infrastructure, namely the extension of broadband connections, to ensure that the right conditions existed for citizens to use the local e-democracy.

Despite these impressive ambitions, the development of e-democracy in Älvkarleby during the following years became quite modest, as did the actual impact of it. When reviewing the objectives from the strategic vision it becomes clear that only a few of these have been implemented. During this time the website has been modernized and some official documents were thereafter presented on it. This can be regarded as a method for strengthening the distribution of relevant information to citizens. An additional e-democratic improvement is a function on the website for strengthening communication and deliberation. A simple method for citizens to ask questions of politicians and administrators at the municipality as a way of enhancing political dialogue was established. A new website was launched in April 2008, which was of great instrumental importance. Both the initiative and the work relating to this project can to a large extent be connected to the IT department of the municipality (Personal Interview 24 May 2010). The previously described function for allowing dialogue between citizens and representatives of the municipality was improved because of the new website. In connection with the launching of this function, a brochure was sent out to all citizens that informed them of the possibility of dialogue on the website and also permitted them to make comments on a form about the municipality's activity (Älvkarleby Kommun 2008b). The civil servants whose mission was to realize the formulated vision and strategies chose this as a suitable and cost-efficient alternative (Älvkarleby Kommun 2007; Älvkarleby Kommun 2008a).

Between 2004 and 2008, the development of e-democracy was more limited than the ambitions formulated by the municipality. One reason for not fulfilling these ambitions was a restricted economy or, as expressed by the coordinator of the IT Department (Personal Interview 24 May 2010): 'Previously we had an investment budget of about 100,000 [Swedish crowns] and that is ten computers... then there have not been any thoughts at all about this with citizens' participation and e-democracy.' This merely verifies earlier research that has stressed the surprisingly ignored facts about the costs related to e-democracy (Viborg Andersen et al. 2007). It seems to be correct to claim that although Älvkarleby brought the information society to the fore at the beginning of 2000, it took several years before this ambition was transformed into actions.

The last years in this analysis, 2008–2010, partly reflected a new political strategy for the municipality's development. This change also had an impact on the work with e-democracy, which was played down by the leading politicians. Among the more long-term goals, work on strengthening democracy was not emphasized as it had been earlier on, other than in terms of a formulation for strengthening citizens' participation and influence in society. But how this should be accomplished was not specified. Interviewing the local councillor only indicates that the political leaders had no clear opinion of how these aims should be reached (Älvkarleby Kommun 2008c; Personal Interview 24 May 2010). In Älvkarleby's annual report for 2009, two goals for developing e-democracy are mentioned. The first is to set up a web-based record for elected politicians. The second is the possibility of introducing a citizens' jury using ICTs to deliberate on issues of importance for the local community (Älvkarleby Kommun 2009). The purpose of providing a record of politicians' contact details was to strengthen the possibility of dialogue between them and the citizens. In general, the administration seems to have acted with a clear focus on the citizens, even though during this period their actions had been restricted due to the economic reality. Two examples of this were a request from citizens for webcasts of the municipality's council meetings and the publication of the municipality's diary on the website. A large number of potential activities for strengthening e-democracy were therefore discussed, mainly by the administration, but during this time few of them were realized. Any web-based record of politicians' contact details was not compiled, nor were any of the other discussed suggestions implemented. The changed vision for the progression of the municipality's democratic work in the long run seems likely to be an explanatory factor for this inaction. Additionally, representatives of the municipality argue that between 2008 and 2010 little demand from citizens could be traced regarding e-democratic functions. Hence, this was quite a different situation to when Älvkarleby first introduced e-democracy. Relating this to the characteristics of a successful democracy, one can argue that the municipality had set up the tools for increasing transparency and dialogue and had thereby addressed such issues as legitimacy, deliberation and effectiveness.

Concluding the exposition of Älvkarleby's work with e-democracy emphasizes that different mechanisms have played a part during the period considered. In the first phase, when early traces of e-democracy through an establishment of the website can be observed, the initiative was expressed through citizens' demands. The reason for such a demand arising at this specific time is difficult to determine but, in line with earlier research (Medaglia 2007; van der Graft & Svensson 2006; Lidén 2011), it is possible that rising socioeconomic standards and education transformed into a demand from citizens for increased political involvement. Closely related to this is the spreading of computer knowledge that took off during the mid-1990s. Nevertheless, no demand from the surrounding society can be traced during the following period. It seems logical to interpret this as the result of the citizens being satisfied with the development of e-democracy. Although the internal vision of the municipality was not in all cases transformed by new innovations, the municipality has, in the long run, continued to strengthen its e-democracy. From 2008 to 2010, the administration seems to have strengthened its control of this development. However, this cannot be regarded as purely self-directed; to a large extent it is due to the indistinct and short-sighted goals of the political leadership. It can, moreover, easily be associated with the ideas of new public management, and some scholars have argued that technology will increase the authority of the administration (van Dijk 2000). The initiative of e-democracy in Älvkarleby, thus, started from conditions and explanations that can be regarded as exogenous in relation to the organization of the municipality. It was implemented by the municipality and thereafter some internal visions were formed. In the following phase, some economic funds were allocated for developing e-democracy but, on the whole, they were insufficient to reach the goals of strengthening democracy. Some key actors, endogenous in relation to the organization of the municipality (cf. Nyhlén & Lidén 2011), have then been crucial for its future development.

Evaluating E-Democracy

It is probably believed by many that e-democracy is one type of e-democratic innovation that could potentially neutralize some of the flaws associated with modern forms of democracy. Whether e-democracy, when existing as a practical method for carrying out democratic processes, actually does so is a completely different question. Just answering such a question is quite challenging and demands consideration of the empirical material that theoretical reflections concerning the advantages of e-democracy do not always take into account. In this section, I will evaluate the quality of e-democracy based on the five dimensions sketched out by Brigitte Geissel in the introduction of this book. To do so, I will mainly draw on the empirical examples presented in this chapter, but I will also add empirical and theoretical contributions that are of particular relevance.

In a seminal article by Arend Lijphart (1997), the inequality in political participation is brought into focus. Accordingly, one can wonder whether e-democracy can assist in creating *inclusive, equal* and *meaningful participation.* The existence of bias at the individual level that is in favour of the highly educated has previously been presented, and other studies have also verified that this group is more inclined to be involved in e-democratic activity (e.g. Norris 2003). Adding the inequality that is due to age makes it quite clear that e-democracy has not proven to be an efficient way to counteract skewed inclusiveness in political participation. There are positive claims, though, one example of which is collected from the use of internet voting. Studies from Estonia, which is a leading country in terms of using internet voting, reveal that this channel has added a small group of voters who otherwise would not have been involved at all (Madise & Maaten 2010). Positive results can therefore be found. An associated question is to what extent incoming issues arriving through the channels of e-democracy matter at all. Even if the internet allows anyone to present their opinions, the suggestions that eventually result in po-litical changes risk being exclusively for actors of certain importance (cf. Hindman 2009). It may be different at the local level, especially in small socie-ties. In the case of Älvkarleby, the initiative to work with e-democracy at all came from citizens and local businesses. At the same time, no crucial evidence has been found that issues processed through e-democratic channels have led to significant changes or strengthened the quality of democracy.

Questions of *legitimacy* and *political support* are very relevant when dis-cussing what impact one can accredit to political processes applied through ICTs. In theory, there is no question that e-democracy, as a democratic innova-tion, could tackle many of the problems related to modern democracy. By its efficient channels of both spreading information and founding discussions, e-democracy really could function as an influential method. If, in addition to these features, there is also the potential to make decisions with the help of modern technology through, for example, voting or taking part in a poll, then e-democracy might be an innovation which could have powerful effects on de-mocracy. However, as shown by the empirical examples, strong doubts must be raised regarding the difference between idealistic views and reality. Inequality in participation hardly increases legitimacy, and since e-democracy, according to many earlier studies, rather reproduces or even intensifies differences among individuals, the picture is not especially bright (Hindman 2009; Norris 2003; di Gennaro & Dutton 2006). One concrete example of this, which is presented in this study concerns how technological skills can be a barrier to strengthened participation. To conclude, in relation to this criterion of quality, legitimacy in e-democratic processes should initially be addressed by tackling the bias in participation.

E-democratic processes that provide an open dialogue and the possibility of framing and understanding questions can have a definite impact on and add to the demand for a transparent political system. Thus, *deliberation* is a deci-sive factor of quality. In their inquiry into online consultation cases in Europe and the US, Åström and Grönlund (2012) find that processes which can be characterized as deliberative multiply by eighteen the potential to affect policy. There are many ways in which political issues that are managed with the as-sistance of ICTs can benefit from the advantages of such forms. Despite the constraints discussed above, ICTs can be very inclusive and far-reaching. But one relevant issue to consider is how often e-democratic processes show traits of being deliberative. A few of the discussions on the electronic forums of local municipalities' indicate that most of these traits cannot be characterized as de-liberative, and therefore any such traits will only result in a few positive effects in terms of strengthening democracy (Öhrvall 2002). This is partly verified by the municipalities' supply of e-democratic functions related to information and discussion that is considered in this chapter; most municipalities have a wider choice of the former type of function than the latter. If a discussion forum does not exist, then it becomes difficult to have even a deliberative process on the internet that is directed by government in a transparent and open way.

Other criteria of quality are innovations that have the potential to contribute to the output of political systems. These innovations regard *effective problem-solving* as turning collective goals into output and *effectiveness* as guaranteeing a high level of success in achieving such goals. It could be argued that these issues are not solely about democracy. Effectiveness in administrative processes is closely related to the concept of e-government. No widely accepted definition of e-government can be found in the literature, but briefly it can be described as the use of ICTs to facilitate and develop the spread of information and service production from government to citizens, businesses and the organizations of civic society (Yildiz 2007). However, in relation to both e-democracy and other innovations, there are associated improvements that could be put in place, for example methods to strengthen accountability. The ability of citizens to consider their interests rises in response to an increase in the transparency of a political system. In the examples of information collected from the municipality of Älvkarleby, citizens considered that following whether or not e-democratic functions were developed through the local website was an urgent priority. Interviews indicated that they were not satisfied until a reasonable level of e-democracy was developed, and that this process seemed to be quite closely inspected by some members of the local population. However, when it was finally introduced to a reasonable extent, the citizens in Älvkarleby seemed to be quite satisfied and had no further demands for its development, which implies that the improvement taken reflected the demands for legitimacy and efficiency.

Turning to the last criterion, one can wonder whether, and if so to what extent, e-democracy can *enlighten citizens* and give them a *democratic education*. From an e-democratic viewpoint, Schuler argues (1998) that if we want citizens who can contribute to the political sphere, we need a high-quality public education system, widespread internet training and numerous public forums. Perhaps some societies can accomplish at least part of this, but far from all, not even in the rich parts of the world. Although the socialization of citizens into democratic values and norms is crucial for maintaining a consolidated democracy, research in the field of e-democracy shows that civic skills are of less importance when it comes to political activity through ICTs than through traditional forms. In the previously discussed article by Best and Krueger (2005), civic skills, measured through civic engagement of a collective character, show no significant influence on online participation, although they are the most important factor for explaining individuals' traditional political participation. Stressing instead the importance of technological skills, these results verify the outcome of the survey discussed in this study. This raises questions. If there is no positive link between civic skills and e-democratic participation, could we really assume that e-democracy leads to an increase in civic skills? Is a different type of democratic education more relevant in an e-democratic context and must we revise our operationalizations to reach more valid measurements? If civic skills do not have an influence on the e-democratic activity of individuals, do they have an influence on the quality of such e-democratic processes? No given answers exist to these queries. A notion that should be brought to the fore, though, is that reflexively differentiating between democracy and e-democracy is hardly a constructive strategy. By contrast, it seems much more relevant to elaborate upon how e-democracy can be a part of the wider concept of democracy and how it is thereby founded on the core values attached to this phenomenon. Such ideas (Lidén 2011; Macintosh et al. 2009) attach a strong theoretical foundation to e-democracy and create a valid departure for empirical research.

Conclusions

How, then, can and should e-democracy be regarded from a perspective that tries to judge its qualities? First, it has been argued that e-democracy does not lead to inclusive, equal and meaningful participation because of its bias at the individual level, where it is in favour of individuals with certain characteristics, such as education. However, e-democracy has proved that it can attract new groups to be involved in political processes. On the basis of accessible data, it seems reasonable to argue that changes in participation can occur, but that other forms of inequality remain and new ones may develop. Second, although political processes managed with the assistance of ICTs can benefit from the advantages of technology and then can be developed into more deliberative processes, it must be remembered that this is by no means confirmation that all e-democratic examples can be characterized as deliberative and transparent. Third, previous research gives no clear answers as to whether e-democracy can actually socialize and enlighten citizens in relation to democratic norms. Studies emphasizing that civic skills are not important for online participation question the fundament for e-democracy.

To conclude, it is crucial to be aware of and cautious about the bias that participation in e-democracy, as well as in other forms of political participation, can lead to. Studying such flaws can increase the possibility of minimizing these imperfections and strengthening the qualities of e-democracy. Allowing e-democratic processes to be as transparent as possible will create better possibilities for an effective, legitimate and publicly supported e-democracy.

References

Barber, B.R., 2003. *Strong democracy : participatory politics for a new age*, Berkeley, Calif.: University of California Press.

Bell, D., 1973. *The coming of post-industrial society : a venture in social forecasting*, New York: Basic books.

Best, S.J. & Krueger, B.S., 2005. Analyzing the representativeness of internet political participation. *Political Behavior*, 27(2), pp.183–216.

Boulianne, S., 2009. Does Internet Use Affect Engagement? A Meta-Analysis of Research. *Political Communication*, 26(2), pp.193–211.

Breindl, Y. & Francq, P., 2008. Can Web 2.0 applications save e-democracy? A study of how new internet applications may enhance citizen participation in the political process online. *International Journal of Electronic Democracy*, 1(1), p.14.

Bucy, E.P., 2000. Social Access to the Internet. *The Harvard International Journal of Press/Politics*, 5(1), pp.50 –61.

Castells, M., 1996. *The information age : economy, society and culture. Vol. 1, The rise of the network society /*, Malden, Mass.: Blackwell.

Castells, M., 2001. *The Internet Galaxy: Reflections on the Internet, Business, and Society*, Oxford: Oxford University Press.

Christensen, H.S. & Bengtsson, A., 2011. The Political Competence of Internet Participants. *Information, Communication & Society*, 14(6), pp.896–916.

Dahl, R.A., 1989. *Democracy and Its Critics*, New Haven: Yale Univ. Press.

Dahl, R.A. & Tufte, E.R., 1973. *Size and democracy*, Stanford: Stanford University Press.

Deutsch, K.W., 1966. *The nerves of government: models of political communication and control*, Free Press.

van Dijk, J., 2000. Models of Democracy and Concepts of Communication. In K. L. Hacker & J. van Dijk, eds. *Digital Democracy: Issues of Theory & Practice*. London: Sage.

Dutton, W.H., 1992. Political Science Research on Teledemocracy. *Social Science Computer Review*, 10(4), pp.505–522.

di Gennaro, C. & Dutton, W., 2006. The Internet and the Public: Online and Offline Political Participation in the United Kingdom. *Parliamentary Affairs*, 59(2), pp.299 –313.

Gil de Zúñiga, H. et al., 2010. Digital Democracy: Reimagining Pathways to Political Participation. *Journal of Information Technology & Politics*, 7(1), pp.36–51.

van der Graft, P. & Svensson, J., 2006. Explaining eDemocracy development: A quantitative empirical study. *Information Polity*, 11(2), pp.123–134.

Hacker, K.L. & van Dijk, J., 2000. What is Digital Democracy? In K. L. Hacker & J. van Dijk, eds. *Digital Democracy: Issues of Theory & Practice*. London: Sage, pp. 1–9.

Hindman, M.S., 2009. *The myth of digital democracy*, Princeton: Princeton University Press.

Huntington, S.P., 1991. *The Third Wave: Democratization in the Late Twentieth Century*, Norman: University of Oklahoma Press.

Karlsen, R., 2010. Online and Undecided: Voters and the Internet in the Contemporary Norwegian Election Campaign. *Scandinavian Political Studies*, 33(1), pp.28–50.

Krueger, B.S., 2002. Assessing the Potential of Internet Political Participation in the United States. *American Politics Research*, 30(5), pp.476 –498.

Lee, C., Chang, K. & Berry, F.S., 2011. Testing the Development and Diffusion of E-Government and E- Democracy: A Global Perspective. *Public Administration Review*, 71(3), pp.444–454.

Levine, P., 2002. Can the Internet Rescue Democracy? Toward an On-Line Commons. In R. Hayduk & K. Mattson, eds. *Democracy's Moment: Reforming the American Political System for the 21st Century*. Lanham, Md.: Rowman & Littlefield.

Lidén, G., 2011. Från demokrati till e-demokrati - En jämförande studie av demokratiutveckling i det moderna samhället, Sundsvall: Departement of Social Sciences, Mid Sweden University

Lidén, G., 2012. Is e-democracy more than democratic? - An examination of the implementation of socially sustainable values in e-democratic processes. *Electronic Journal of e-Government*, 10(1), pp. 84-94.

Lijphart, A., 1997. Unequal Participation: Democracy's Unresolved Dilemma. *The American Political Science Review*, 91(1), pp.1–14.

Macintosh, A., 2004. Characterizing e-participation in policy-making. In *System Sciences, 2004. Proceedings of the 37th Annual Hawaii International Conference on*. Hawaii, USA, p. 10 pp.

Macintosh, Ann, Coleman, S. & Schneeberger, A., 2009. eParticipation: The Research Gaps. In Ann Macintosh & E. Tambouris, eds. *Electronic Participation*. Berlin: Springer Berlin Heidelberg, pp. 1–11.

Madise, Ü. & Maaten, E., 2010. Internet Voting in Estonia. In D. Rios Insua & S. French, eds. *e-Democracy: A Group Decision and Negotiation Perspective*. Dordrecht: Springer Netherlands.

Medaglia, R., 2007. Measuring the diffusion of eParticipation: A survey on Italian local government. *Information Polity*, 12(4), pp.265–280.

Min, S.-J., 2010. From the Digital Divide to the Democratic Divide: Internet Skills, Political Interest, and the Second-Level Digital Divide in Political Internet Use. *Journal of Information Technology & Politics*, 7(1), pp.22–35.

Nam, T., 2011. Whose e-democracy? The democratic divide in American electoral campaigns. *Information Polity*, 16(2), pp.131–150.

Norris, P., 2001. *Digital divide? : civic engagement, information poverty, and the Internet worldwide*, Cambridge: Cambridge University Press.

Norris, P., 2003. Preaching to the Converted? *Party Politics*, 9(1), pp.21 –45.

Noveck, B.S., 2009. *Wiki government : how technology can make government better, democracy stronger, and citizens more powerful*, Washington, D.C.: Brookings Institution Press.

Nyhlén, J. & Lidén, G., 2011. Decision-making in a Governance Context: An analytical Framework. Presented at the Nordic Municipality research conference, 24-26 November 2011, Göteborg.

Personal Interview, 24 May, 2010. Personal Interview.

Personal Interview, 9 June, 2010. Personal Interview.

Putnam, R.D., 2000. *Bowling alone : the collapse and revival of American community*, New York: Simon & Schuster.

Rheingold, H., 1993. *The virtual community: homesteading on the electronic frontier*, Reading, Mass: Addison-Wesley.

Rose, R., 2005. A Global Diffusion Model of E-Governance. *Journal of Public Policy*, 25(01), pp.5–27.

Saglie, J. & Vabo, S.I., 2009. Size and e-Democracy: Online Participation in Norwegian Local Politics. *Scandinavian Political Studies*, 32(4), pp.382–401.

Schmitter, P.C. & Karl, T.L., 1991. What Democracy Is . . . . and Is Not. *Journal of Democracy*, 2(3), p.75.

Schuler, D., 1998. Global Communication and Community Networks: How Do We Institutionalize Democracy in the Electronic Age? In ITS'98. Stockholm.

Selwyn, N., 2004. Reconsidering Political and Popular Understandings of the Digital Divide. *New Media & Society*, 6(3), pp.341–362.

Smith, M.R. & Marx, L., 1994. *Does technology drive history? : the dilemma of technological determinism*, Cambridge, Mass.: MIT Press.

Statistics Sweden, 2005. *Älvkarleby Kommunfakta 2005*, Available at: www.scb.se [Accessed May 6, 2010].

Sylvester, D.E. & McGlynn, A.J., 2010. The Digital Divide, Political Participation, and Place. *Social Science Computer Review*, 28(1), pp.64–74.

Sørensen, G., 2008. *Democracy and democratization : processes and prospects in a changing world*, Boulder, Colo.: Westview Press.

Taewoo, N., 2012. Dual effects of the internet on political activism: Reinforcing and mobilizing. *Government Information Quarterly*, 29, Supplement 1(0), pp.S90–S97.

Ward, S. & Vedel, T., 2006. Introduction: The Potential of the Internet Revisited. *Parliamentary Affairs*, 59(2), pp.210–225.

Vedel, T., 2006. The Idea of Electronic Democracy: Origins, Visions and Questions. *Parliamentary Affairs*, 59(2), pp.226 –235.

Verba, S., Schlozman, K.L. & Brady, H.E., 1995. *Voice and equality : civic voluntarism in American politics*, Cambridge, Mass.: Harvard University Press.

Viborg Andersen, K. et al., 2007. Costs of e-participation: the management challenges. *Transforming Government: People, Process and Policy*, 1(1), pp.29–43.

WII, 2010. *Metodbeskrivning Svenskarna och Internet*

WII, 2008. *Svenskarna och Internet: Dataset 2008*.

WII, 2009. *Svenskarna och Internet: Dataset 2009*.

Wohlers, T.E., 2009. The Digital World of Local Government: A Comparative Analysis of the United States and Germany. *Journal of Information Technology & Politics*, 6, pp.111–126.

Wojcieszak, M.E. & Mutz, D.C., 2009. Online Groups and Political Discourse: Do Online Discussion Spaces Facilitate Exposure to Political Disagreement? *Journal of Communication*, 59(1), pp.40–56.

Yildiz, M., 2007. E-government research: Reviewing the literature, limitations, and ways forward. *Government Information Quarterly*, 24(3), pp.646–665.

Åström, J. & Grönlund, Å., 2012. Online Consultation in Local Government: What Works, Shwn, and Why? In S. Coleman & P. M. Shane, eds. *Connecting Democracy: Online Consultation and the Flow of Political Communication*. Cambridge, Mass.: MIT Press.

Älvkarleby Kommun, 2008a. Administrativa avdelningen, 15 February.

Älvkarleby Kommun, 2008b. Förslag till riktlinjer för synpunktshanteringen, "Tyck om Älvkarleby".

Älvkarleby Kommun, 2008c. Kommunfullmäktige, November 26.

Älvkarleby Kommun, 2001. Kommunfullmäktiges Mål och Budget för åren 2002-2004.

Älvkarleby Kommun, 2007. Kommunstyrelsen, 3 December.

Älvkarleby Kommun, 2009. Årsredovisning 2009. Available at: www.alvkarleby.se [Accessed May 6, 2010].

Älvkarleby Kommun, 2002. Älvkarlebys Vision 2010. Available at: www.alvkarleby.se [Accessed February 17, 2010].

Öhrvall, R., 2002. *Det digitala torget - en studie av kommunala debattforum på Internet*, Uppsala: Statsvetenskapliga Institutionen, Uppsala Universitet.

Conclusions – an Evaluation of Democratic Innovations in Europe

Marko Joas

Since the wake of the new social movements in the 1960's and 1970's that contested the traditional political cleavages in Western democratic societies, there has been a growing discussion about the failures of representative democracy. Erkki Berndtson (1984: 145) stated almost 30 years ago that *'(t)here seems to prevail a strong opinion that Western democracies are in some kind of a crisis'*. This finding has been one of the leading discussions in political science ever since then, at times stronger and at times weaker, but constantly present. However, as Berndtson (1984: 145) also stated, the very nature of this crisis was already then, and still is, *'much more unclear'*. What is clear, however, is that demands by the people and political institutional actors outside the traditional democratic governance bodies on prevailing democratic institutions have accelerated over the past decades. The gradual awareness of this change has forced existing democratic institutions to take the different forms of democratic demands into account.

This volume gives the reader a clear view of this on-going process of change. Democracy, as all social processes, is under constant development: *"Democracy is a variable not a constant"* (Newton 2012: 3). This development is based on gradual, slow processes within the existing institutional structures or, very occasionally, on forced changes in institutional structures by internal or external forces. The development takes place in constant, mostly stepwise, gradual, small movements towards a multi-channelled democracy, not replacing but clearly completing traditional democratic institutions. As noted by Ken Newton (2012: 11): *"There is something wrong with this assumption that the new and the old are incompatible and alternative forms of government. New forms of direct democracy – whether referendums, co-governance, or citizen juries and mini-publics – are inevitably developed within and by the institutions of old forms of representative democracy."* Traditional democracy meets and helps innovative democracy forward.

As the theoretical and empirical articles in this volume have shown, the introduction of new democratic elements into existing democratic institutions has been happening in real life as well as on our theoretical drawing boards. In a large number of case-studies we have seen that small-scale and local democratic innovations can be found all over the world, even in countries not necessarily governed by democratic rule on a national level. This volume is, however, about changes in established, stable democracies. The authors have shown that this process of change is also highly vivid in Europe, in countries seen as the homelands of traditional representative democracy.

Democracy is not only developing through practical innovations in politically governed institutions. It is, in fact, at least as often re-designed on the laptops of democratic theorists, in small-scale experiments and theoretical models. This development is thus by nature an on-going dialogue between theory and practice. This feature is also evident in our volume. The articles included are both empirical and theoretical, all however with an analytical approach fitted into our frame of reference.

Back to the Analytical Framework

The introduction of democratic innovations is often addressing the problems with existing traditional forms of democracy. Therefore, it is obvious that democratic innovations must be evaluated against the very same criteria as traditional forms of democracy.

In this concluding chapter, we are conducting an overall evaluation of all the cases presented in this volume, against the analytical framework presented in the introductory chapter. Our analytical framework was not meant to be complete; in fact, we fully believe in the notion expressed by Graham Smith (Smith 2009, 10) that *"democratic theories and models tend to be incomplete"*. Despite this, we must be able to look at our basic societal institutions, including democracy, through constant evaluation.

The basic rationale of our framework is discussed in detail in the introduction of this book, highlighting five central principles of democracy: *participation, legitimacy, deliberation, effectiveness* and, finally, enlightenment of citizens. It can be assumed that these criteria emphasize different aspects in our case-studies of democratic innovations, as different types of democratic innovations affect our framework in an individual manner. Certain innovations, certain forms of democracy, address specific features of democracy and, therefore, also emphasize specific problems with democracy.

However, it is also obvious that all innovations can, and finally must, be evaluated against all critical principles of democracy.

Not all the empirical or analytical papers in this volume do explicitly deal with all the variables discussed in the framework. The individual analyses are conducted in their individual settings, and all innovations are not expected to have an effect on all of our indicators. Our analysis is based on an overall judgement on the specific cases presented by the authors, i.e. on our interpretation of how the individual authors see and evaluate the key aspects of our framework against their cases.

In the empirical cases, the authors have explicitly considered a number of the main evaluation criteria described by Geissel (in this volume). The individual empirical work by the authors has not in all cases included an analysis that could cover all our criteria. This is also the case with the non-empirical articles in this volume. This has forced us to base some of our concluding analysis on assumptions made by us or by the authors themselves. Nevertheless, we do consider the empirical evidence strong enough, especially as it is derived from several independent case studies, for us to draw general conclusions about how different types of innovations respond to our criteria.

Table 12.1 Evaluation Framework for Democratic Innovations (Geissel, this volume)

Criterion	Intentions of Procedure	Possible Indicators (Examples)
Participation	Inclusive participation	Inclusive participation of affected groups and stakeholders, participation of minorities
	Meaningful participation	Agenda-setting options for participants, transformation of participants' preferences into policies
Legitimacy	Improvement of perceived legitimacy	Attitudes towards - political representatives - the political system
Deliberation	High-quality public deliberation	Rational debate, willingness to listen, respectful exchange of arguments
Effectiveness	Improvement of effectiveness	Identification of collective goals, achieving collective goals, output in line with collective interests
Democratic citizenries	Enlightenment of citizens	Improvement of knowledge, improvement of tolerance, enhanced public spiritedness

Cooperative Governance

Perhaps the most used and also most differentiated types of innovations discussed in this volume are the numerous different cooperative governance procedures that are available especially within local governments. These are very different in scope and character, more or less institutionalised and therefore used in various ways in different countries and even different local settings. Many co-governance structures are, in fact, part of everyday political and administrative life in Europe. Co-governance democratic innovations emphasize user- and interest-based participation in small-scale decision-making, in local level budgeting, in local planning and end-user settings (such as schools and other local government services).

The empirical cases selected for this volume are based mostly on evaluations of Participatory Budgeting processes. In addition, the Spanish cases presented by Font and Navarro highlight more broadly different participatory processes.

A general observation about these empirically evaluated participatory processes is that the authors are relatively cautious in their judgements of these innovations against our criteria. Their observations do, however, mostly indicate small-scale steps taken in local governments to involve limited groups of actors in decision-making processes. It seems obvious that different co-governance innovations are not meant to change the local basic political settings in Europe, but rather to indicate the stepwise change in everyday political and administrative action.

Röcke and Putini indicate slightly positive effects for our participatory indicators; however, it is still obvious that the examined institutions fulfil the criteria of inclusiveness and meaningfulness only to some extent. Font and Navarro judge the inclusiveness of their cases even as slightly negative.

The level of legitimacy is not analysed by the case study authors, but according to Röcke, the level of legitimacy could potentially reach a higher level during participatory democratic processes, based on the very nature of the innovation. She points out that institutional design is crucial for this aspect: '*If participation is restricted to very local questions without any link to the broader political agenda, the risk is high that the participatory process becomes only a "legitimatory cloak" for a political system that remains at a great distance from the needs and priorities of local people*' (Röcke in this volume).

All case study authors judged that the quality of deliberation was very low in the presented empirical cases. Talpin even indicated, as the only empirical point he analysed, that real theoretically defined deliberation actually almost never happened. Still, there is potential for deliberation in co-governance processes, but it is clear that the institutional design must not only allow but also encourage deliberation. In fact, as Talpin points out in this volume, there is rather naturally a '*clear trade-off between (quantitative inclusion) and deliberative quality. While a higher number of participants increase the legitimacy of a democratic innovation, it reduces its capacity to foster deliberation*'. However, Font and Navarro found some evidence in their multi-case analysis that some forms of co-governance innovations could, in fact, also raise the quality of deliberation. This was, however, not within the scope of their study.

Finally, the authors were also very cautious about the effectiveness and enlightenment of the citizens, but both authors who looked into these aspects still considered that there are some benefits to achieve both concerns the level of knowledge and the level of effectiveness, as defined in the framework of this book.

Table 12.2 Empirical Evaluation of Cooperative Governance Procedures (NA = not analysed)

Cooperative Governance:	Participatory Budgeting			Participatory Processes
Intention of Innovation	*Röcke*	*Putini*	*Talpin*	*Font & Navarro*
Inclusive participation	Positive / neutral effect	Positive / neutral effect	NA	Negative / neutral
Meaningful participation	Positive / neutral effect	Positive / neutral effect	NA	NA
Improved perceived legitimacy	Optional positive effect – Institutional design matters	NA	NA / Optional negative effect	NA
Public deliberation with and among non-state actors	Clearly Low Quality	Clearly Low Quality	Scarce and clearly low quality – Institutional design matters	NA / Optional positive effect
Improvement of effectiveness	Positive / neutral effect	Positive / neutral effect	NA	NA
Enlightenment of citizens	NA / Optional positive effect	Positive / neutral effect	NA	NA

Deliberative Procedures

Deliberative democratic procedures highlight a different type of democratic approach, i.e. the debate and arguments in democracy, aiming at consensus for the best argument. This does, once again rather naturally, have specific effects in relation to our indicators.

Two of our case studies address deliberative instruments, so far only in experimental usage, though.

By analysing the participating groups the authors of both case studies can show a fair degree of inclusive participation. This is possible to achieve through the selection process of the participants, in that a certain feature can be designed to guarantee inclusive participation. Even if the empirical cases could not tell us about the level of meaningful participation, it can be seen that deliberative institutions can be designed so as to have an effect, as well.

Furthermore, deliberative poll was considered to have a clear legitimating effect on the participants, something that can also easily be deducted from the theoretical literature. This effect was, however, not visible in the virtual polity experiment.

The quality of the deliberation was also judged differently in these two forms of deliberative innovations. The discussions, within the virtual polity, were considered by Strandberg and Grönlund as positive, but at least partly negative, within the deliberative poll, by Fiket and Memoli. This might indicate, as also the methodological paper by Himmelroos highlights with clarity, that the institutional design is very important in order to achieve high quality deliberation.

Effectiveness can be considered in the same manner as meaningful participation; institutional design is crucial in order for these institutions to take the step from guiding discussions to decision-making platforms.

Finally, the level of knowledge can be expected to rise, at least within the specific groups taking part in these exercises, a feature which was also visible in the deliberative poll case. As Dahl (1998: 185) states, enlightened understanding is a basic criterion and a challenge for democracy, not for democratic innovations alone. However, the virtual polity did not show the same development, therefore leaving this indicator on a somewhat loose ground.

Table 12.3 Empirical Evaluation of Deliberative Procedures (NA= not analysed)

Deliberative Procedures:	Deliberative Poll	Virtual Polity
Intention of Innovation	*Fiket & Memoli*	*Strandberg & Grönlund*
Inclusive participation	Clearly positive effect	Clearly positive effect
Meaningful participation	NA / Optional positive effect	NA – Institutional design matters
Improved perceived legitimacy	Clearly positive effect	No change in legitimacy
Public deliberation with and among non-state actors	Partly negative	Clearly positive effect
Improvement of effectiveness	NA / Optional positive effect	NA – Institutional design matters
Enlightenment of citizens	Clearly positive effect	No change in knowledge

Direct Democratic Procedures

Setälä and Smith analysed two direct democratic innovations, referenda and re-call institutions. Direct democratic innovations, once again, emphasize other criteria than co-governance and deliberative innovations. Even though a refer-endum can hardly be called a democratic innovation, it can (in certain settings beside institutions of representative democracy) be considered innovative. Democratic innovations are often something already existing in some political settings that are brought into new political settings, other political systems.

Recall as a political institution is new in certain political settings, too. In Europe, it has been introduced in several fairly new democracies in Eastern Eu-rope as a way of working against corruption. In his paper, Smith analyses some empirical cases, in Poland and Slovakia, of recall institutions on the local level.

Table 12.4 Empirical Evaluation of Direct Democratic Prodcedure (NA=not analysed)

Direct Democratic Procedures:	Referenda/Popular Initiative	Local Recall
Intention of Innovation	*Setälä*	*Smith*
Inclusive participation	Clearly positive effect	Clearly positive effect
Meaningful participation	Clearly positive effect	Clearly positive effect – Institutional design matters
Improved perceived legitimacy	Clearly positive effect	Clearly positive effect – Context matters
Public deliberation with and among non-state actors	Partly negative effect	NA
Improvement of effectiveness	Clearly positive effect	Clearly positive effect – Institutional design matters
Enlightenment of citizens	Partly negative effect	NA

The analytical overview presented by Setälä and the empirical cases presented by Smith clearly show that democratic innovations have potential to bridge several of the problems with contemporary representative democracy.

Traditionally, direct democracy is seen as one of the main options of dealing with the political dissatisfaction with parties and political elites. In her analysis, Setälä (in this volume) concludes that *"[d]irect democratic institutions, especially referendums, appear to provide inclusive and effective participation. Referendums also seem to have strong legitimizing impacts. Popular initiatives allow citizens to raise political issues on the agenda and, if the thresholds are not too high, this should improve the inclusiveness of the policy-making process."* Therefore, it is fairly clear that referenda have positive effects on the participation criteria. Participation is inclusive, with high if not universal coverage of adult population, as well as meaningful in the sense that even guiding referenda normally result in high level of implementation.

The same positive judgement applies also to the recall institution. The option to react upon policy choices by the elected representatives is normally universal and in that sense inclusive and also meaningful, provided that the institutional design of the instrument is of such a character that it can be used in a meaningful manner. The number of citizens required to initialize this is decisive, however, for the judgement of how meaningful this institution is in real life.

It is also obvious that the level of legitimacy of this form of democratic innovation is rather high. How the innovation is used is naturally quite dependent on the context, as is also pointed out by Smith (in this volume): *'Differing institutional contexts can also shape residents' behavior in the recall process. This does not mean that the recall is not a useful tool for restoring public legitimacy, but it does suggest that recall outcomes and whether public legitimacy is indeed in crisis depend very much on local conditions and context'.* Referenda and recalls should not be used for too obvious political reasons, with the risk of lower levels of legitimacy and, thus, adding to political distrust.

The quality of deliberation, the quality of the political debate prior to referenda, is not on a high level in referenda processes. Quite logically, the same also applies to the criteria of enlightened citizens: *"Especially in terms of criteria such as deliberation and enlightened citizen participation, direct democratic institutions may first appear defective"* (Setälä in this volume). Poor discussion and media coverage, highlighting issues other than content arguments, do not educate the electorate.

Finally, also fully logically, both of the described direct democratic innovations can be judged as being effective in so far as collective, common goals are both identified and achieved as a result of the institution.

E-Democracy – A Tool Rather than an Innovation

To evaluate the effects of e-democracy – or e-governance – according to the criteria for democratic innovations is very difficult. On one hand, it is clear that e-democratic innovations have effects on our criteria but, on the other hand, e-democratic innovations cannot be considered as an innovation proper. They can rather be seen as tools or channels for innovations to be distributed on to participants, to citizens. It is, as noted by Lidén, much more important and *"relevant to elaborate upon how e-democracy can be a part of the wider concept of democracy and how it is thereby founded on the core values attached to this phenomenon".* E-democracy can thus be utilised in all forms of democracy – traditional or innovative.

As regards channels for democratic procedures – innovative or already existing within a society – we can fully support the conclusion drawn by Lidén (in this volume): *"Allowing e-democratic processes be as transparent as possible will create better possibilities for an effective, legitimate and publicly supported e-democracy".* Thus, it is obvious that a well-designed, transparent, e-democratic institution can support legitimate, effective and even inclusive democracy. It is also possible that e-democratic tools can make deliberation easier for larger groups compared to other forms of political dialogue but, once again, it is the design of the tool and especially the institution that makes the difference, not the existence of the on-line tool itself. It is also unclear, whether e-democracy as such can enlighten citizens. In his article above, Lidén asks himself and the reader: Considering that *"there is no positive link between civic skills and e-democratic participation, could we really assume that e-democracy leads to an increase in civic skills?"*

To conclude, then, e-democracy can help us reach the democratic goals described by the set of criteria we use in this volume. Still, it must be emphasized that e-democracy and e-governance are only tools which aid societies in administering complicated and, at times, innovative democratic processes; therefore, we will leave them outside the following overall assessment of the democratic innovations highlighted in this volume.

An Overall Assessment

As recent literature shows, Participatory Budgeting alone is used in more than 1500 local governments, in at least 11 European countries, and there are thousands of other similar processes all over the world (Pihlaja and Sandberg 2012: 158). The change that we are talking about in this book is thus already happening in local governments, which offer citizens options of political participation through other channels than elections. These changes may somewhere be called experiments; they might include a limited number of participants and/or issues, but, nonetheless, they are real democratic institutions. Often, but not always, these new democratic innovations are introduced in local governments. Citizens today, as noted by Leighninger (2006: 1-2), have more knowledge and will to participate also directly in the governance of common issues: *"[C]itizens seem better at governing, and worse at being governed, than ever before"*. This raises a clear pressure to reform our contemporary democratic institutions. There is an obvious demand for new participatory elements in public decision-making, and there are public officials and politicians who are willing to introduce new elements, new input, into the political system. The effects of this change are still to be seen in public policies, though, as noted by Geissel (2012: 211), for example: *"[P]articipatory innovations have had little or even no impact on public policies"*.

We have displayed only a small number of different types of cases, but already this limited selection shows us the potential – as well as the limitations – of these innovations. In an overall assessment of the individual empirical cases, a pattern seems to emerge (Table 12.5 below).

On one hand, it looks as if the theoretical notions about the strong and weak sides of the direct democratic institutions are clearly enhanced in our study. These types of innovations are strong in participation, both regarding inclusiveness and meaningfulness, they do enhance the overall legitimacy of the decision-making process and also the effectiveness of the process. This is clearly noted by Smith (2009: 186) in his case-study analysis of democratic innovations, mostly outside Europe: *"The design of direct legislation places most weight on the realisation of inclusiveness and popular control"*. However, as Bengtsson and Mattila (2009: 1033) show, we must also be aware that inclusiveness, too, might be a problem: Participation in direct democratic institutions tends to attract the same types of citizens as are already privileged.

Table 12.5 Empirical Evaluation of Democratic Innovations - An Overall Assesment

Principles of Democracy	Intention of Participatory Innovation:	Cooperative Governance	Deliberative Procedures	Direct Democratic Procedures
Partici-pation	Inclusive participation	+/-	++	++
	Meaningful participation	+	(+)	++
Legitimacy	Improved perceived legitimacy	(+)	+	++
De-liberation	Public deliberation with and among non-state actors	--	++/-	-
Effective-ness	Improvement of effectiveness	+	(+)	++
Enlightened citizens	Enlightenment of citizens	+	+	-

Institutional design, thus, matters in order to achieve progress along these criteria. It is easy to understand that non-binding forms of referenda, for example, are not as effective or considered as legitimate, as binding forms of referenda. This finding is fully in line with Budge's (2012: 25) notion *"that many of the critical arguments against direct democracy are valid against its unmediated forms, but not against its mediated forms."*

The quality of the political debate (deliberation), and therefore also the education of the broad public (enlightenment of citizens), are both considered by Setälä as weaker features of direct democracy, at least to some degree. This conclusion is in accordance with a similar finding by Michels (2011: 287-288) who, however, also found some evidence of positive effects on knowledge (about some specific question under ballot), as well as on skills and virtues, even though less than what she found in other participatory forms of democratic innovations.

Deliberative and co-governance institutions are, on the other hand, not as clear-cut in their strengths and weaknesses in relation to our criteria, even though in general, both forms show somewhat similar patterns. In many of our case studies, the authors point out that institutional design is crucial in order to obtain positive effects on the criteria that we analyse. There is obviously a very high potential in designing the institutions in such a way that effects on almost all of our criteria can be seen as positive. To emphasize institutional design prior to the introduction of new co-governance institutions, as well as other democratic innovations presented in this volume, can be seen as a clearly outspoken result from the studies in this book. Unfortunately, in real life, the design of both experiments and small-scale practices still show clear weaknesses in their institutional construction.

On one hand, participation criteria – both inclusion and meaningfulness – are highlighted in the case studies as at least optionally positive. This means that participating individuals or groups can be selected so that inclusiveness is taken into account and so that the institutions have a proper role in the political and administrative system (for example power to decide over budget funding within limits). Legitimacy is also considered as a criterion that to some extent can be evaluated stronger if participatory democratic institutions are introduced. The same careful optimism regarding effectiveness and enlightened citizens is visible in the case studies presented in this volume, even if this mostly applies for the involved groups.

The quality of deliberation – political debate in deliberative settings – on the other hand, is by no means on the level that theorists assume might be possible to achieve. There is always a trade-off between inclusiveness and quality of deliberation, for example between co-governance and deliberative institutions. It is the *"law of time and numbers"*, as defined by Dahl (1998: 109), which makes perfect participatory institutions almost impossible: *"The more citizens a democratic unit contains, the less that citizens can participate directly in government decisions and the more that they must delegate authority to others."*

It is a trade-off between different democratic criteria; there is no one-size-fits-all as an option in institutional design for democratic innovations. This overall notion about the importance of the design is also made by Michels (2011: 290) – the type of innovation matters for the effect on different democratic evaluation criteria. We can make a contribution to the quality of democracy with a careful design of innovations that will enhance existing democratic institutions within our societies. But, as Michels continues (2011: 290-291), the effects can mostly be seen for those selected citizens who participate; the effects of small scale, exclusive innovations can thus not fully be transferred to democracy as a whole. *"No design is perfect"*, as stated by Smith (2009: 193), but we can easily make our prevailing institutions better by introducing well-designed elements, democratic innovations that make the malaises of contemporary democratic institutions less harmful.

The study of democratic innovations should, by now, go into a second phase, with more systematic analysis using empirical methods and covering a much larger sample of case studies. Without this, we will continue to work with too little over-arching knowledge about what could be achieved through democratic innovations, not only potentially but also in real life – especially as they are part of our everyday lives already today.

References

Bengtsson, Åsa and Mattila, Mikko 2009, Direct Democracy and its Critics: Support for Direct Democracy and 'Stealth' Democracy in Finland, *West European Politics*, Vol. 32, No. 5, 1033-1048.

Berndtson, Erkki 1984, Contemporary Crisis of Democracy. Conditions for Change – but What Kind of Change?, in Anckar, Dag and Berndtson, Erkki (eds.), *Essays on Democratic Theory*, The Finnish Political Science Association, Tampere.

Budge, Ian, 2012, Implementing Popular Preferences: Is Direct Democracy the Answer? in Geissel, Brigitte and Newton, Kenneth (eds.), 2012, *Evaluating Democratic Innovations: Curing the Democratic Malaise?*, Routledge, 23-38.

Dahl, Robert A., 1998, *On Democracy*, Yale University Press.

Geissel, Brigitte and Newton, Kenneth (eds.), 2012, *Evaluating Democratic Innovations Curing the Democratic Malaise?*, Routledge.

Geissel, Brigitte (2012), Democratic Innovations Theoretical and Empirical Challenges of Evaluation, in Geissel, Brigitte and Newton, Kenneth (eds.), 2012, *Evaluating Democratic Innovations Curing the Democratic Malaise?*, Routledge, 209-214.

Leighninger, Matt, 2006, *The Next Form of Democracy: How expert rule is giving way to shared governance... and why politics will never be the same*, Vanderbilt University Press.

Michels, Ank, 2011, Innovations in democratic governance, in: *International Review of Administrative Sciences* 77(2), 275-293.

Newton, Ken, 2012, Curing the Democratic Malaise with Democratic Innovations, in Geissel, Brigitte and Newton, Kenneth (eds.), 2012, *Evaluating Democratic Innovations Curing the Democratic Malaise?*, Routledge, 3-20.

Pihlaja, Ritva and Sandberg, Siv, 2012, Alueellista demokratiaa? Lähidemokratian toimintamallit Suomen kunnissa (Regional democracy?), Ministry of Finance Publications 27/2012.

Smith, Graham, 2009, *Democratic Innovations: Designing Institutions for Citizens Participation*, Cambridge University Press.

The Authors

Irena Fiket Irena Fiket is a Post-doctoral fellow at Department of Political Science and Sociology (Dispo), University of Florence and affiliated researcher at CIRCap (Center for the Study of Political Change), University of Siena. Her research interests include Democratic innovations, Deliberative Democracy, European Public Sphere, and Western Balkans and she has published for Oxford University Press, Transitions Review, Stato e Mercato and others.

Joan Font Fàbregas is a senior researcher at IESA-CSIC (Córdoba, Spain). He has conducted research about elections, surveys, local participation processes, citizen juries, deliberative polls and referendums and has published in journals like European Journal of Political Research, Public Administration, International Journal of Urban and Regional Research or Southern European Society and Politics.

Brigitte Geissel, Goethe University Frankfurt a.M. (Germany), Professor for Political Science and Political Sociology, Head of Research Unit 'Democratic Innovations', Speaker of ECPR Standing Group 'Democratic Innovations'; fellowships, research and teaching positions at various universities/institutes such as Harvard Kennedy School (USA), Social Science Research Center Berlin, Åbo Akademi (Finland), Universities of Darmstadt, Muenster, Berlin, and Illinois (USA). Her research interests include democratic innovations, new forms of governance (European Union, national, subnational), political actors (new social movements, civil society, parties, political elites, citizens).

Kimmo Grönlund is a Professor of Political Science and the Director of the Social Science Research Institute at Åbo Akademi University, Finland. He is the Principal Investigator of the Finnish National Election Study and convenor of the ECPR Standing Group on Democratic Innovations. His major research interests include political behavior and political knowledge, participatory democracy, the role of social and institutional trust in democracy, as well as experimental research. He has published on the topics in journals such as the European Political Science Review, Political Studies, Scandinavian Political Studies, Electoral Studies and the American Review of Public Administration.

Staffan Himmelroos holds a PHD in Political Science from Åbo Akademi University. His thesis focuses on the quality of deliberation in citizen forums. His primary research interests are public deliberation and experimental research methods, especially with regard to the study of political reasoning and opinion formation. He is also a founding member of the Finnish Institute for Deliberative Democracy, an association that brings together researchers, practitioners, public officials and organizations with an interest in promoting public deliberation in Finland.

Dr Marko Joas is Professor in Public Administration at Åbo Akademi University, Department of Political Science (Turku, Finland). His main research interests include (local) environmental governance, often seen from a democratic point-of-view, innovative democracy and comparative sustainable development, all these in national, regional and European contexts. Furthermore, he is a Steering Board member for Democracy: A Citizen Perspective - A Centre of Excellence on Democracy Research at Åbo Akademi University. He has been partner in several empirical European and Finnish Research projects and published within his areas of research peer-reviewed articles, edited volumes as well as monographs, for example Governing a Common Sea (Earthscan 2008 together with Detlef Jahn and Kristine Kern) , Governing Sustainable Cities (Earthscan 2005 with Bob Evans, Kate Theobald and Susan Sundback) and Informed Cities - Making Research Work for Local Sustainability (forthcoming Earthscan 2013/2014 with Kate Theobald, David McGuinness, Cristina Garzillo and Stefan Kuhn).

Gustav Lidén is a Post-doctoral Fellow at the Department of Social Sciences at Mid Sweden University (Sweden). His dissertation focuses on the explanations of societies' success in e-democracy. His research is comparative and carried out in the fields of democratic theory and e-democracy but also covers theories of migration and decision-making. Concerning e-democracy he has recently been published in journals as Information Polity and Electronic Journal of e-Government.

Vincenzo Memoli is an Assistant Professor at Università degli Studi di Catania in Italy. He has worked on topics including public opinion, party system, and democracy. His articles have appeared in British Journal of Political Science, Acta Politica, and International Political Science Review, among other journals.

Clemente J. Navarro, Universidad Pablo de Olavide (Spain). Professor of Political Sociology, Head of the Centre for Urban Political Sociology and Policies, and the Local Government Observatory. Visiting professor in various universities such as Firenze, Rio de Janeiro, Buenos Aires, Autónoma de Chile, Consiglio Nazionalle della Ricerca, The Harris School of Public Policy Studies, University of Chicago. His research interests include multi-level governance, local policies and politics, and specially, the public participation policy.

Antonio Putini, research fellow in Political Sociology at the Department of Political Science (Sapienza University, Rome), lecturer in Sociology of Public Administration at University of Tuscia; member of various scientific societies (AIS, Associazione Italiana di Sociologia, Section of Political Sociology; ECPR, European Consortium for Political Research; ISA, International Sociological Association; IIS, International Institute of Sociology). His research interests include participative and deliberative democratic theories, digital democracy, democratic innovations (participatory budgets) and political actors (civil society and cyber-parties)."

Anja Röcke, Assistant Professor at Humboldt-University, Berlin (Germany). She has been member of the Berlin Graduate School of Social Sciences and the Marc Bloch Center, Berlin, before writing her PhD at the European University Institute, Florence (Italy). Her dissertation deals with the topic of "Framing Citizen Participation. Participatory Budgeting in France, Germany and the United Kingdom", published with Palgrave (2013, forthcoming). She worked as researcher for a European comparative project on Participatory Budgeting, of which the results have been published in several languages. Her research interests include democratic innovations, sociological theory and most recently sociology of education.

Maija Setälä is Professor of Political Science at the University of Turku. She gained her PhD from the LSE in 1997. She has been a visiting research fellow at the Columbia University and the Australian National University. Setälä specializes in democratic theory, political trust, direct democracy and democratic innovation and has published a number of articles and books on these topics. Setälä is also involved in projects applying experimental methods in the analysis of democratic mechanisms.

Michael L. Smith is a Senior Researcher at the Institute of Sociology, Academy of Sciences of the Czech Republic. He is also a Senior Researcher at the Institute for Social and Economic Analysis in Prague, as well as a Lecturer for the Comparative History of Ideas Program at the University of Washington, Seattle. He received his Ph.D. in political science in 2008 from the New School for Social Research in New York with the dissertation 'Making Direct Democracy Work: Politics of Local Referendums in the Czech Republic'; He publishes and conducts research in the areas of political governance and transparency, social inequality, and social and political change in the countries of Central and Eastern Europe, primarily on the basis of research grants from the Czech Science Foundation and other institutions.

Kim Strandberg holds a PhD in Political Science and is a Senior Researcher and Associate Professor at the Social Science Research Institute at the Department of Politics and Administration at Åbo Akademi University (Finland). His primary areas of research are political communication, citizen deliberation and political uses of the Internet. He has published on these topics in journals such as Party Politics, New Media & Society, Information Polity, Scandinavian Political Studies and Journal of Information Technology and Politics.

Julien Talpin is a research fellow at the Centre National de la Recherche Scientifique (CNRS, France), member of the Research Center on Administration, Politics and Society (CERAPS/University Lille 2). He has been a Visiting Fulbright fellow at the University of Southern California (USA). He received his PhD from the European University Institute (Florence); his dissertation focuses on the effects of Participatory Budgeting on actors, published at ECPR Press: Schools of Democracy. How Ordinary Citizens (Sometimes) Become Competent in Participatory Budgeting Institutions. His research interests include democratic innovations, community organizing, democratic processes within social movements, and poor people forms of participation.

Index